CW01175956

Marjorie Merriweather Post

The Life Behind the Luxury

Marjorie Merriweather Post

The Life Behind the Luxury

Estella M. Chung

Hillwood Estate, Museum & Gardens, Washington, D.C.
in association with D Giles Limited

© 2019 Hillwood Estate, Museum & Gardens

First published in 2019 by GILES
An imprint of D Giles Limited
66 High Street
Lewes, BN7 1XG
gilesltd.com

Library of Congress Cataloging-in-Publication Data

Names: Chung, Estella M., author.
Title: Marjorie Merriweather Post : the life behind the luxury / Estella M. Chung.
Description: Washington, D.C. : Hillwood Estate, Museum & Gardens, in association with D Giles Limited, 2019. | Includes bibliographical references and index.
Identifiers: LCCN 2019006530 | ISBN 9781911282457
Subjects: LCSH: Post, Marjorie Merriweather. | Philanthropists--United States--Biography. | Women philanthropists--United States--Biography. | Women art collectors--United States--Biography. | Rich people--United States--Biography. | Hillwood Museum and Gardens--History.
Classification: LCC HV28.P6 C473 2019 | DDC 361.7/4092 [B] --dc23 LC record available at https://lccn.loc.gov/2019006530

ISBN (hardcover): 978-1-911282-45-7

All rights reserved

No part of the contents of this book may be reproduced, stored in a retrieval system, or transmitted in any form or by any means, electronic, mechanical, photocopying, recording, or otherwise, without the written permission of the Trustees of Hillwood Estate, Museum & Gardens and D Giles Limited.

For Hillwood Estate, Museum & Gardens:
Kate Markert, Executive Director
Estella M. Chung, Director of Collections

For D Giles Limited:
Copyedited and proofread by Jenny Wilson
Designed by Alfonso Iacurci
Produced by GILES, an imprint of D Giles Limited
Printed and bound in China

Front cover
Marjorie Post strides ahead at the races, Belmont Park, New York, ca. 1932–35

Back cover
Marjorie Post's massage and hairdressing room, filled with tokens of appreciation to the philanthropist

Frontispiece
Marjorie Post as Marie Antoinette, First Prize for costume, Everglades Ball, 1926

Contents
Boin-Taburet tea and coffee service used at Marjorie Post's gatherings

Contents

Foreword — 7
Kate Markert, Executive Director

Acknowledgments — 9

Introduction: — 13
The Life Behind the Luxury

Business — 41

Service — 75

Travel Luxe — 105

Giving — 135

Legacy — 167

Notes — 176

Selected Bibliography — 188

Photographic Credits — 190

Hillwood Collection Objects — 194

Index — 196

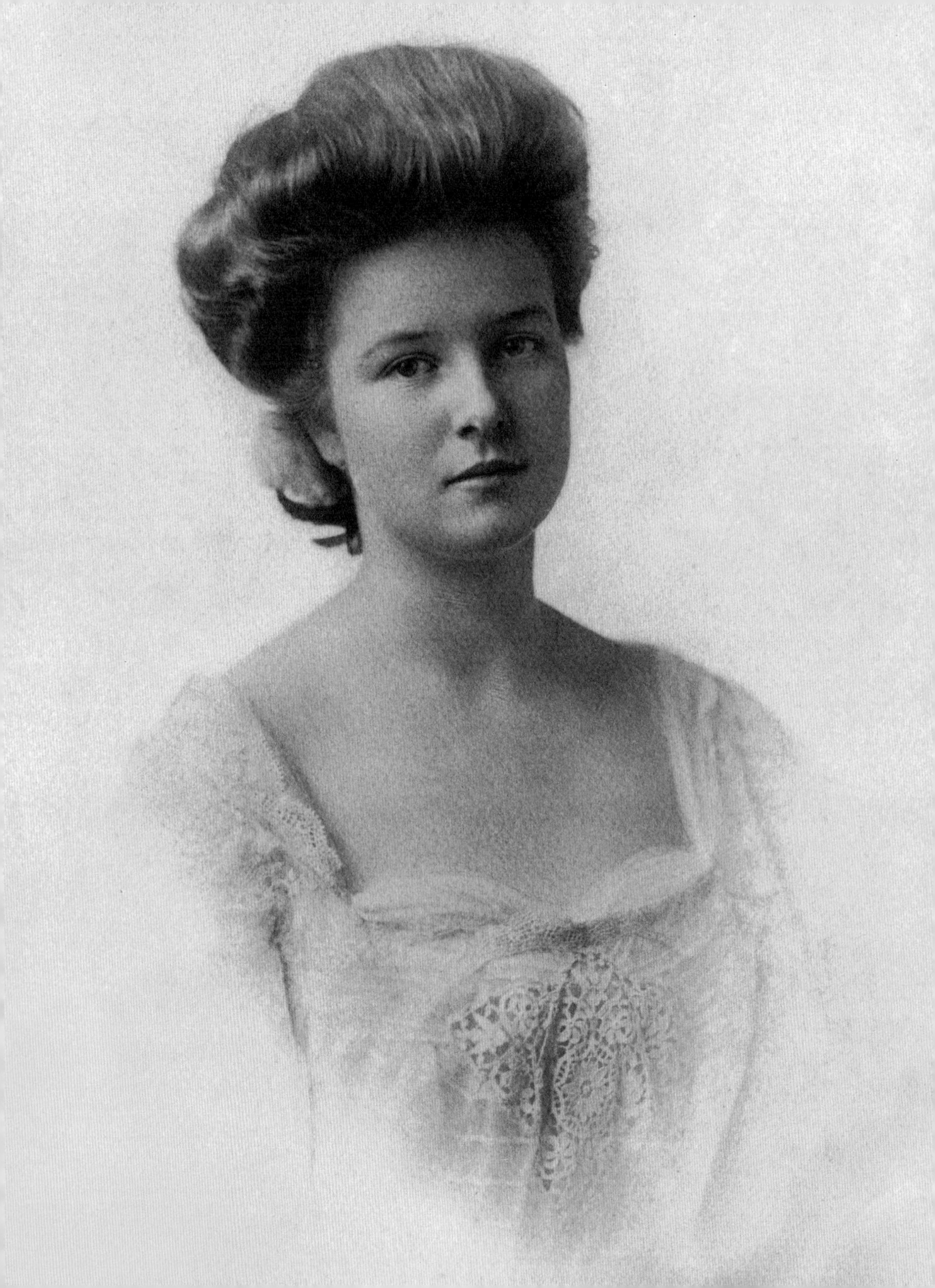

Foreword

The last time a biography of Marjorie Merriweather Post appeared was in 1995. That book, *American Empress* by Nancy Rubin, followed Post's life chronologically and relied heavily on society press coverage as source material to tell the story. It is still in print, but almost twenty-five years later, Estella M. Chung has taken a very different approach to Marjorie Post's life, reviewing it thematically through the prism of Post's multifaceted interests and accomplishments.

Estella Chung has studied Post for more than ten years, beginning when she was hired in 2007 as a historian and curator of American material culture at Hillwood Estate, Museum & Gardens. Fred Fisher, the wise executive director who hired her, had identified a Post biography as a key future project for the new hire. Fisher convened a blue ribbon committee to help shape a strategic vision for Hillwood, and committee members ultimately recommended emphasizing the story of the museum's remarkable founder as a central theme in achieving Hillwood's institutional mission.

Chung thrilled at the relatively rare opportunity to explore the life of a female museum founder and conveyed to Fisher in her cover letter that Post was especially interesting because of her personal blend of the "ordinary and extraordinary" as a woman making her way in the twentieth century. The more Chung learned about Post, the more interesting she became. Post was modest regarding her many good deeds, so such instances were ripe for further research. In the process, Chung discovered Post's deep well of remarkable humanitarianism in times of need and war, and an exceptional generosity throughout her long life.

Living Artfully, a 2013 publication and exhibition at Hillwood curated by Chung, tracked a calendar year in Post's life—from spring at Hillwood to summer at Camp Topridge, her Adirondack home, then back to Hillwood in the fall and finally to Mar-A-Lago, the extravagant Palm Beach, Florida, estate that she built and where she wintered. The publication's many reprints suggest significant interest not only in Post's remarkable homes, gardens, and lifestyle, but also in her obvious aptitude for organizing such a complex way of life.

Post entertained and cared for others in the memorable settings of her homes, where she created unusually rich and beautiful surroundings for her own life, including phenomenal art collections. Readers of *Living Artfully* were left with admiration for Post's tremendous ability to handle a myriad

Marjorie Post, ca. 1902–3

of daily and long-term details with unique thoughtfulness and grace, while exhibiting a down-to-earth approach to problem solving and nurturing a close working relationship with her large staff.

In *Marjorie Merriweather Post: The Life Behind the Luxury*, Chung shows us the grand and gracious Post that many met in *Living Artfully*, adding an array of delightful details, my favorite being from the "Travel Luxe" chapter. Who among us would not have loved to accompany Post on a Mediterranean excursion aboard her yacht, the *Sea Cloud*, or to have popped up to Camp Topridge on her plane for a "little weekend"? Post's life was indeed one of luxury and elegance. Chung goes further, however, in revealing Post to be an astute business executive, a deeply caring and generous humanitarian, and a philanthropist.

For an institution to commit to a project such as Post's biography is no small endeavor. It is quite different from Hillwood's usual business of organizing exhibitions and related catalogues, as complex as those campus-wide undertakings can be. A biography necessarily requires an extended commitment and giving a key staff member the time and environment to conduct research, to organize material, and then to write. Even authors who are able to work full time on such projects can spend years on the task. While Chung pursued her research and developed a deeper understanding of Post, she also took on more responsibilities at Hillwood, adding head of oral history and director of collections to her portfolio. Along the way, she curated the exhibition *Deco Japan* in 2015, in addition to *Living Artfully* two years earlier, and *A Photographic Journey of the Ambassador's Daughter: Moscow, 1937–38* in 2010. It is a testament to Chung's commitment, as well as the appeal of her subject matter, that she was able to maintain her focus on Post's biography over the past decade.

We appreciate the support for this project provided by Hillwood's board of trustees. Many thanks are especially owed to Kristen and Tom Roberts, the current owners of Hogarcito, Post's first home in Palm Beach, for their generosity in helping to publish this volume.

Kate Markert
Executive Director
Hillwood Estate, Museum & Gardens

Acknowledgments

Not many people get to snoop, professionally or otherwise, among someone else's correspondence, photographs, and possessions for a decade. Nor are many afforded the opportunity to do so at their subject's 25-acre estate, with a home containing some of the most splendid objects the world has to offer. This, however, is the peculiar realm inhabited by the museum curator, estate historian, and biographer—my callings for the past decade at Hillwood. I have clicked along the same garden paths that Marjorie Merriweather Post walked, smelled the bountiful blossoms in her cutting garden, and taken visual delight in not just the intricate details but also the abundance of decorative arts with which she filled her mansion. I have scanned her guest lists, read her mail, and even set out her cereal bowls.

To experience Post's creation—an estate that stimulates and pleases all the senses—is to come to appreciate a person of extraordinary capabilities, not only in regard to her tasteful eye, but also in her capacity to simultaneously focus on the practical. Before my tenure at Hillwood, many who enjoyed Post's estate yearned for more information about the creator of this oasis in the nation's capital. It was, therefore, my good fortune that in 2007 Hillwood sought a cultural historian and curator interested in biography, oral history, domestic staff history, art and material culture, women's studies, and international cultural history.

The publication *Living Artfully: At Home with Marjorie Merriweather Post* (2013) shared Post's incredible three-estate lifestyle, which she maintained with the help of a top-notch staff. Now, with the publication of *Marjorie Merriweather Post: The Life Behind the Luxury*, we can see a portrait of Post's abilities to manage her wealth, enjoy it, and share it with others. However, in the research for this publication, certain aspects of her generosity and skillfulness proved difficult to uncover, leading me to seek the assistance of a number of individuals and institutions. They have helped immeasurably in making this book possible.

I must start with two Hillwood executive directors, not only for their steadfast commitment to recording the history of the estate and its founder, but also for providing the particular resources required to complete a book such as *The Life Behind the Luxury*. Thus, I thank Fred Fisher, retired director of Hillwood, and I thank the current executive director, Kate Markert, for her extraordinary support for this publication. Moreover, I have to express my gratitude not only for being given the resources to complete this publication, but also for being able to work as director of collections, thus furthering my appreciation of Post's legacy at Hillwood.

Among others deserving of gratitude in Washington are the Library of Congress's Manuscript Division staff, the Smithsonian Archives of American Art, the Special Collections Research Center at George Washington University, and the historian "P.B." at the National Capital Area Council of the Boy Scouts of America.

Additional thanks go to the Historical Society of Palm Beach County, Long Island University Post, Eliza's Quest Foods, Post Holdings, and the Historical Society of the Town of Greenwich. Also, a note of gratitude goes to curator Jennifer Gaudio at the United States Coast Guard Museum in New London, Connecticut; the staff at the Schlesinger Library at Harvard University; and individuals DeWitt Chapple, John Irelan, Barbara Schmir, and Pamela Nichols Howe. To Terrence J. McDonald, Diana Bachman, and Malgosia Myc at the University of Michigan's Bentley Historical Library, a very special thank you.

My appreciation also goes to those who sat for Hillwood oral history interviews in this century and the last. It must be said that you have made valuable contributions to the estate's historical record. Many of your interviews are cited throughout *The Life Behind the Luxury*. Moreover, thank you to prior Hillwood oral historians Nancy Harris, Kathi Ann Brown, and Stephanie Brown. I am thankful to visitor services staff and volunteers alike for alerting me to guests at Hillwood who revealed that they had personally interacted with Marjorie Post, allowing us to identify additional oral history candidates.

At Hillwood, my appreciation also goes to board members, staff, and interns who supported and shared in this endeavor: Ellen Charles, president emerita; Marcia DeWitt, president of the board of trustees; Brian Barr, director of horticulture; Samantha Hernandez, director of human resources; Jan Jensen, head of development; Audra Kelly, director of interpretation; Doug Rose, director of finance; Lynn Rossotti, director of marketing, communications, and visitor services; Ed Vreeland, director of operations and technology; and Wilfried Zeisler, chief curator. My gratitude also goes to Hillwood alumni Angie Dodson and Michael Dudich, as well as to those curators no longer with us, namely Anne Odom and the dearly missed Liana Paredes.

Acknowledgments

A very special thanks for the whole-hearted teamwork by the collections and curatorial divisions: Kayla Baker, Megan Martinelli, Ariel Caruso, Manuel Diaz, Kathryn Fay, Linda Heinrich, Manuel Rouco, Abby Stambach, Rebecca Tilles, and Peter Tsouras. A separate mention of acknowledgment goes to Beth Blackwood, Kathryn Fay, and Abby Stambach for managing the images for this publication. Interns Elizabeth Artlip, Verena Calas, Isabel Mann, Isabel Matthäus, and Lauren Raffensperger willingly combed through years of accumulated research and certainly made their mark on this book with their projects.

To the team at D Giles Limited, in England, many thanks for yet another enjoyable and fruitful publications partnership. I must also express my gratitude to John Dean, Erik Kvalsvik, Edward Owen, and Brian Searby, the photographers who documented Hillwood's many objects and spaces. I would also like to thank my parents, my husband, son, extended family, and dear friends for their support, delicious meals, and fun distractions. Cheers to members of the Biographers International Organization, headed by James McGrath Morris, and the Washington Biography Group, long guided by Marc Pachter and Pat McNees, for making what could be the very lonely conundrums of writing a biography into a shared discussion about the craft, connecting authors in Washington and around the world.

Last but far from least, thank you to the board of trustees of Hillwood Estate, Museum & Gardens and the present-day owners of Post's Palm Beach home of Hogarcito, Kristen and Tom Roberts, for their generous funding and sponsorship of *The Life Behind the Luxury*.

When Marjorie Post was honored in a 1966 radio program, the commentator Roy Meachum remarked, "I can't count all the things that she has done for this city.... I'd take the odds she can't even remember them." With the help of the many people listed here, there is now a new accounting of Post's good works and a greater understanding of her many legacies.

Estella M. Chung
Director of Collections
Hillwood Estate, Museum & Gardens

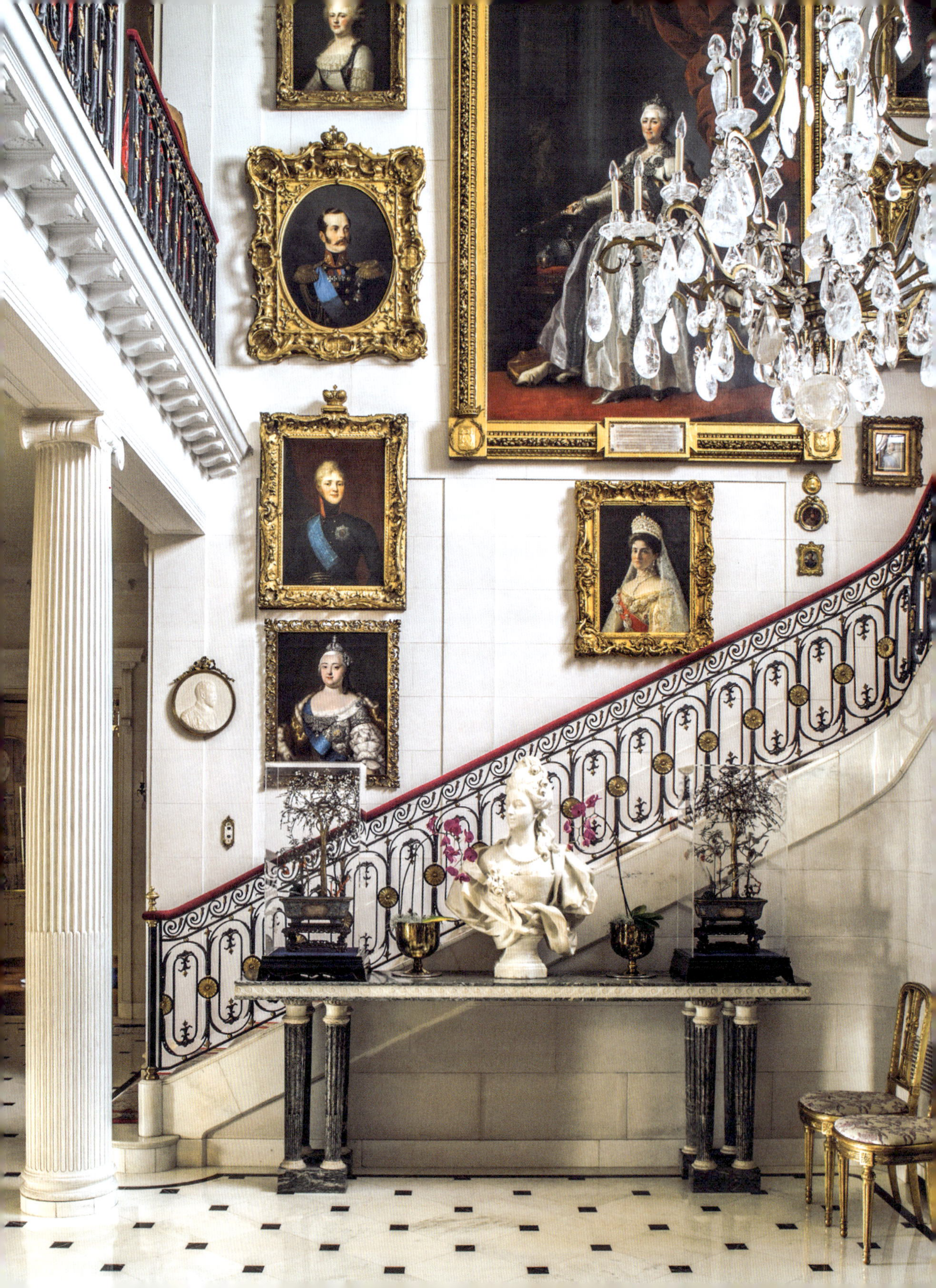

Introduction: The Life Behind the Luxury

Marjorie Merriweather Post was in full command of her wealth from the sales of the coffee substitute Postum and Post Grape-Nuts cereal. She also wielded financial oversight of mansions on multiple estates, a yacht, fabulous jewelry, and an impressive art collection, capably creating and managing a twentieth-century life of luxury, complete with a butler, footmen, gardeners, and personal maids. All that said, it was not Post's ability to read a spreadsheet for which she was often noted in newspapers and magazines. While Post's good works made the news, announcements of her social gatherings, what she wore, her four marriages and four divorces, and her father's suicide got more ink. Her life—in all its honorable, glamorous, and painful moments—was syndicated news, and not a private matter.

"It was a big organization … even though it was her personal life," said Betty Cannella, who served as Post's financial secretary.[1] At times in her adult life, Post employed one hundred to three hundred people across her residences in full-time, part-time, and seasonal positions, depending on the year's activities.[2] Today, her Hillwood estate, occupying twenty-five acres in Washington, D.C., is a museum, with Post's style on display for the public's perusal. Her gardens, greenhouse, clothes closets, mid-century modern kitchen, and place settings in the formal dining room are all on view.

"It's as if Mother could walk in and sit down to dinner," explained the actress Dina Merrill, born Nedenia Hutton, the youngest of Post's three children, upon the opening of the museum.[3] Sumptuous Sèvres porcelain, fabulous Fabergé eggs, and a dazzling quantity of bejeweled objects fill Hillwood's hallways, display cabinets, and rotating exhibition galleries. Post once wrote in a letter, "I do like beautiful things and it has been my privilege to be able to enjoy them.... Also, I like a smoothly running organization."[4]

Mixing the envisioned grandeur of European estates with top mid-twentieth-century American functionality, footmen in tuxedos worked in the pantries of Post's modern kitchens with stainless-steel work surfaces. Should the nation's capital encounter a nuclear threat, over sixty people could be accommodated in Hillwood's well-stocked fallout shelters.[5] Post's pampered pet, a schnauzer named Scampi, accompanied her aboard the *Merriweather*, her private plane. The means for acquiring and sustaining Post's mansions originated with a coffee substitute and cereal business in Battle Creek, Michigan. "Postum cereal factories were growing up around us," she said, referring to her childhood in Battle Creek.[6]

Marjorie Post was born on March 15, 1887, in Springfield, Illinois, but by the early 1890s, the family had moved to Battle Creek, where her father, Charles William "C.W." Post, was experimenting with formulas for a coffee substitute that he would later market as Postum. He and his wife, Ella

Scampi and Marjorie Post at Hillwood, 1965

Introduction: The Life Behind the Luxury

C.W. Post (1854–1914),
Marjorie Post's father

Ella Merriweather Post
(1852–1912), Marjorie
Post's mother

Letitia Merriweather, would have only one child, a daughter they named Marjorie Merriweather Post.[7]

In light of her father's interest in the latest trends for healthy living, Marjorie Post fondly recalled how she and her parents "learned to go barefooted in the snow, or wander around on the lawn in the evening or early morning dew … dad, mother, and I, in our nighties … [making] all kinds of shadows in the moon light."[8] She described her mother, whom she adored, as "first and foremost … the most beautifully groomed woman…. I had never seen [her hair] in disorder…. She tended to it herself. She didn't go to hairdressers." Ella Merriweather was also a great one "for canning, making jams and jellies…. Being an only child, I [excitedly] entered into all those things," said Post.[9] Ella Merriweather was also "a marvelous needleworker," sewing and knitting for the family, remembered Post. "I used to bring children [to my] mother, when I thought they were not very well dressed because their family could not afford many things, [and mother would] outfit them," she recalled.[10]

However, the Post family also faced challenges. "Mother had a really very bad time of it. Father was ill so long, so much, and she was always waiting on him, fussing and stewing and fretting on it," Post said of her parents.[11] It was C.W. Post's illness that led the family to Battle Creek and also to Christian Science.[12] Marjorie Post stayed with Christian Science until her death, frequently communicating with a practitioner who lent a good ear, offering guidance and suggesting passages to read from Mary Baker Eddy's *Science and Health*. Maintaining a positive outlook on life, monitoring negativity, and sharing encouraging sentiments with other Christian Scientists remained a part of Post's lifelong habits. Avoiding doctors and alcohol, however, did not.

Post saw various physicians, and although not much of a drinker—heavily intoxicated people displeased her—she would on occasion have a little scotch or Seagram's V.O. with water. She served cocktails, wine, spirits, and champagne at her functions.[13] Ella Merriweather, in addition to C.W. Post, suffered from bad health at times. "There were many, many [childhood] trips alone with my father [when mother was not too well]," Marjorie Post noted.[14]

"I think it is a very valuable experience to be thrown [together] with girls one's own age from all walks of life. I certainly adored Mount Vernon Seminary," Post reminisced about attending boarding school in Washington, D.C. "[Children] learn to adjust themselves to people and get along…. It is really a schooling for getting out into the world."[15] Her report cards from 1902 and 1903 show that she took classes in botany, geology, arithmetic, algebra, English literature, composition, rhetoric, and American history, and received two unexcused "T"s, for tardiness.[16]

Dinner doubled as a meal and a class in conversation, as students were required to competently discuss science, fine arts, and current events while eating.[17] As prim and proper as it might sound, Mount Vernon Seminary also offered opportunities ahead of the times for young women to obtain a higher education from the late 1860s onward. At the school's 1966 convocation, the educator Gordon Hoxie, a guest speaker, remarked, "One cannot today comprehend the distrust and hostility with which women's education was then greeted."[18] Post remained a staunch advocate and supporter of the school.

C.W. Post and Ella Merriweather divorced in October 1904. When C.W. Post told his seventeen-year-old daughter that he planned to marry Leila Young, then employed as his secretary, Marjorie Post first confirmed that they had no plans to have children and then flatly replied, "Well, I think your choice is awful." Young was just ten years her senior. "I was furious," Post recounted.[19]

C.W. Post and Leila Young married in November 1904, and in his annual December address to Postum employees, he stated, "I am going to take a personal subject ... for my family affairs have been made public in perhaps every newspaper in America." He continued, "The first Mrs. Post and I ... lacked mature judgement in the selection of a life partner ... therefore we found it better to live apart most of the time." C.W. Post then explained how Leila Young had originally been hired as a governess to look after the young Marjorie Post at lunch and dinnertime, and her duties transitioned into her becoming his secretary. Now, he said, he was introducing Leila Young Post as his wife.[20] Thereafter, Marjorie Post often spent time with her mother or with C.W. Post and Leila Young Post.[21]

In 1905 Marjorie Post married Edward Bennett Close, who hailed from a tradition-minded family. C.W. Post could not help referring to Close as a "bundle of old clothes."[22] Such sentiments aside, he bestowed the Boulders—a staffed estate in Greenwich, Connecticut—on his daughter, as a wedding present, and set about teaching the new bride the financial art and responsibilities of running a large property.[23]

Exchanging letters addressed to "Dear Budge" and "Dear Dada," father and daughter, respectively, wrote about the financial matters of household staff, automobiles, and basic principles of business correspondence. "Hereafter, when you write business letters, you had better not mix the business with the personal affairs.... Generally a business letter should be filed for future reference and it should not contain personal matters," instructed C.W. Post, before sweetly concluding, "So you can write Daddy two letters instead of one."[24] Marjorie Post toiled over the accounting, and when she got it right he wrote, "I want to tell you again how pleased I was at the last

Edward Bennett Close
and Marjorie Post
married in 1905

investigation of your books, to observe you have your affairs in hand."[25] It was fortuitous that she did. Ella Merriweather died in October 1912, and C.W. Post died by his own hand in May 1914. In December 1915, Marjorie Post became owner of the Postum Cereal Company. She was twenty-eight.

Post's married life—four marriages and four divorces—spanned from 1905 to 1964. The last marriage lasted six years, while her earlier unions ranged from fourteen to twenty years. As a 1905 magazine article commented on the culture at that time, "Divorce is a topic that very frequently occupies the center of the stage."[26] Some visitors to Post's estate have been known to ask museum guides, "Why four divorces?" One guide was said to reply, "Madame, I was not under the bed, I cannot tell you."[27]

As early as 1920, newspapers kept a running tally of Post's marriages and divorces, along with those of other prominent women of her time.[28] The columnist Betty Beale remarked about the practice, "Most news people, if the person had been married before … [reporters] would write it down every single time…. They would say 'who was formerly married to' and 'who had two husbands before'…. Well—that wasn't news."[29]

Post herself offered this frank summation on her love life: "I've been very smart about most everything in my life. But, I'm not smart about men."[30]

Edward Bennett Close, Marjorie Post, and their daughter Adelaide, ca. 1909

Recalling her engagement party to Edward Bennett Close, she said, "I was right up in the stratosphere."[31] Though she also noted, "Of course, when Ed Close and I were married [in 1905] we were a pair of children."[32] Post was eighteen at the time.

Soon after the wedding, Close wanted her to give up Christian Science. "That didn't start us off too well," Post explained, adding, "Ed felt that the traditional things were the things that were to be done." As for her, she noted, "Of course I wasn't raised that way, and it was difficult."[33] Ultimately, Post and Close had two daughters together, Adelaide and Eleanor Close. The couple generously gave their money and their time to World War I relief efforts. Their marriage ended in divorce in November 1919.[34]

Post and the financier Edward Francis "E.F." Hutton wed in July 1920. They built landmark homes, designed a breathtaking yacht, fed the hungry, and ushered the food business that C.W. Post started into a new era.[35] A little love note Post saved from Hutton read, "Care to lunch with the one man who simply adores [you?].... What say-o?—Ned."[36] They had a daughter, Nedenia Hutton, who would act under the stage name Dina Merrill. With Hutton's infidelity came divorce in September 1935.[37] "It was her pride that was hurt," assessed Dina Merrill. "It's sad the way it went."[38]

E.F. Hutton (Ned) and Marjorie Post

E.F. Hutton, Marjorie Post, and their daughter, Nedenia Hutton (later known by her stage name, Dina Merrill), ca. 1924–25

Post married Joseph Davies in December 1935. With Davies's appointment as U.S. ambassador to the Soviet Union and later to Belgium, the couple served their country *en poste* and shared the pleasure of collecting Russian icons and decorative arts. When they found themselves apart, they wrote love letters with such sentiments as, "My dearest—how I love you, can't wait to see you!"[39] Dina Merrill recalled, "The only time I've ever seen Mother in tears was when Joseph Davies sailed [back to Belgium] when World War II was imminent.... She thought he was going to get killed, or sunk, or something."[40]

In later years, passions flowed differently. "Joe Davies and his stupid jealousy," as Post described it, proved to be problematic. One related incident occurred when Post was fox-trotting with a friend at a dance. "All of a sudden they struck up a tango. [My dance partner] liked to tango, and so do I, so we danced." She continued, "Going home in the car I was upbraided for making an exhibition of myself, dancing two dances with the same man.... That kind of thing went on and on most of the later years of our marriage."[41] Waiting

Introduction: The Life Behind the Luxury

Marjorie Merriweather Post

Joseph Davies and Marjorie Post, from their honeymoon album "Marjoe Cruise," 1935–36
Marjorie Post and Joseph Davies, ca. 1944–47

Herbert May and Marjorie Post, ca. 1959–1960

for her divorce briefing and case in March 1955, Post wrote to a friend from Sun Valley, Idaho, "Tomorrow is the shampoo; the next day is the briefing; the following day is the case!" [42]

Last was Post's marriage to Herbert May. They wed in June 1958, and May retired from his senior vice presidency at the Westinghouse Air Brake Company in 1959.[43] They entertained and hosted philanthropic events together, donating their time and money to support education and the arts. Daughter Dina Merrill thought May to be the perfect companion and husband for Post's later years, as he also loved to dance and entertain like her mother. Post found herself shocked to learn that Herbert May was gay. They divorced in August 1964. She was seventy-seven.[44]

"Mother was not the type of person not to be married," said Dina Merrill. "She always liked to have a man in her life."[45] One neighbor recalled, "If you were walking down the street, all men's heads would turn because she was so beautiful and her carriage so stately."[46] During Post's fifty-five years of marriage, she took her husbands' names, making her at times Marjorie Close, Marjorie Hutton, Marjorie Davies, and Marjorie May. After what would be her last divorce, she officially returned to Marjorie Merriweather Post. For the purposes here, she is always Marjorie Post, no matter her marital status.

Post's business activities, service as an engaged citizen, and acts as a philanthropist, as well as her magnificent way of living, continued, regardless of her love life. "She was very determined and liked it her way," remarked granddaughter Ellen Charles about Post's marital woes, also revealing Post's capacity to carry on.[47]

"My daughters are so different," chuckled Post. "On one hand, I have to make Adelaide spend money … [while] on the other Eleanor goes through money like it's water."[48] Adelaide Close, born in 1908, pursued her interest in animals to become a fine dog and horse breeder. She also enjoyed gardens and the outdoors.[49] Eleanor Close, born in 1909, collected art objects and developed into a Francophile, taking up residence in Paris. "I have always had such a thing for France…. Everybody teases me…. I adore France," she said.[50] Nedenia Hutton, fourteen years younger, was born in 1923. As noted, she took the stage name Dina Merrill, slightly altering the spelling of Merrall, a name in the family. She acted on television, the big screen, and Broadway, passing in 2017. Eleanor Close preceded her in death in 2006 and Adelaide Close in 1998. Each daughter supported various philanthropic causes, among them juvenile diabetes research, feeding the hungry, humanitarian emergency medical relief, and seeing-eye dog training.[51]

Post fondly recalled memories of the young Adelaide and Eleanor at their home in Greenwich, Connecticut. "That place, the Boulders, was really a lovely place to raise children," she observed. At one point, Ella Merriweather gave granddaughters Adelaide and Eleanor a puppy. "That little puppy grew up with the children and was their shadow…. That dog is in the portrait which hangs in my bedroom of Eleanor and Adelaide in pink dresses," Post noted.[52] The travels of Post, Hutton, and their daughter Dina Merrill aboard their yacht, with a crew of seventy-two, made for unforgettable

Marjorie Post with daughters Adelaide and Eleanor Close

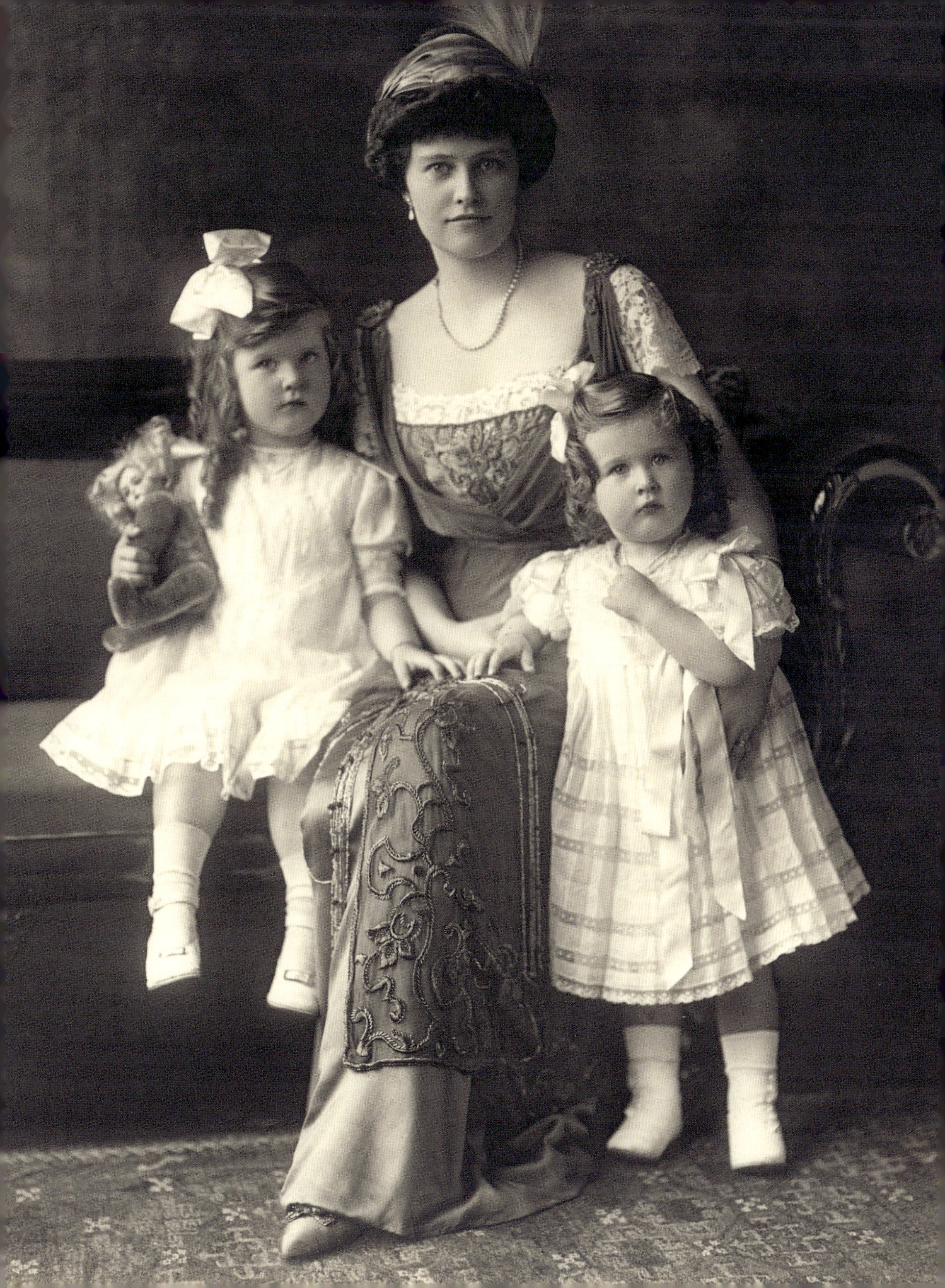

Eleanor Close, Marjorie Post, and Adelaide Close, 1923

family adventures. "I was full of curiosity about all the places we went to," recalled Dina Merrill.[53] In terms of personality, Post was rather formal, as opposed to cozy. "She was very busy," said Merrill.[54]

Post brought that formality to grandparenting. She taught her grandchildren how to play backgammon, but she would not let them just have the win. They actually had to best her in strategy.[55] Daunting for young teens, when Post spoke with them, she preferred serious conversation, touching on the realms of politics and the arts.[56] Her formidable presence proved useful at times. For instance, when young family members needed to be quiet and sit still, Post could turn them to stone, unmoving and silent, with a few magical words and her commanding presence.[57]

Introduction: The Life Behind the Luxury

Post and her children, Adelaide, Nedenia (Dina Merrill), and Eleanor, 1927

Nedenia Hutton (Dina Merrill) as flower girl at her sister Adelaide Close's wedding, 1927

When it came to the household staff, granddaughter Ellen Charles, describing the kind yet demanding Post, said, "I never heard her raise her voice. She never had to." Charles added, "You knew she expected a certain level of behavior."[58] Donald Handelman, a financial consultant to Post, said, "Now, there's a difference between being in charge and meddling, and she did not meddle … [using] whatever channel of command she had established."[59] He continued, "I don't think there were many people in her position who had as good an overall knowledge of business and financial matters…. She didn't flaunt it…. Social friends did not see the business side of her."[60]

From the mid-1950s onward, Post lived primarily at Hillwood, enjoying spring and autumn in Washington, and traveled to Mar-A-Lago in Palm Beach, Florida, for the winter season, and to Camp Topridge in the Adirondacks near Lake Placid, New York, to escape the heat of summer. Post and Hutton completed Mar-A-Lago in 1927, and she kept the property until the end of her life, in 1973. By that time, the estate was "one of America's most elaborate twentieth-century mansions" still in the hands of the original owner.[61] With ample outdoor activities and well-appointed cabins, Topridge was a

Adelaide and Eleanor Close portrait by Pierre Tartoué

family favorite. The camp also served as a retreat for government officials hosted by Post.[62]

Looking at possible future uses for these estates, Post proposed that Mar-A-Lago become a place of respite for official foreign visitors to the United States government. For example, dignitaries could rest up at Mar-A-Lago for a few days before departing for formal meetings in Washington.[63] Post envisioned an educational use for Camp Topridge, which she also held from the 1920s until her death.[64] These two properties would eventually end up in private hands.

Post's other great estates before 1955 included the Boulders, in Greenwich, Connecticut; the Burden mansion, in Manhattan; Hogarcito, in Palm Beach, Florida; a triplex apartment at 2 East 92nd Street, also in Manhattan; Hillwood, in Roslyn, New York; and Tregaron, in Washington, D.C. She owned Hogarcito, her first Florida property, during the era of fantastic fancy dress balls in Palm Beach. Her triplex in New York marked her time as a leading philanthropist in the city and a member of café society.[65] Daughter Dina Merrill fondly remembered the triplex, recalling,

Adelaide Close (1908–1998)

Eleanor Close (1909–2006)

"I loved it there when I was little.... [The roof terrace] had a sandbox ... and I had a tricycle that I rode around in a circle."[66]

In addition to the above homes, Post resided and entertained at the U.S. embassy in Moscow from January 1937 to June 1938 and at the U.S. embassy in Brussels from July 1938 to November 1939. From time to time, there were also other temporary but grand places to call home, as her life required, such as well-appointed apartments in New York and Washington.

"My first interest in collecting was the decorative arts of eighteenth-century France," Post wrote in 1965.[67] After she purchased the Burden mansion in Manhattan, decorated by the firm of Jules Allard, its Louis XVI style led her to acquire French furniture from the art dealer Sir Joseph Duveen in 1921. She not only became a Duveen client, but also took advantage of his mentoring to develop a sense of taste and a collector's eye of her own. Her first love was for eighteenth-century French furniture, gold boxes, and Sèvres porcelain.[68] "If she liked something, she bought it. It was exciting to her," said granddaughter Ellen Charles.[69]

Post began her Russian collection in the late 1930s, while posted to Soviet-era Moscow. After making her first purchases there, she remained dedicated to building the collection over the next thirty years, acquiring important pieces and the bulk of her holdings through auctions in Western

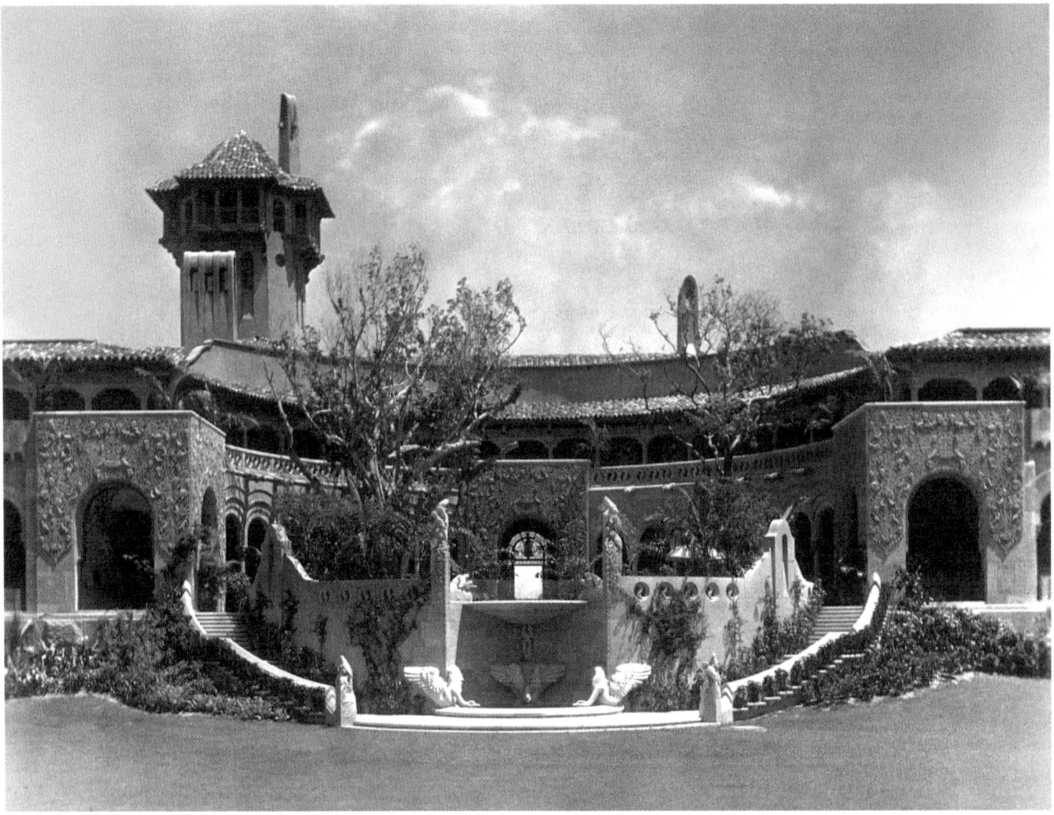

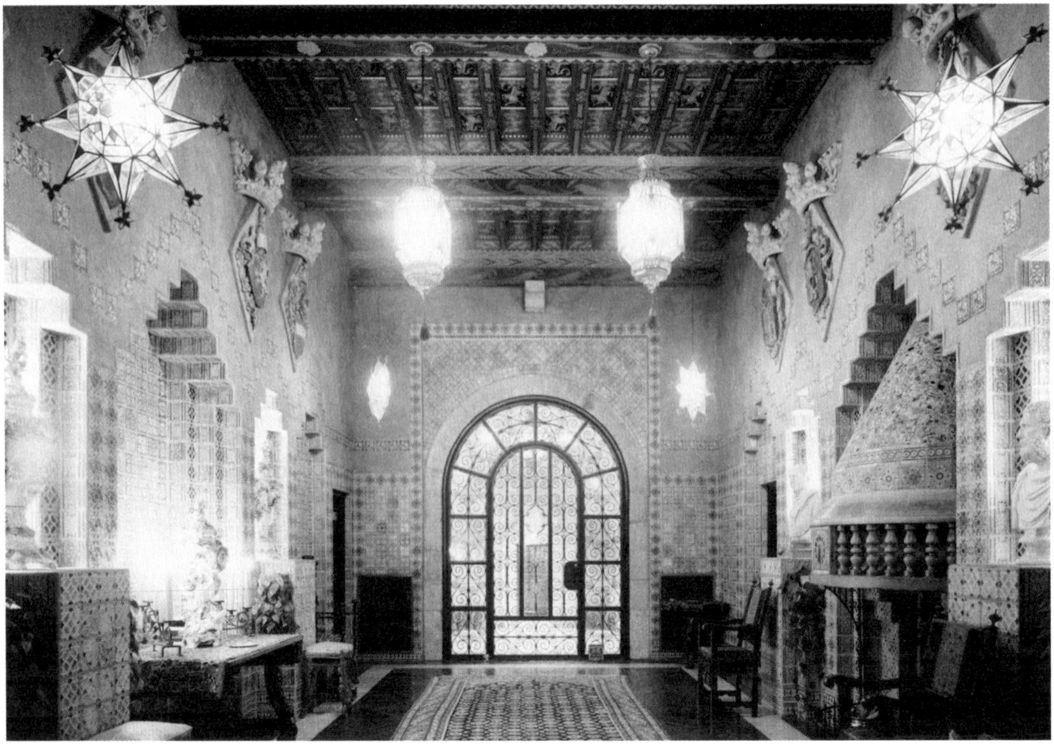

opposite
Mar-A-Lago,
Marjorie Post's Palm
Beach home, 1928;
entrance hall, 1967

Mar-A-Lago,
living room, 1967;
dining room, 1967

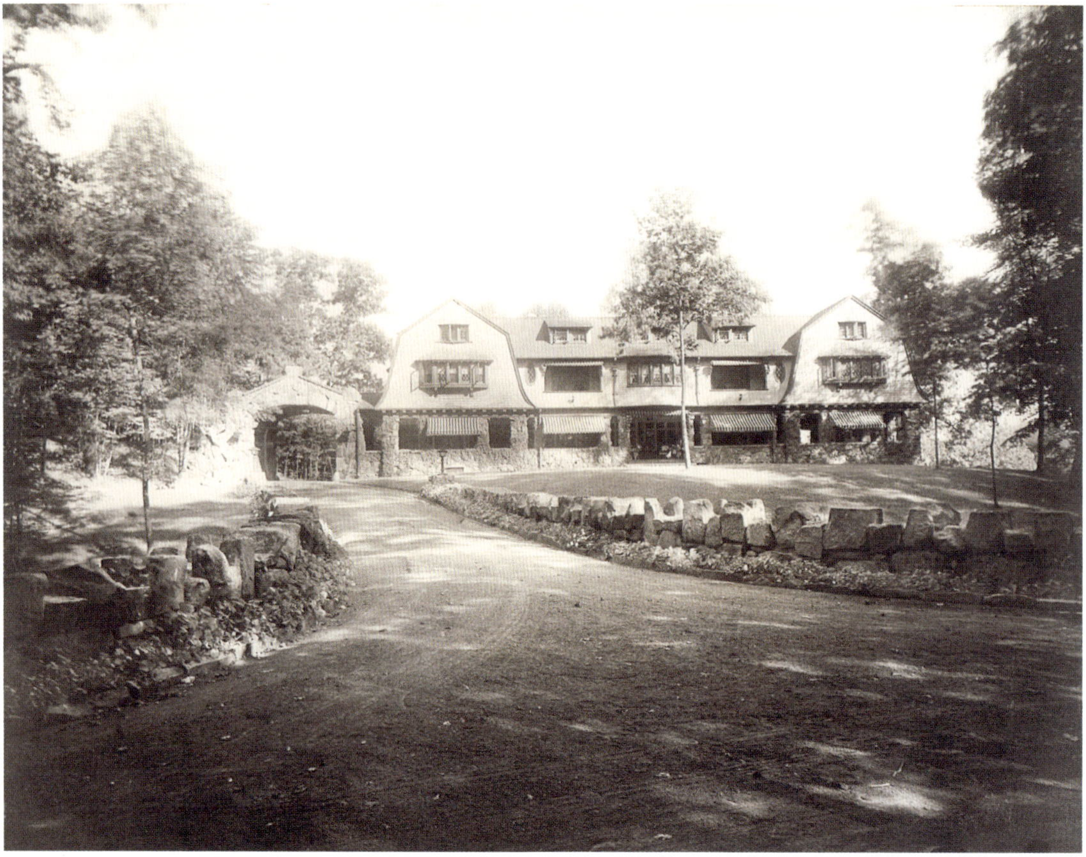

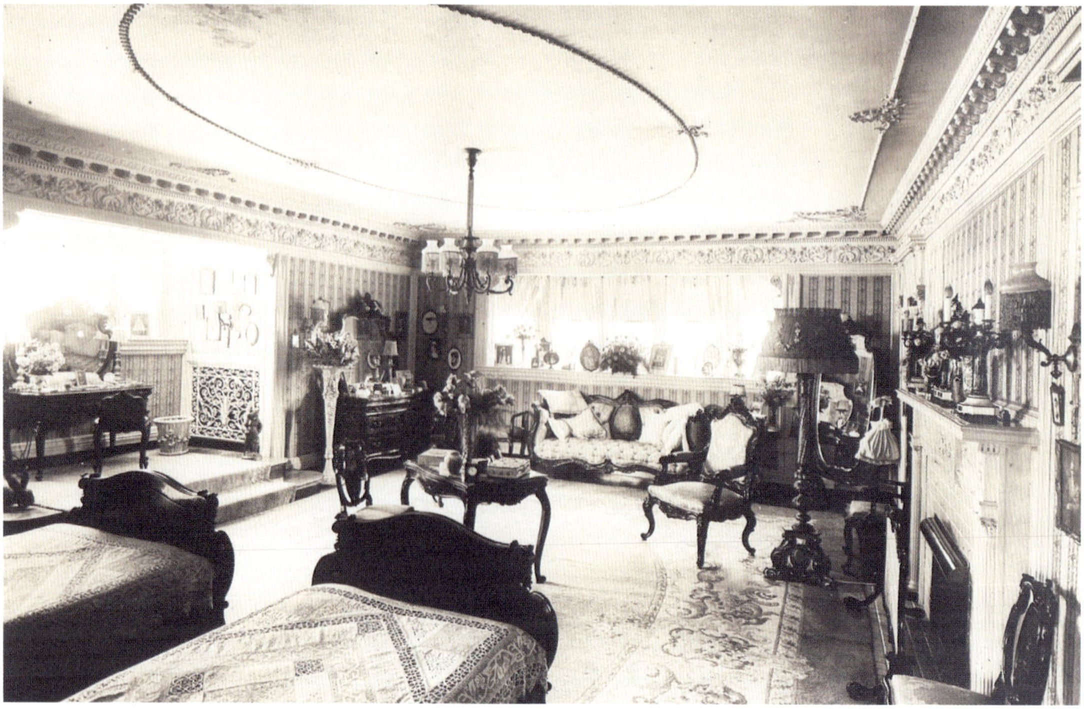

The Great Hall of Camp Topridge, Marjorie Post's home in the Adirondacks, near Lake Placid, New York

Europe and the United States.[70] Post did not originally set out to assemble a Russian collection. When she and husband Joseph Davies were *en poste* in Moscow, however, they were invited to Soviet-run commission shops, and at times, because of their diplomatic status, to the state storerooms.[71]

To fund industrialization, these Soviet shops were used to sell off Russian art and heritage objects commandeered from aristocrats and imperial palaces. By the time Post encountered the shops, they had been up and running for years, well-combed through by others.[72] Describing one of her experiences at a commission shop, Post recalled, "We found chalices looking like pewter—filthy dirty all pushed under a table. We were allowed to poke and dig…. Chalices—old, new, jeweled or not—were a ruble a gram, weighed on a feed store scale."[73] This was the start, Post said, "and since, I have continued the search."[74]

Over her five decades of collecting, Post amassed holdings of remarkable objects of beauty, superior craftsmanship, and historical association. She herself identified her main interests as "the art of eighteenth-century France and that of Imperial Russia—painting, porcelain, glass, jeweled articles, textiles and furniture."[75] By the mid-1950s, it became clear to Post

Hogarcito, Marjorie Post's home in Palm Beach, Florida

that this personal passion could become a philanthropic legacy in the form of a museum. Hillwood could be a historical document of a way of life. "I want young Americans to see how someone lived in the twentieth century and how this person could collect works of art the way I have," Post said. "I want to share this with the rest of the world. Maybe it'll be an incentive to some people. Maybe it won't, but at least they'll get a chance to see how I lived."[76]

Opening her homes for educational and charitable activities—parties with a purpose—or treating guests to a memorable long-weekend retreat brought Post "delight [and] real fulfillment," said columnist Betty Beale.[77]

Marjorie Post, as Marie Antoinette, on the steps of Hogarcito

Introduction: The Life Behind the Luxury

Triplex apartment

One dazzling aspect of Post's dinner parties at Hillwood was viewing her decorative arts collection, on display throughout the mansion and pieces of it also used for dining.[78] "Oh, yes, it was wonderful," said Clem Conger, a deputy chief of protocol at the White House who knew Post from presidential and state department functions. "[She hosted] dinners where everything was served on Sèvres porcelain."[79]

Post's guests often viewed her gatherings as flawless. Conger reminisced, "[At Hillwood] everything was right, always on the dot. It was like going to an embassy or the White House…. Oh, yes, it was perfect service…. Beautiful flowers you took for granted, superb gourmet meals you took for granted."[80] Of course, a closer look would reveal that not everything

Triplex apartment, breakfast room

was perfect. While things were generally managed well, at times household staff took advantage, occasionally pinching supplies and petty cash.[81] The owner of professional projection equipment, Post often showed first-run films to guests. One of her struggles later in life was with hearing loss, and to compensate she began to show the same films over and over, while her kind-hearted guests sat through multiple viewings.[82]

Post was of the same generation as Rose Kennedy. They knew each other socially, and Post's daughter Dina Merrill was close in age to Jacqueline Kennedy, Rose's daughter-in-law and first lady.[83] The inaugural committees for Presidents Roosevelt (1941), Truman (1949), Eisenhower (1953, 1957), Kennedy (1961), Johnson (1963), and Nixon (1969) all "requested the

Hillwood, Marjorie Post's home in Roslyn, New York

honor" of Post's presence at the ceremony and related events.[84] She also invited military service members to her homes. Among them were soldiers wounded in Vietnam and convalescing at the Walter Reed military hospital in Washington. They arrived in wheelchairs, on stretchers, and using crutches to enjoy a day of refreshments amid Hillwood's garden setting.[85]

Shortly after Post's death on September 12, 1973, she was recognized in the *Congressional Record* as a philanthropist and business executive who "derived particular joy out of her ability to give happiness to others."[86] She did so by tending to business, giving graciously, and indulging guests. Over her lifetime, as the chapters that follow detail, she prepared coffee substitute ingredients, knitted, rolled bandages, honored the aviatrix Amelia Earhart, fed the hungry, relocated 535 hand towels, and not only had a concert venue named in her honor, but a body of water as well. Also, she was portrayed in a Warner Brothers feature film. As granddaughter Ellen Charles recalled, Marjorie Merriweather Post "certainly enjoyed herself most of the time."[87]

Eros sculpture in the motor court, Hillwood, Washington, D.C.

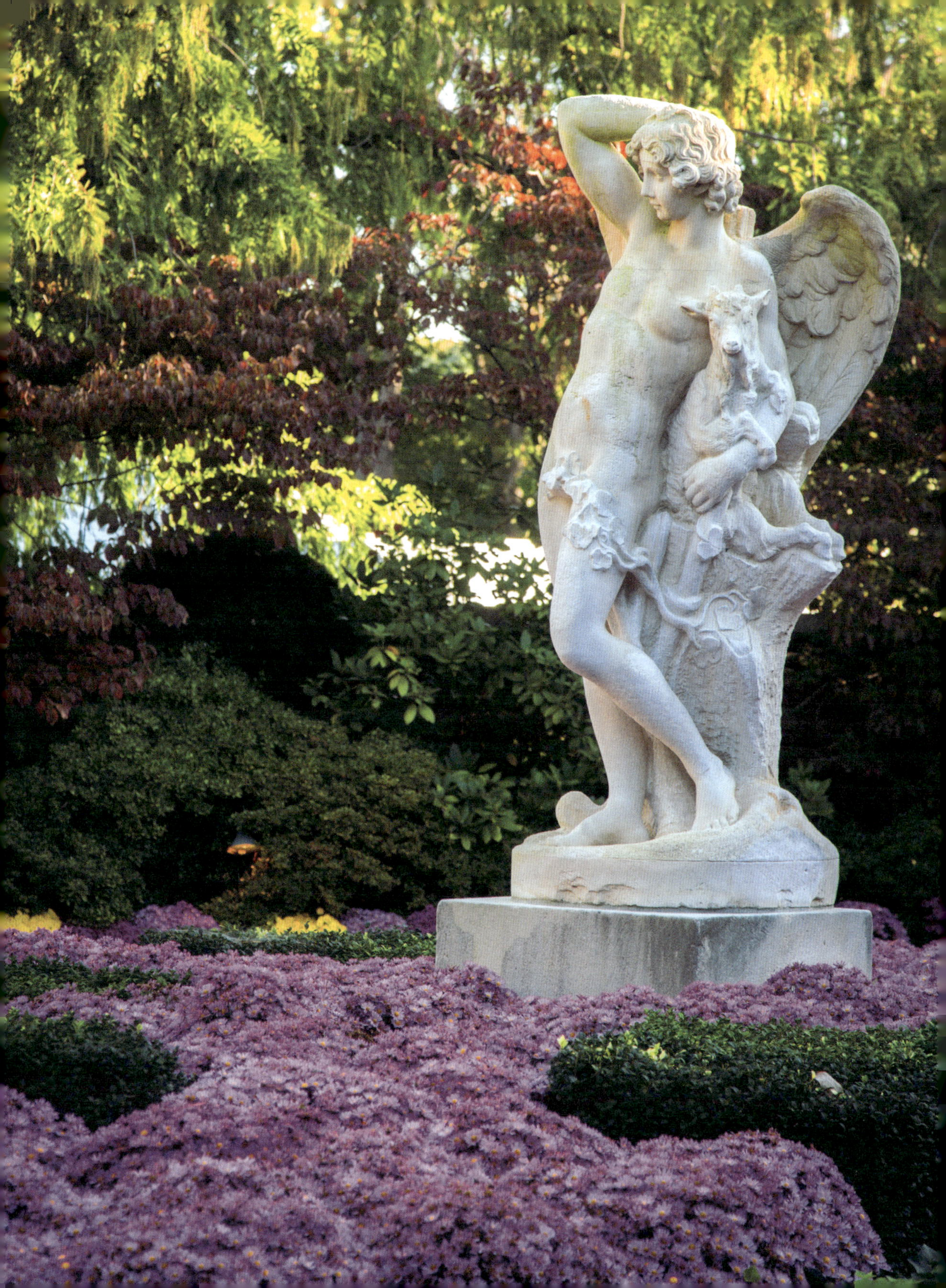

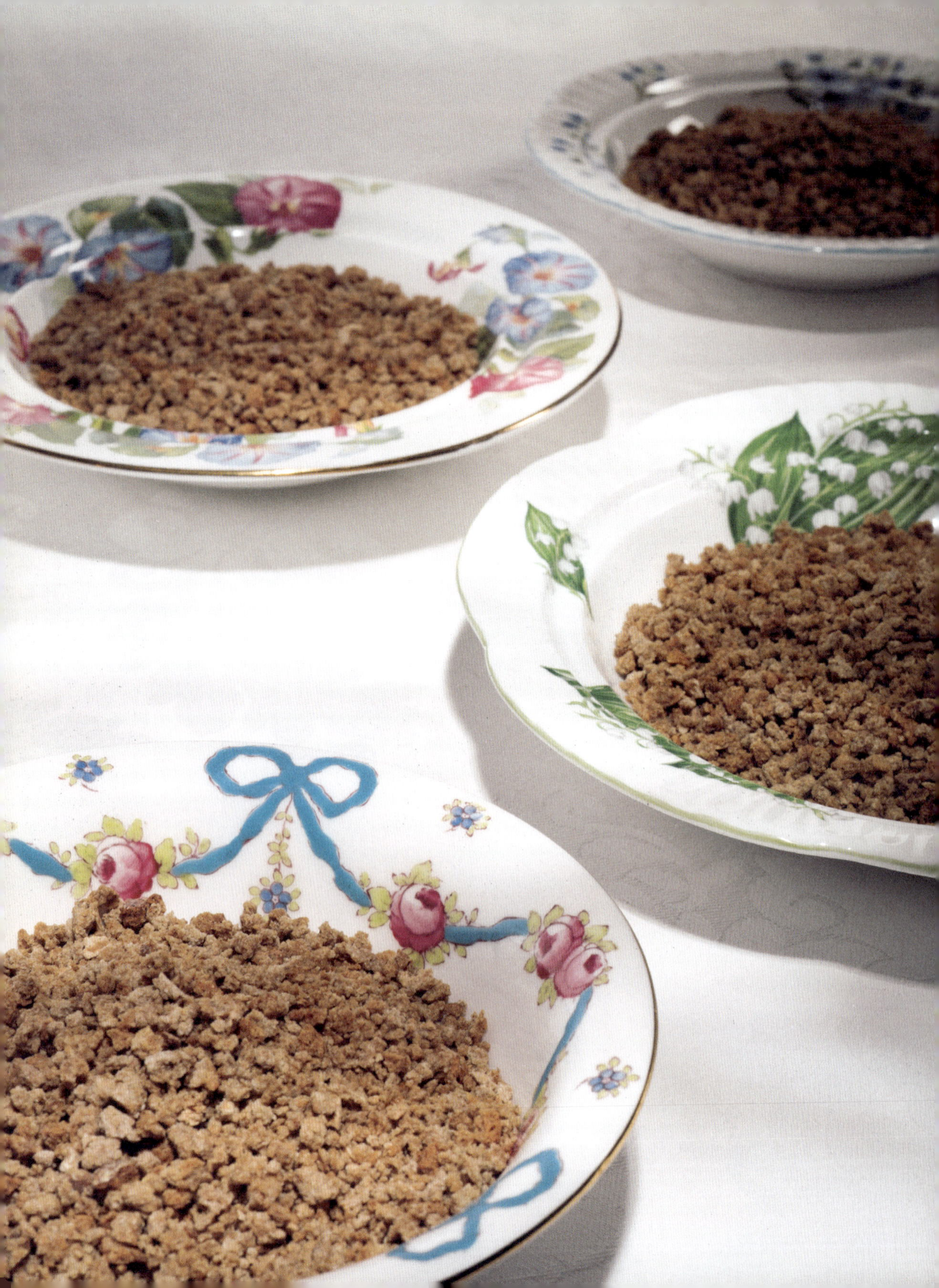

Business

"I knew the processes in our own company," Marjorie Post stated. "[It] was intended [that] I see how other companies handled their businesses, and so we would go through all sorts of factories."[1] She added, "First and foremost, this was Dad's idea of training me in his own business…. I must say I went with him all over the United States at one time or another, up to the time I was married."[2] Post believed that since she was an only child, her father likely realized, "The time might come when I would have to pick-up where he left off," and she noted, "That did happen."[3] After C.W. Post, the founder and advertising strategist for the Postum Cereal Company, took his own life in 1914, "Things became very active for me since I had to take over the many irons he had in the fire," Marjorie Post explained.[4]

In a sense, illness is what brought her father to start the business in the 1890s. Weak to the point of being wheelchair-bound, C.W. Post checked in at the Battle Creek Sanitarium, in Michigan, in 1891. Dr. John Harvey Kellogg offered healing diet options there, and the sanitarium presented talks and an atmosphere intended to boost well-being. C.W. Post's health did not improve, so his wife at the time, Ella Merriweather, took him to a consultation with Elizabeth Gregory, a Christian Science practitioner in Battle Creek. After listening to Gregory, C.W. Post insisted on remaining under her care. Within a few weeks, he had gained weight and had begun to walk again.

C.W. Post walked away from Gregory's care feeling inspired by the power of mind over matter and proper diet. By 1892, with money belonging to Ella Merriweather, he had established La Vita Inn, which hosted patient-guests and conducted research on nutritional foods for good health. In 1893, Ella Merriweather transferred all stock in the inn to their daughter, making six-year-old Marjorie Post the owner, with C.W. Post serving as trustee.

At La Vita, C.W. Post worked on a formula for a coffee substitute.[5] The recipe for what became Postum, consisting largely of wheat berries, bran, and molasses, was inspired "by what Dad saw when he was a cowboy as a young man out on the Western plains," recalled Marjorie Post.[6] When people

Marjorie Post's cereal bowls

Marjorie Merriweather Post

The First Cup of **POSTUM** is not always good, for cook fails to boil it long enough
Try again!

The Second Cup followed directions (easy) and secured a fascinating delicious coffee with the mild flavor and color of Java
Such Fun!

The Third Cup of **POSTUM** no more shaky nerves, dyspepsia, etc. from coffee
Can Eat and Sleep!

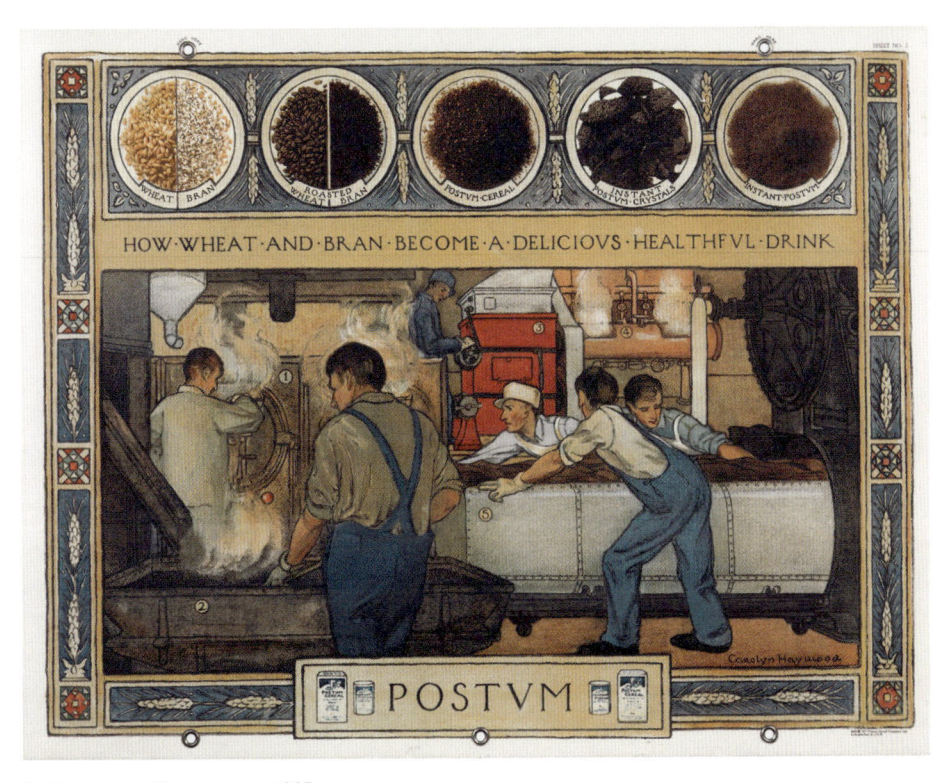

Postum production process, 1927

ran out of coffee, they roasted chicory or wheat to make a warm beverage. C.W. Post intended his version of the drink as a substitute for people who could not sleep after consuming coffee or could not stomach it at all.[7]

In the early days a barn was repurposed as the roasting room, and a hired helper nicknamed Shorty let the young Marjorie Post rake the ingredients in the fire. "I used to love to do that, it was fun as a child," Post reminisced. She would then go upstairs to "help glue things up." "Shorty did the roasting … then we had one girl upstairs doing the packaging, but it was no time at all before the number one factory was built," Post said.[8] Business records show that C.W. Post sold $5,000 worth of his coffee substitute in 1895. One year later, the growth in sales made it worth measuring income by the month, with Postum bringing in $6,000 in October.[9] By 1897, the operation employed 450 people.[10]

C.W. Post introduced and promoted Postum by initially advertising in a targeted area and making it available at local stores, sometimes having to convince retailers to carry it on consignment. After the product gained

Advertisement for coffee substitute Postum

America's Foremost Ready-To-Eat Cereal

Grape=Nuts

REGISTERED IN UNITED STATES PATENT OFFICE.

Made of Wheat, Corn and Barley.

MANUFACTURED BY

Postum Cereal Company, Battle Creek, Mich., U.S.A.

A FOOD

Containing the natural nutritive elements of Wheat, Corn and Barley thoroughly cooked by scientific baking.

ECONOMY

Four heaping teaspoonfuls of GRAPE=NUTS for the cereal part of a meal is sufficient for an ordinary person. More may be used if desired.

"THERE'S A REASON"

When war called for the saving of wheat, Grape=Nuts stood ready with its superb blend of cereals, its wonderful flavor, fullest nourishment, and practical economy.

Grape=Nuts
The Food For The Times

Evils of Coffee, Tobacco and Alcohol (1913), an entry in a national competition held by C.W. Post

momentum, he would move on to another area and repeat the process.[11] Even when the business had grown to warrant an executive management team, which C.W. Post called the Cabinet, advertisements still had to go through him for approval. He adopted the slogan "There's a Reason" to convey to consumers the usefulness, health benefits, and convenience of the Postum Cereal Company's products.[12]

C.W. Post would leave "word that the minute I was home from school, I was to come to the office, and I would be pushed over into a corner to listen, and then after the conference was over, he would ask me if I had understood what it was all about," Marjorie Post said. "[If I didn't] … it would be diagramed for me, as to the whys and ways of merchandising, [and] advertising methods." She further explained, "So far as the products were concerned, I was as familiar with them as he." Marjorie Post also noted, "I was always taken on many of the business trips, but I could not make the trip if I did not make my grades … so the books would go along with me."[13]

Grape-Nuts, the food for the times, 1918

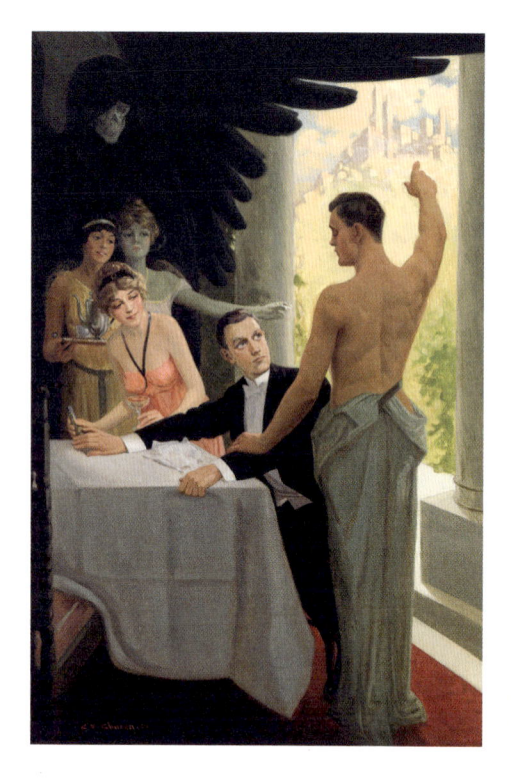

Evils of Coffee, Alcohol and Tobacco, by Charles F. Church (1913), Third Place winner, national competition held by C.W. Post

By 1907, the factory, grounds, and main office building of Postum Cereal Company in Battle Creek were welcoming visitors to take tours of the facility. A message painted in large letters on the side of one of the buildings read: "Visitors shown through works and offices with pleasure, enquire for guide at main office." The offices were decorated with works of art, and the grounds were landscaped, blending aesthetics and business, indoors and out. By 1914, the general public was familiar with and buying Postum, Instant Postum, Post Toasties cereal, and Grape-Nuts in substantial quantities.[14]

To assist workers, the Postum Cereal Company built the Post Addition, a housing development covering some five miles of streets. Homes in the Post Addition were available for monthly payments of 1/100th the purchase price. Under those terms, a $1,500 home would require a $15 monthly payment. A company brochure boasted that workers paid "a sum no greater than a good rental … [and] 81% of Postum employees own their homes and good ones."[15] On the matter of financial health, C.W. Post told the Postum workforce in 1906, "[Those] who work with their hands, faithfully, and have not had opportunity to train their minds in the ways of making money, should have honest help." He urged staff to save and grow the 5 and 10 percent

POSTUM ROASTING ROOM
One of two rooms of great capacity in which the wheat used in Postum is roasted, ground and blended.

Postum Cereal Company, roasting room, Battle Creek, Michigan

bonuses they earned, adding his endorsement of a "board of advisors established by our workmen to help any employee decide on safe investments." The bonuses were awarded weekly and deposited into a bank account accruing 4% interest. The employee received the bankbook at the end of the year. C.W. Post declared, after promoting homeownership among his employees, "Next, I want to see every one become a combined workman and capitalist."[16]

At the management level, the Cabinet that C.W. Post directed consisted of a vice chairman, treasurer, secretary, superintendent, sales manager, advertising manager, counsel, and head of the paper box company.[17] One

> INSTANT POSTUM FILLING MACHINE
> Each of these machines fills a tin of Instant Postum every three seconds and brushes off any extra powder on the tin.

A tin of Instant Postum filled every three seconds

of his memos addressed "to the cabinet" read, "I have for a long time been under a growing impression that the bread cutting machine is seriously detrimental to our best interests."[18] What followed were details on how to troubleshoot the matter, how long to try out the new solution, and how to make the workspaces more comfortable for the bakers. In another instance, Post wanted a manager who showed favoritism to particular employees to be told "his failing and insist that he correct it … [but also that] we esteem

Postum Cereal Company, administrative offices

[him] very highly for his [otherwise] very valuable traits." The memo closed, "I trust these instructions will be put in force promptly."[19]

The role of the Cabinet was to deal with day-to-day operations of the company and thereby enable C.W. Post to address other matters, such as unions and their impact.[20] Marjorie Post recalled, "We had an open shop all during my father's life, and it was many years after he died that they finally unionized," adding that Postum offered the highest wages in Michigan, along with housing and health-care benefits and bonuses.[21]

Although Postum's shop remained open, C.W. Post was keenly aware of the power of labor unions and closely observed their ability to shut down works through strikes, lockouts, and destruction of equipment. He knew of plans for a shutdown of Postum in 1905 and of a boycott in 1906.[22] He wrote in 1907, "I do not object to organizations of labor, when they are conducted peaceably and according to law and common sense."[23] He was nationally known for being vocal on the subject, writing pieces for trade publications and printing pamphlets to present his views. "Real workmen like peace and 52 pay envelopes in a year," he asserted. "That keeps [the]

Marjorie Merriweather Post

PRIVATE OFFICE OF C. W. POST

A BLENDING OF ART AND COMMERCE

family out of debt and the children in school."²⁴ To employees, he said, "We are attacked at times by people seeking to wreck us," adding, "They have aimed directly at your bread and butter."²⁵

On May 9, 1914, a telegram arrived for Marjorie Post, addressed to her as Mrs. E.B. Close, at the Boulders, her estate in Greenwich, Connecticut. It read, "Your father died suddenly at ten this morning."²⁶ That day and for several to come, newspapers from New York to San Francisco reported on C.W.'s death and the cause of it: "C.W. Post—Breakfast Food Millionaire—Takes Own Life," "Charles W. Post of Cereal Foods Fame Shoots Self," and so on.²⁷ He died in his Santa Barbara, California, home, which he shared with his second wife, Leila Post. Recovering from an appendicitis operation, he sharply shifted from a state of despair, to good cheer, and back to anguish.²⁸

The *Kalamazoo Progressive Herald* ruminated on C.W. Post as a person "having everything in this world of a material nature that money can buy," proclaiming his death by suicide "beyond comprehension."²⁹ The *Virginian*

Postum Cereal Company, administrative offices, blending art and commerce

Marjorie Merriweather Post

The Post Addition, housing development for Postum employees, 81 percent of whom owned their home

Postum Cereal company personnel

C.W. Post

opined, "[For a] tireless worker … a shattered constitution was the price."[30] The *Battle Creek Journal* reported that the passing of its city's "most highly esteemed citizen … [casts] a pall of gloom over the entire community."[31] Looking back fifty years after losing him, Marjorie Post simply stated, "I was beside myself."[32]

A second telegram on the same day to Marjorie Post read, "[Leila] leaves [Santa Barbara] with remains for Battle Creek at once."[33] Marjorie Post thought it would be fitting for the Cabinet members to be the pallbearers and for heliotrope ribbon and flowers to be placed on portraits of C.W. Post and the doors of the business offices while closed for mourning.[34] Leila Post agreed and finalized matters.

On the day of the funeral, May 14, 1914, syndicated reports noted, "Every store in the city was closed, street cars stopped running, [and] factories shut down."[35] In tribute, Postum Cereal Company employees, standing eight deep,

C.W. Post's monogrammed porcelain, Royal Doulton and Company

flanked both sides of the entrance to the Independent Congregational Church. They sent a flower arrangement shaped like the white barn, repurposed as the roasting room, where Shorty and the young Marjorie Post raked Postum ingredients.[36] People from industry and elsewhere sent bountiful arrangements of sweet peas, lily of the valley, orchids, and magnolia. For her beloved Dada, Marjorie Post ordered an arrangement of roses circulating a broken column of pink carnations from the Fleischman Floral Company, Chicago.[37]

    Reverend Roswell Post, a relative, addressed the mourners, saying, "There is no human who can play Atlas to the world … to uphold the many enterprises … the minutest details…. His genius was his undoing."[38] C.W. Post's parents, Charles Rollin Post and Caroline Lathrop Post, wrote to a relative that day, "We would not have chosen the way that our dear Charles was permitted to take in order to get out [of] the poor suffering human body, and we would not have wished him to live on with that disordered mind." They also made note of "his awful load of this world's burdens all left behind for others to carry."[39]

C.W. Post's will went into probate in the same month as his passing. Newspapers announced that he had left half of the Battle Creek company to daughter Marjorie Post and the other half to wife Leila Post.[40] Regarding shares of common stock in the Postum Cereal Company, the will stated, "I give, bequeath, and devise in equal shares to my wife ... and to my daughter."[41] Yet, resolution of ownership of the business would take more than a year and a half. "Post millions seems likely to cause a fight," one paper reported.[42] Meanwhile, assertions to the contrary on behalf of Leila Post and Marjorie Post included statements of "no sensational situation to arise" and "the suit in question is a friendly one."[43]

The *Grand Rapids Herald* reported that Marjorie Post had initiated the suit to establish title to Postum Cereal Company.[44] According to the *Detroit Free Press*, however, the State of Michigan had brought the suit to collect inheritance tax and in the process had uncovered a statement of interest made by C.W. Post in bankruptcy court. It reported that C.W. Post had told the court that Ella Post, his first wife and Marjorie's mother, had provided $750 that was then put under daughter Marjorie Post's name. Acting as Marjorie Post's agent, he then used that $750 to build the Postum Cereal Company. The *Free Press* summarized, "This has never been corrected, according to the record," which therefore made Marjorie Post, at the age of twenty-eight, the sole owner of the Postum Cereal Company in December 1915.[45] In short, in the eyes of the law, the Battle Creek cereal business was built as a subsidiary of La Vita Inn, which was owned by Marjorie Post, with her father growing the business as her trustee. Thus, she had owned the company from age six.[46]

As settlement, Leila Post received $6,000,000, the *New York Times* reported. Newspapers followed the story from Hamilton, North Dakota, to Nashville, Tennessee, and from Waterbury, Connecticut, to San Francisco, California.[47] The *Times* noted that Leila Post's concerns were "not over the money, for she had been left an abundance of that ... but of the constant rumors of trouble."[48] Still, dramatic headlines announced the closure of the matter, among them "Widow Sells Out" and "Mrs. Post Ends Estate Battle."[49]

Regarding the workers at Postum, Marjorie Post stated, "Their devotion to [my father] was something unbelievable." In addition to being dynamic, she said, he also had a "humanitarian something.... He was interested in their problems."[50] She knew most of the long-standing employees by

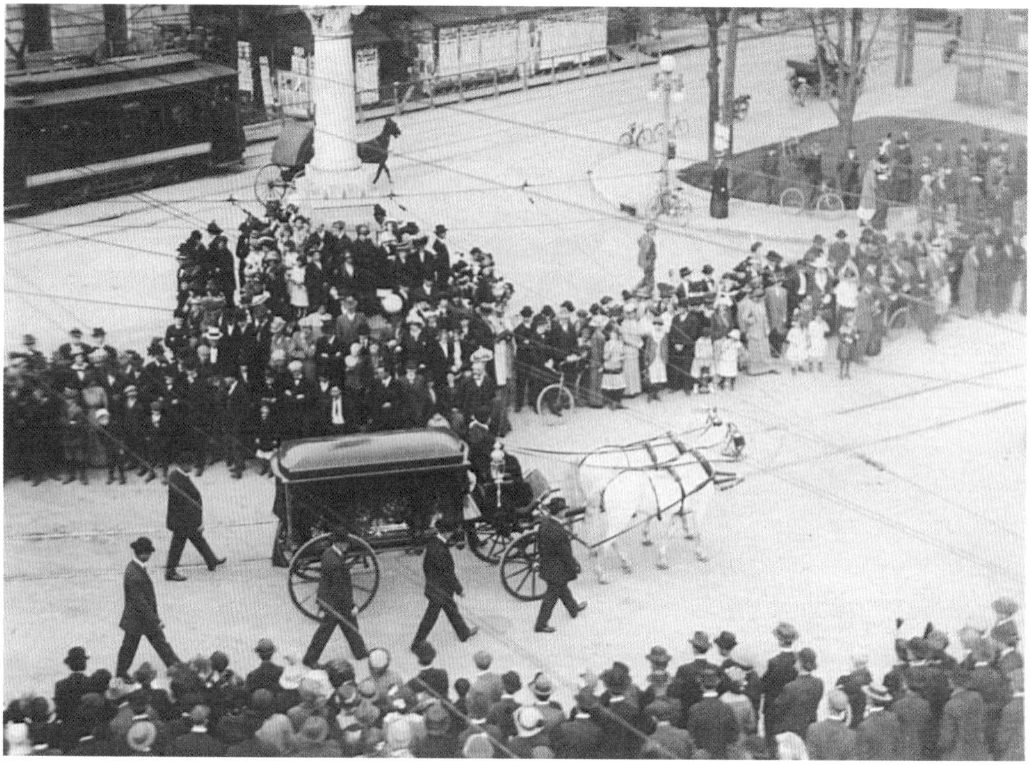

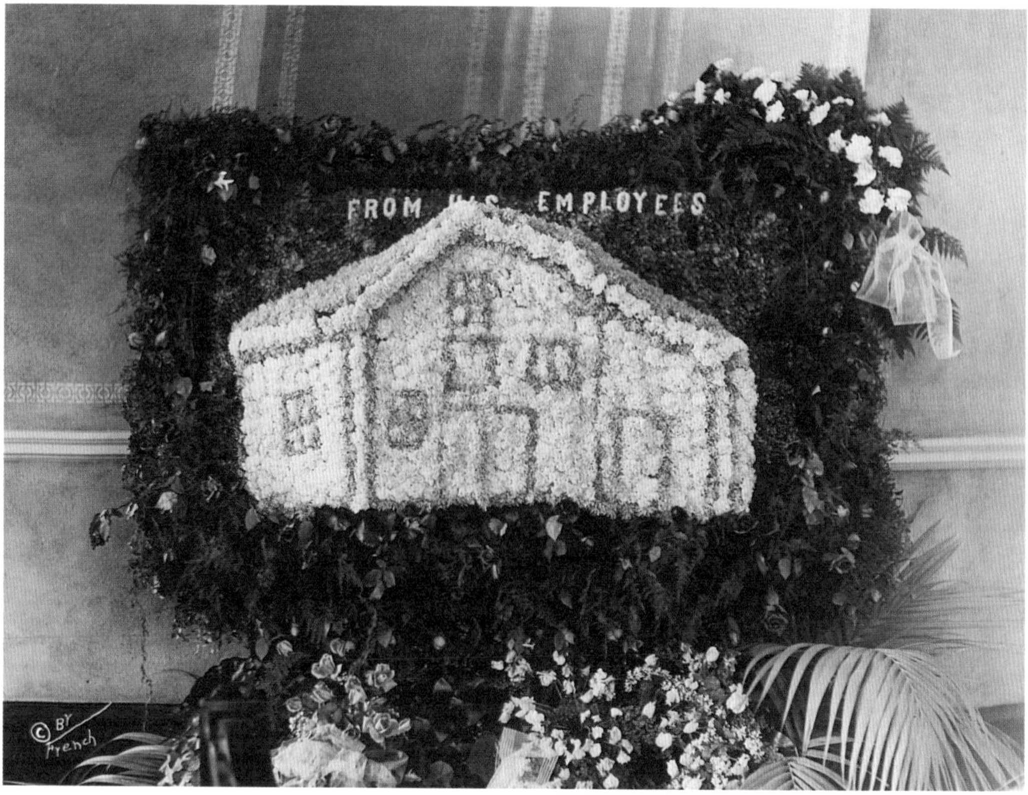
FROM
EMPLOYEES
© BY French

Business

C.W. Post's funeral,
May 14, 1914, Battle Creek

Marjorie Merriweather Post

C.W. Post's funeral, a broken column of pink carnations from Marjorie Post; a floral pillow from Adelaide and Eleanor Close, 1914

name.[51] "Ah, all the [workers'] family problems," she remembered. "They were brought to me after he died, and I must say I suffered with them."[52]

In terms of the company itself, due to shortages, with the government using corn flour as a substitute for wheat during World War I, palatable alternatives had to be found to keep the business running.[53] In addition, the managerial Cabinet loomed on Marjorie Post's mind, now that her father was no longer directing it, and it was understood that running the cereal business was not of interest to—or the right occupation for—her husband Edward Bennett Close, who was trained in law and had wartime duties. In the early 1900s, it would have been assumed that her husband would or could have a strong hand in her family's business.

"Very shortly after our marriage [in 1905], Ed who had graduated from law school, decided to go on my father's advice into the Postum plant to learn the business," Post recalled.[54] At that time, the couple lived on Maple Street in Battle Creek and took summer breaks at the Boulders in Greenwich, Connecticut. "But Ed decided he was going back into law, which he did, so that kept us in the vicinity of New York," she explained.[55] After C.W. Post's death, both Marjorie Post and Edward Bennett Close attended to business affairs in Battle Creek, traveling to and from New York from the time of the funeral into 1916.[56] Then, as *Fortune* magazine put it, in 1919 Marjorie Post "suddenly became an active volcano."[57] Post divorced Close, ending an unhappy marriage that had further deteriorated after Close's military service.[58] Four years after assuming ownership of the Postum Cereal Company, she brought in Colby Chester to serve as assistant treasurer. Schooled at Yale, and considered competent and trustworthy, Chester would grow into the role of company president.[59]

Post knew that her father had had plans for expanding the business. "Shortly before my father died, he had been talking about joining with other companies," she recalled.[60] The basic concept C.W. Post shared with his daughter was to buy products that were already available to the public and doing well.[61] Wartime, with World War I's demand on supplies and command of the nation's attention into late 1918, was not the right moment to implement such a plan. With the war over, however, the moment came to expand. Moreover, Post, with her marriage in July 1920 to Edward F. Hutton, head of the brokerage firm E.F. Hutton & Company, now had a spouse interested in the family business and finance at large.[62]

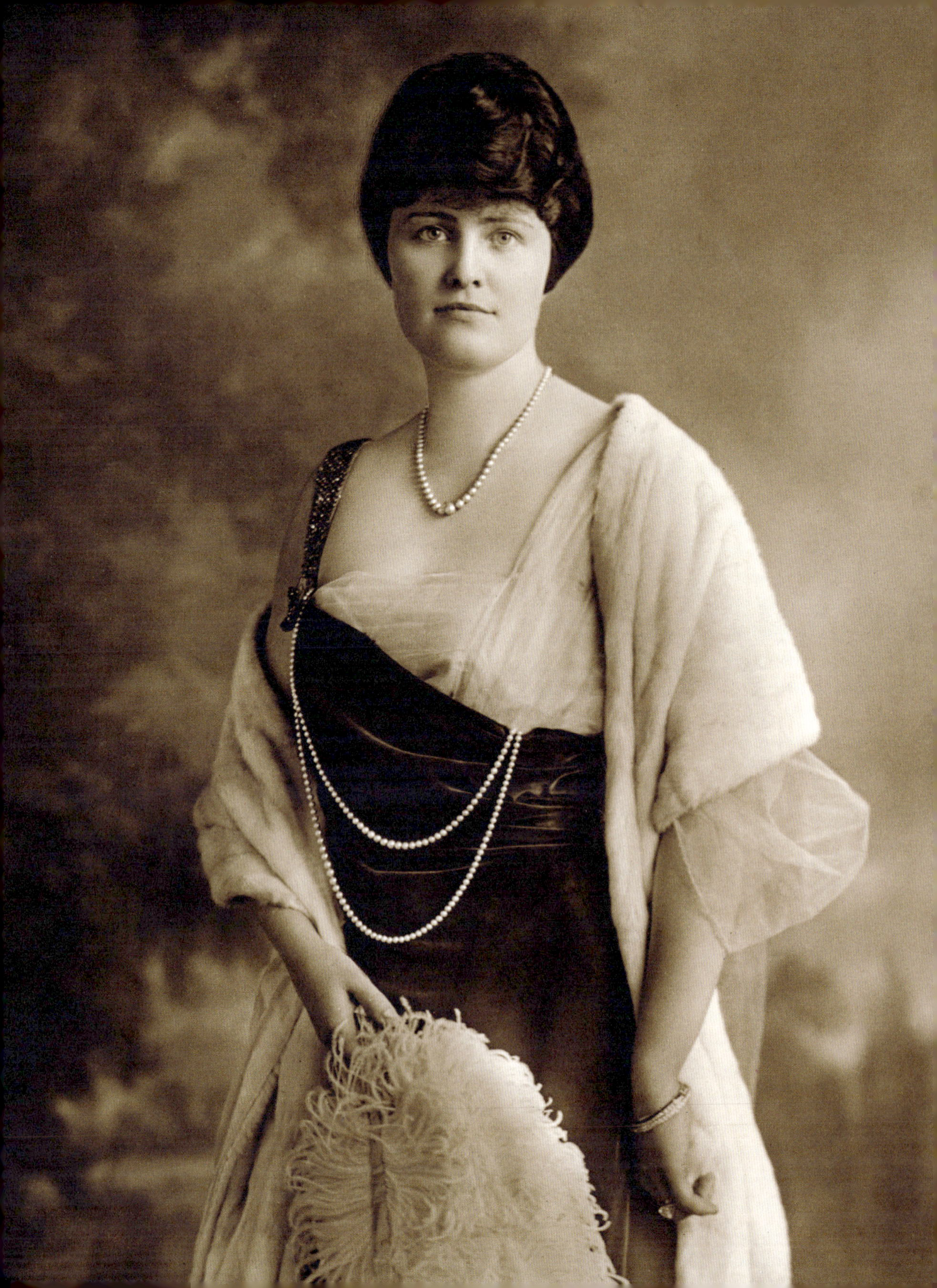

Business

Postum Cereal Company executives, 1916

Postum Cereal Company Incorporated stock appeared on the New York Stock Exchange in 1922, with the business showing over $17 million dollars in sales, and over $2 million dollars in profits for 1921.[63] "He didn't like stockholders telling him what to do, but ... he wanted it listed on the exchange," explained Post, regarding her father's thinking. "He made some chit-chat with some bankers, but it was after I married Mr. Hutton that it did get on the exchange."[64] The company's corn mill, able to grind fifteen thousand bushels of corn per day, became one of the largest in the nation. The plant in Battle Creek encompassed 18 acres, 33 buildings, and 25 grain tanks. Meanwhile, the Canadian plant, making products for the United Kingdom, added six buildings and four storage tanks to the total. While nearly mortgage-free, the company disclosed one debt—$4,300 for an undeveloped piece of land. The company's signature products—Postum, Grape-Nuts, Post Toasties, and Instant Postum—were deeded "firmly established and of proved earning capacity."[65]

E.F. Hutton had become chairman of the board by 1923, and Colby Chester the company's president by 1924.[66] "We decided that we might look around and see whether it might be a good idea to broaden our base," said Marjorie Post.[67] The company purchased Jell-O in 1925. "It was the first thing we bought, and it's been a very, very satisfactory business," she declared.[68]

The Postum Cereal Company's acquisition of products already successful on the market was notable, as was the concept for their distribution.[69] Marjorie Post and E.F. Hutton's daughter, Dina Merrill, recalled, "Colby Chester and daddy decided that they should take advantage of the distribution system that the cereal people had."[70] Each product kept its name and consumer identity.[71] By 1928, Swans Down Cake Flour, Minute Tapioca, Walter Baker's Chocolate, Log Cabin Syrup, and Maxwell House Coffee had all become part of the business.[72] "[Maxwell House Coffee] nearly finished me off," Post said. "I had been raised with the idea that coffee was just like taking dope, so I nearly died at the thought of buying a coffee company, and we paid $45 million for it!"[73] With a wry sense of humor, Post continued, "Well, it wasn't too long after that we also bought Sanka, so we had utter purity [caffeine-free Postum], we have half-dose [Sanka], and the works, Maxwell House."[74]

In July 1929, Postum stockholders approved the purchase of Frosted Foods, just before the great stock market crash in October of that year.

Mark Kurlansky, the author of *Birdseye: The Adventures of a Curious Man* (2012), found that the $23.5 million purchase of Frosted Foods also included patents. As Kurlansky analyzed the business deal and available documentation, he came across various iterations of a well-recounted tale of Marjorie Post and a Birds Eye frozen goose that he found problematic.[75]

In brief, the business legend as told in many publications suggested that in the mid-1920s Marjorie Post and E.F. Hutton had eaten and enjoyed a Birds Eye frozen goose aboard their yacht.[76] Post was so impressed with the taste and technology that she pestered her husband about purchasing the business.[77] As Kurlansky observes, there are not only problems in the details of the story, but it also paints Marjorie Post as "self-indulgent" and acting "on a whim."[78] Rather, Kurlansky saw a story about Post and Hutton brokering the deal and finding the funds to pay for it.[79] Likely, the business acumen of Colby Chester, who worked closely with Post and Hutton, also played a part in reaching an agreement.[80]

In 1929, after the Frosted Foods purchase, the Postum Cereal Company became the General Foods Corporation.[81] By 1936, *Barron's* newspaper was reporting on the public's acceptance of frozen foods, with the availability of more effective and lower-cost cold storage equipment, noting the substantial use and business generated through large food service venues, such as medical care facilities, cruise ships, and passenger trains.[82] Three decades later, General Foods chairman Charles Mortimer noted, "Marjorie had the most wonderful and instinctive way of putting her finger on an opportunity … showing how astute [she] is, in my opinion, to be able to recognize, even before the case is proven, what can be an excellent commercial opportunity."[83]

At General Foods' annual stockholders meeting in April 1936, Post was elected as a director. "A woman who is thoroughly schooled in the traditions of business has become a director of General Foods Corporation," declared one newspaper, noting that Post had been looking after the business since 1914, through various phases of its development.[84] Furthermore, since General Foods counted more than 30,000 women shareholders, the article marveled, "It is only appropriate and fitting that a woman represent their viewpoint on the board."[85] Post's high profile, combined with the announcement of Natalie J. Van Vleck becoming a director at the Colgate-Palmolive-Peet Company, generated buzz about "the gals beginning to

Marjorie Merriweather Post

When the heat of Summer weather
Makes you wonder what to eat,
Polly says, "We'll have **Post Toasties**
And enjoy **a Royal Treat.**"

Business

Grape-Nuts Stereo 383–385.
6 in. across 2 cols. wk. end. Oct. 14/05.

Re-building a Brain

Only can be done by Food which contains Phosphate of Potash and Albumen.

That is nature's way and the only way.

That is the Mission of

Grape=Nuts

Note the users of **Grape-Nuts**. They are brainy, nervy, clever people. Keen brains make money, fame and success.

They **must** be fed.

opposite
Post Toasties, 1913

Grape-Nuts, 1905

Marjorie Post's dressing room suite, also used as her home office, 1970s

inch their way into big business."[86] Both women were large stockholders.[87] Announcements noted that Post and Hutton had divorced in September 1935, but that Hutton, no longer chairman, was also elected as a director at the April 1936 meeting. Reports at the time of Post's election to the board also mentioned that more than 1,200 retail stores now carried Birds Eye Frosted Foods and that stockholders had approved a profit incentive program for employees.[88]

By 1940, General Foods had been producing products on the market for forty to fifty years, yet it could not rest on its laurels due to competition for consumers by the National Biscuit Company and General Mills.[89] For Marjorie Post, her company's earlier products had a "sentimental and a nostalgic value to her life history." Charles Mortimer explained, "She has always been very keen about Grape-Nuts and the original products…. Birds Eye has been one of her pets."[90]

Furthering company tradition, in December 1941 the Battle Creek operation, plus eleven other U.S. locations, acknowledged employees. That year,

MENU

Gelatin Mould with Crab Meat

Filet of Beef

Dutchess Potatoes

Artichoke Bottom with Puree of Peas

Mushroom — Asparagus

Salad — Cheese Tray

Vanilla Ice Cream — Strawberries

Cookies

Pommard 1955

HILLWOOD
April 29, 1962

Hillwood menu, including a savory gelatin with crab meat, 1962

a meal in their honor featured the company's products, with a Birds Eye turkey as the main course. In Battle Creek, 222 employees received recognition for fifteen years of service, 176 workers for twenty years, and 94 for twenty-five years with the company.[91] With nearly thirty years of service in various roles since December 1915, Post as a director held the most shares of common stock. She held more than 281,000 shares in 1945, while the next closest General Foods director had just over 33,000 shares.[92]

As for stock ownership, a 1945 study conducted by Harvard University's Graduate School of Business Administration included a statement by an unidentified director of General Foods. The director told Harvard that stock ownership was not the only requirement of directorship, also citing "obligation for service…, sense of business ethics and public responsibility…, plus long-range foresight as distinguished from dependence on expediency" as key qualities in leadership. "Shrewd," is how Charles Mortimer, by then a former chairman of General Foods, described Post. "[She called] the shots in respect to the company when she had a great interest." He recalled Post inviting him to her New York apartment for lunch. "It turned out that what she wanted to do was to tell me first-hand her particular ethics…. [That is,] the company never cut corners … for a quick buck…. [We were not to] lose sight of certain values." Post maintained her strong interest in succession planning, installing the right leaders at the helm of the business, maintaining integrity, quality control, and the original Postum line, while also developing new products.[93]

Post's work with General Foods, and her role as ambassadress in Moscow in 1937 and 1938, eventually led to unwanted attention in 1949. A group contacted General Foods to say that they planned to protest Post becoming a director given her "friendly communistic activities."[94] Post provided a statement to General Foods about the directive that President Franklin Roosevelt had given her and her husband, Ambassador Joseph Davies, "to build friendly relations between the two countries." In the end, however, it was Post's role as honorary chairman of the Women's Committee that was the concern. The committee consisted of a group of American and Soviet women, with "the idea of having a better understanding of the two countries which would further the project of peace."[95] Post directed General Foods to share with the protesters her resignation from the Women's Committee, which specifically addressed their point of contention.[96]

MENU

Caviar and Blinis

Roast Butter Ball Turkey
Chestnut Dressing   Lingonberry Sauce
Sweet Potatoes Marshmallow
Vegetable Jardiniere

Mixed Green Garden Salad
Brie

Apple Jello Ring with Assorted Fruit
Filled with Balls of Strawberry
Sherbert

Cup Cake   Cookies

Vodka
Chassagne Montrachet 1953
Moet Chandon Dom Perignon 1952

HILLWOOD
October 17, 1963

Hillwood menu with apple "Jello", 1963

Meanwhile, the corporation promoted itself by publicizing new ways to use General Foods products, such as distributing dessert recipe pamphlets like "Miracles with Minute Tapioca," involving puddings, pies, and tarts. For pies, "the miracle is plenty of luscious juice kept where it belongs by Minute Tapioca magic," explained one pamphlet from 1948.[97] With illustrations of mountains on the cover, a 1949 guide on how to use Swans Down Cake Flour suggested ways to bake "tender, feathery-moist" cakes when the kitchen is 5,000 feet above sea level.[98] Among its many other pamphlet offerings, General Foods provided a 1952 "guidebook to chocolate cookery" using Baker's chocolate.[99]

After a visit to the Battle Creek plant in 1953, including two hours touring and inspecting the Sugar Crisp and Post Toasties operation, and another two hours in the Postum and Grape-Nuts facilities, Post remarked, "[It is] interesting to me that we are making many of those machines in our own plant again.... This is the type of thing we did so much of in years past ... as there were no machines on the market that would in any way fit our requirements."[100] Regarding a 1957 gourmet line of foods, she frankly stated, "The ham is not worth being brought into this country.... We have much better ham, more tasty and attractive, right here, so why bother."[101]

Dina Merrill and Cliff Robertson's wedding meal, Hillwood, 1966

Business

Marjorie Post's breakfasts included Post cereals; a favorite breakfast service, by Shelley Potteries, England

Weighing the other side of the coin, she added, "Certainly, the other items [in the gourmet line are] very different and very interesting, to my mind."[102]

General Foods products were regularly served in Post's homes. She had Grape-Nuts and other Post cereals for breakfast, preferring the assortment packaged in little boxes.[103] With quality control on her mind, when a box of Sugar Crisp cereal arrived stale, she sent it to the research manager at General Foods.[104] The same went for unsatisfactory packets of Maxwell House. She returned them to General Foods with the directive, "You better give them to the man in charge of this particular division so he can find out what on earth has happened.... I would be interested in knowing [the conclusions]."[105] The response: the problem had been caused by a packaging subcontractor no longer in service to the corporation. General Foods had since installed equipment to package its products itself.[106]

Post's household staff prepared Postum, Sanka, and Maxwell House for guests, often presenting the beverages in exquisite coffee services and cups from her decorative arts collection. Those having lunch with Post at Hillwood might find themselves serving as taste testers for a new or experimental flavor of Jell-O or a General Foods International Coffee.[107] In 1966 Jell-O was served on a silver platter by footmen at the wedding meal for Post's daughter Dina Merrill and the actor Cliff Robertson. The gelatin was a regular item on the menu for formal dinners at Hillwood and lunch at the rustic Camp Topridge. Post told a guest, "Jell-O is a wonderful product, because of course it's used by all levels of income ... and it's good for all times."[108] She certainly used it that way.

In 1958 Marjorie Post became director emeritus of General Foods. She wrote to the company, "My association with the board of General Foods over all these past years has been very close to my heart, as you must know, and my first interest shall always be the company and its activities."[109] Documents show that she continued to evaluate products into the 1960s.[110] "Modern Women," a syndicated newspaper article from 1936, identified Post as one of the twenty-three richest women in the nation. Thirty years later, in 1967, Post remarked that she knew there were others wealthier than her. "The only difference," she said, "is that I do more with mine.... I put it to work."[111]

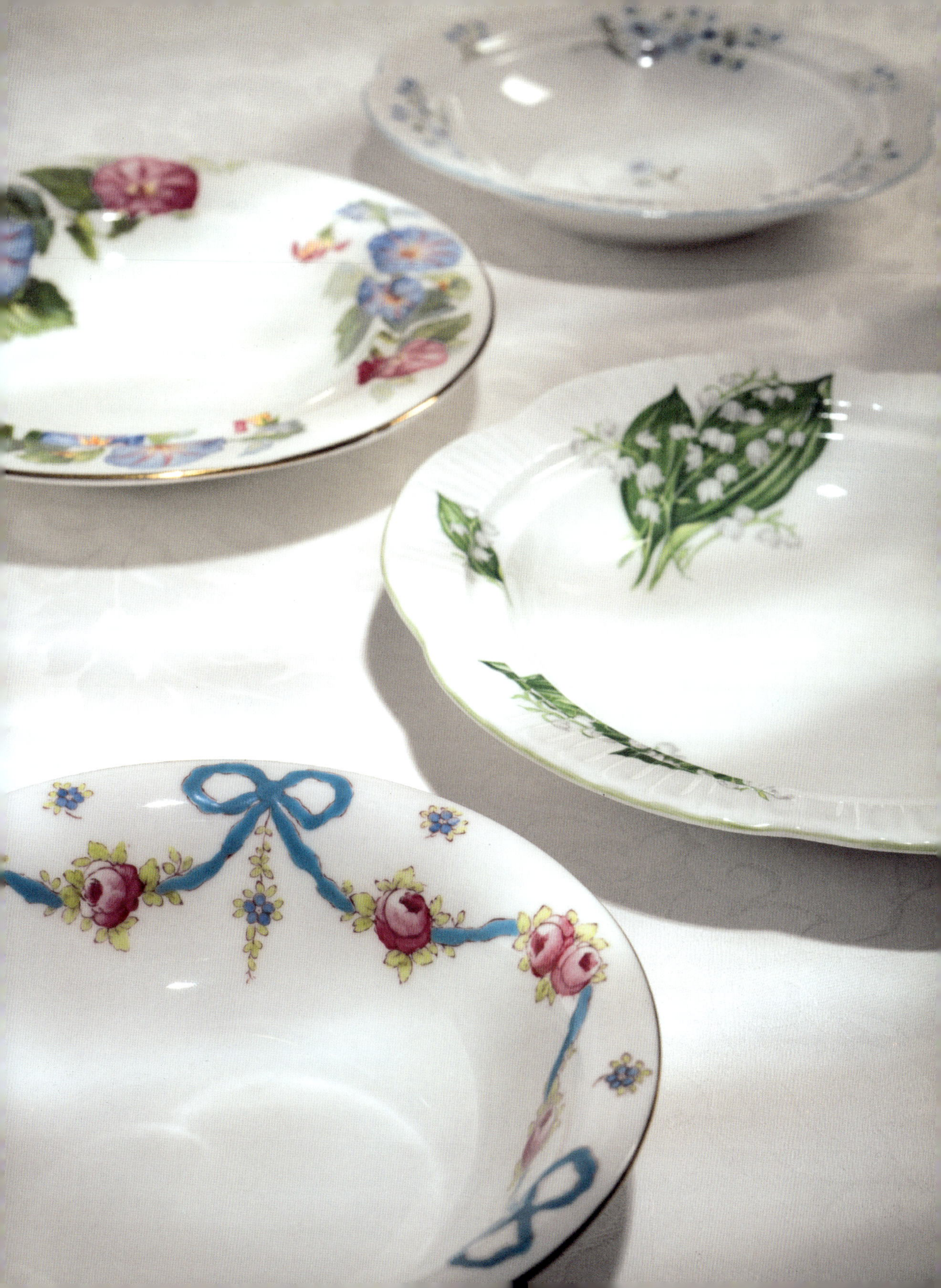

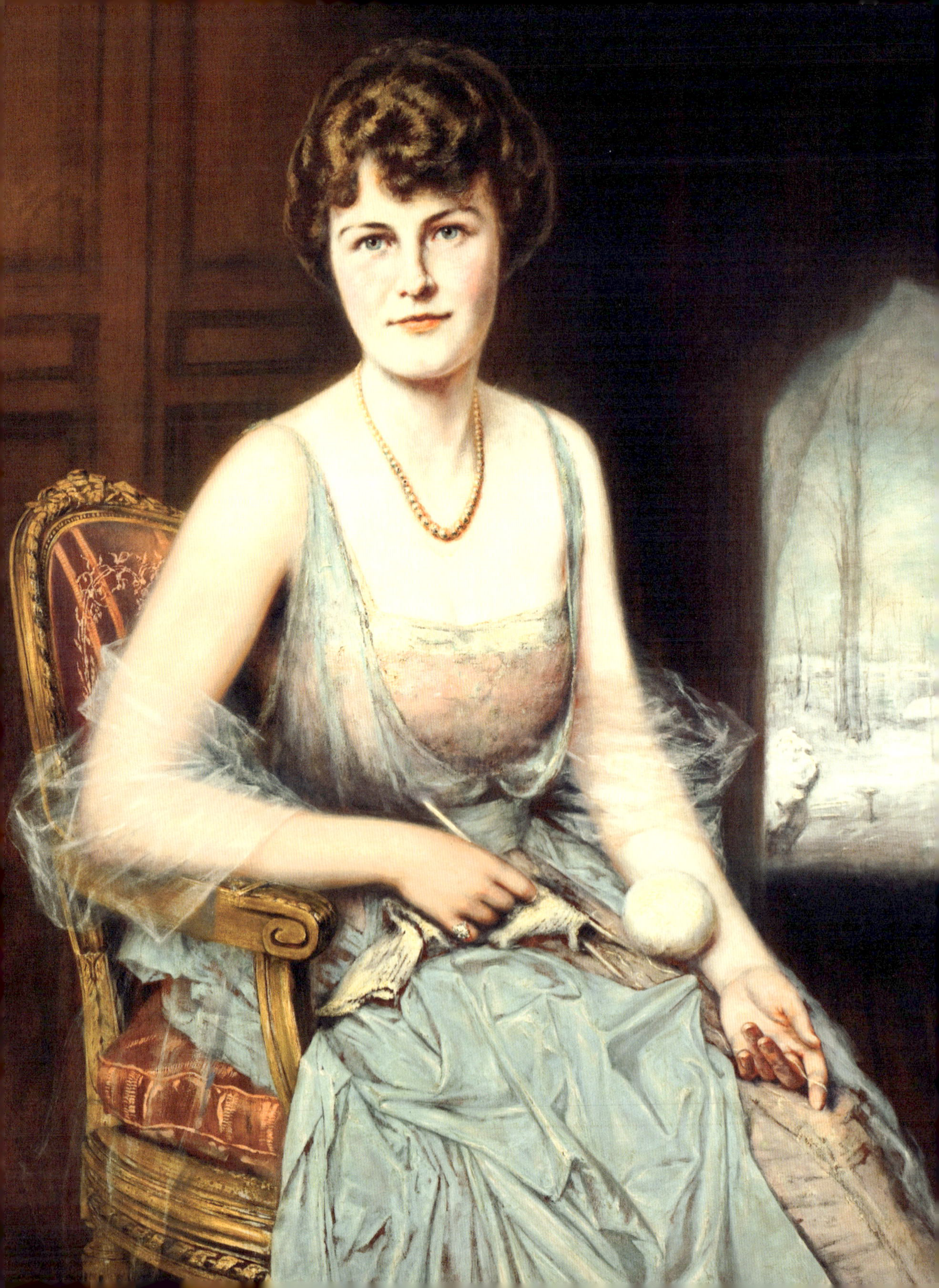

Service

Marjorie Post knitted. She then rolled bandages.[1] With World War I underway, a newspaper reported in 1916, "Red Cross work is gaining new impetus daily, with an interest and zeal that can only result in glorious success."[2] The number of wartime Red Cross chapters increased in the United States from 107 to 3,864, with some 20 percent of Americans getting involved in its activities.[3] "At yesterday's luncheon," shared society writer Cholly Knickerbocker in 1917, "guests sat at a round table on which was a red cross of roses."[4] Marjorie Post hosted three luncheons at the Greenwich Country Club in Connecticut, setting out place cards, napkins, and cakes sporting red crosses. Attempting to charm Greenwich residents into World War I aid projects, Post supplied each guest with a box of surgical dressings for a contest.[5] The person at each table who turned the materials into the greatest number of proper bandages took home the prize—a crystal and enamel vase, provided by Post. Throughout Post's life, when it came to times of war, large-scale hunger, and opportunities to be an engaged citizen, she chose to be involved, donating her time, money, and thoughtfulness.

In 1917 *Vogue* lauded American women's "solid base of organization" and "example of preparedness" in their World War I efforts.[6] Women knitted for the Navy, using government-provided wool and following an instructor to complete vests, scarfs, and caps for enlisted men at sea. Women gathered in Red Cross groups to collect clothes and money and to make surgical dressings.[7] This work amounted to approximately 371 million "relief articles"—bandages, hospital gowns, clothing—not only for soldiers, but for displaced persons in Europe as well.[8]

Post's contribution far exceeded the boxes of bandages made over lovely luncheons. In fact, she funded a boatload of surgical dressings big enough to outfit a base hospital. The supplies had been loaded onto the USS *Saratoga* in New York, after which the vessel was accidentally rammed while still in the harbor. Nearly all the equipment and property on board suffered damage. Quickly, Post funded a second ship, and seven days later, on August

Marjorie Post with her knitting needles, ca. 1905–19

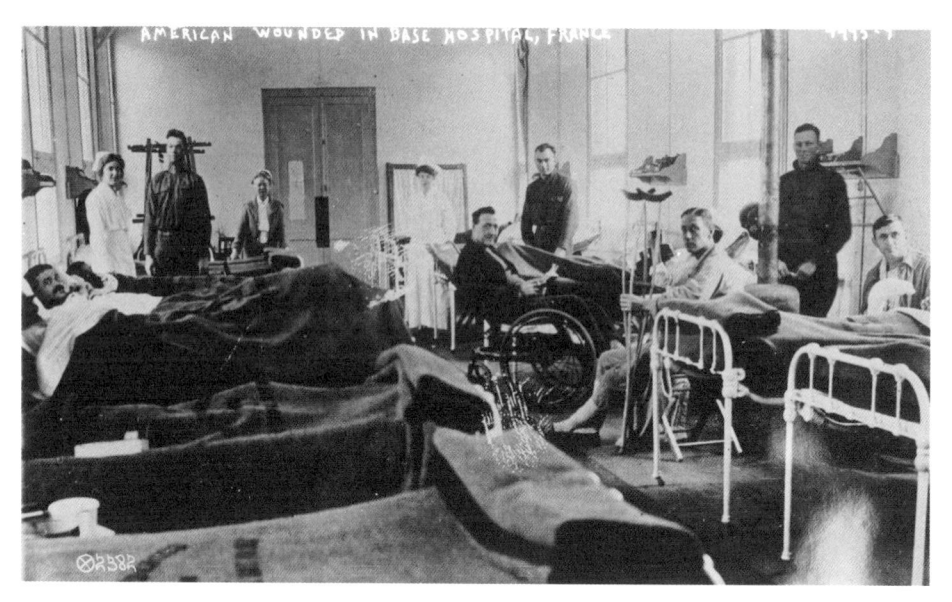

American wounded at a base hospital, World War I, France

7, 1917, the SS *Finland* departed with supplies, arriving in France thirteen days later. In a white stone school building, the first hospital in Savenay, France, was begun. It was officially called Base Hospital No. 8.

The hospital began receiving patients in September 1917. Starting in August 1918, it focused on patients being evacuated to the United States. Auxiliary buildings gave Base Hospital No. 8 a capacity of 2,460 beds plus surgical units. By November 1918, it had evolved to the point of the American Expeditionary Forces calling it "one of the largest and most important hospital centers in France."[9] By the end of its run in January 1919, Base Hospital No. 8 had cared for 35,244 sick and wounded. Post reflected on the effort in the 1940s, remarking, "The hospital did magnificent work and I have always taken great pride in the splendid accomplishments of its personnel."[10]

Meanwhile, as Base Hospital No. 8 conducted its good works in Europe, back in the United States, Post joined a delegation of women who met with President Woodrow Wilson on October 25, 1917 to discuss the matter

Set by Wedgwood & Sons to raise money for an Allied charity, 1917

of women's suffrage. She would later affix her "Votes for Women" pin and bright yellow ribbon representing the New York State Suffrage Party in her personal scrapbook. Post matter-of-factly told family biographer Nettie Major that women's suffrage "was a cause she believed in," but this simple statement belied to what extent. A list published in the *New York Times* showed Post to be a large contributor to the suffrage party of New York state.[11]

On June 20, 1932, Post honored another pioneering woman, declaring to the aviatrix Amelia Earhart in front of two thousand people in New York City, "We women of the country are especially proud of you," adding that Earhart "exemplified … [the] courage of American Womanhood."[12] In Bryant Park just after 12:30 p.m., the fire department band played "Stars and Stripes Forever," after which the audience sang "America" in honor of Earhart receiving the United States Flag Association's Cross of Honor. Post, as chair of the women's national council of the flag association, presented the award in front of the multitudes gathered to get a glimpse of the first

Marjorie Merriweather Post

Suffragettes, ca. 1916

Marjorie Post's suffragette suit

woman to fly across the Atlantic solo—a flight she had completed just one month earlier.

The Cross of Honor, awarded by the flag association for outstanding patriotic service, would be awarded to Post herself at the White House, by First Lady Eleanor Roosevelt, in December of the following year. The first lady said the citation was for Post's "rendering during the year 1932 greater service than did anyone else to the United States Flag Association in its efforts to foster American patriotism and otherwise make stronger and more secure the foundations upon which the Republic is established."[13]

Days after the award ceremony, newspapers learned of Post's next project. One headline declared, "Women to Fight Crime in Nation-Wide Crusade."[14] Post remarked in an article about the initiative, "Unworthy men are permitted to gain office, and racketeering runs rampant, exacting a toll of $15 billion yearly from hard-working men and women."[15] She then called on women to raise citizens able to evaluate and elect responsible officials. The articles on the matter acknowledged that this goal could take decades to accomplish.

While stamping out crime, Post ruminated on sharing as well. A resident of Manhattan, in 1933, she pressed a ceremonial button to illuminate the "I Will Share" sign affixed to the New York Central Building on Park Avenue.[16] With the United States in the depths of the Great Depression, Post told journalists, "Everyone with money owes a duty to our generation to prevent illness that results when children are undernourished."[17] As vice chair of the emergency relief drive for the unemployed, Post gave speeches and appealed for funds, explaining that amid the devastating unemployment, "Wealth would be a burden on my soul if I did not spend much of my time sharing it."[18] In a talk to Staten Island relief workers, she remarked, "We women have a very special place in meeting the present crisis.... I know that it is a hard job."[19]

Dina Merrill, Post's daughter with E.F. Hutton, explained, "She was very conscious, and he was too, of people who were in a bad position. She was quite an amazing [person]. So was dad, he really was."[20] The Salvation Army's *Unemployment Relief Work* report from 1931 stated, "The sight of a long column of men lining the sidewalk in all weathers, patiently waiting their turn for a bowl of stew and a hunk of bread is abhorrent.... A hungry man is a desperate man, and the experience gained during the past year

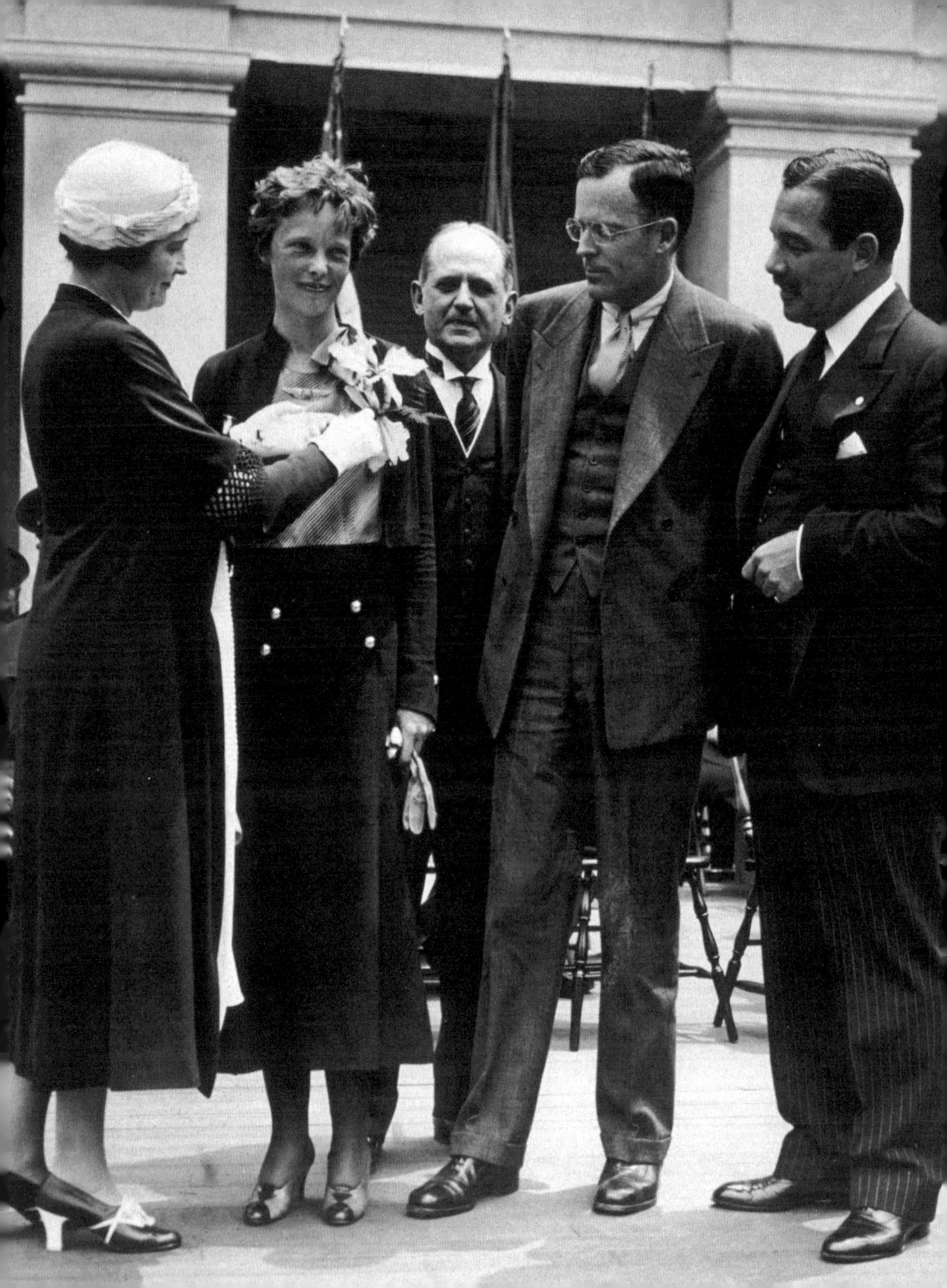

The Cross of Honor awarded to Marjorie Post in 1933

shows that these food stations often acted as front line trenches against possible disorder and riot."[21]

The E.F. Hutton Emergency Food Depot for the Salvation Army offered "food free to all in need" and "without distinction of race, color, or creed."[22] In 1932 Hutton also funded 100,000 Thanksgiving baskets filled with two weeks of "balanced ration" for five people.[23] Meanwhile, Salvation Army trucks displayed banners for the "E.F. Hutton Welfare Box[es]" that were distributed to the families of the unemployed.[24]

By 1931 fourteen Salvation Army stations were in operation in the greater New York City area, serving 48,000 meals per day, with some also offering breakfast for "those who tramped the streets from dawn looking for work."[25] Men waited outdoors in food lines, but the Salvation Army did not believe "in subjecting women and children to the harrowing experience of having to eat the bread of charity in public."[26]

A newspaper reported, "The Marjorie Hutton Post canteen is the only institution in the City of New York where women and children are provided full course meals entirely free…. Through the provision of Mrs. Hutton, the guests sit at tables arranged for family groups … and eat from clean, starched linen."[27] In the first six months, the Marjorie Post Hutton Food Station for Women and Children at 455 Tenth Avenue had fed more than 120,000 women and 55,000 children.[28]

Marjorie Post presents the Cross of Honor to the aviatrix Amelia Earhart, 1932

First Lady Eleanor Roosevelt presents the Cross of Honor to Marjorie Post for outstanding patriotic service, 1933

Women with college degrees, those who formerly lived off stock holdings, and unemployed schoolteachers found aid at the canteen. The food station report referred to the guests as "persons who have worked hard all their lives, and who now are unable to find work…. There are few, if any 'professional' charity cases…. Most of them, upon a return to normal economic conditions, will find work and support themselves…. Now, however, they are destitute, and if denied the opportunity to eat at this food station, might starve."[29] Along with the goal of eliminating the indignity of waiting outside in a breadline, which was accomplished by setting up two large waiting rooms, the canteen fulfilled Post's wish that "no one be embarrassed by asking for food, no one is asked to show a ticket when appearing for meals, everyone who enters the building is served without question."[30] For breakfast, available from 6:30 to 8:30 a.m., guests had cereal, jam, bread, and butter, and "as much tea or coffee as he or she desires."[31] Dinner, served from 4:00 to 6:30 p.m., provided meat, vegetables, fish on Fridays, baked beans on Saturdays, and a dessert of bread or rice pudding.[32]

Marjorie Merriweather Post, 1933

By 1936, the canteen had moved to 30 East 29th Street and had added sleeping accommodation for about fifty women. "Many of these young women find themselves in financial distress through sickness, loss of positions, and other causes," the canteen report stated. The staff offered education and "inspirational services … however, in some instances freedom from attention and an opportunity to quietly gather up the broken threads of life unobserved and without comment is the kindest treatment possible," the report noted.[33] Post underwrote the canteen for six years, in part by adjusting her personal finances: She put her gem collection in a vault and directed the money saved on insurance premiums to the canteen.[34]

On top of Post's charitable spirit and compassion, her affection also caught the attention of the press. A newspaper headline from November 1936 reported, "Wife Breaks into Solemn Event and Kisses Mate Twice." The

Salvation Army distributing E.F. Hutton welfare boxes, New York City

story was about the swearing in of Post's third husband, Joseph Davies, as U.S. ambassador to the Soviet Union.[35] In the office of Secretary of State Cordell Hull, she had kissed Davies on each cheek and stepped back, refusing to repeat the moment for the press's cameras. It was President Franklin Roosevelt who signed and issued Davies's commission as ambassador.[36]

As Davies described in his book *Mission to Moscow*, he understood that the work at hand, beyond the usual portfolio of American security and other interests, was to aid in negotiations to renew a trade agreement due to expire and to decipher Soviet policy in regard to Germany and Hitler. Potential war loomed in Europe. In this matter, Davies was to assess the Soviet Union in terms of its industrial and military capabilities.[37]

"Joe was offered France," Post said, "but there were reasons why I could not go to France with ease; the older children's father [Edward Bennett Close] was living in Paris and his one delight was to be able to go to the American Embassy." She further stated, "There were other reasons why Joe, himself, did not want to take France as a post—because the commercial

[work] for the embassy in Paris is drastic [and was undesirable]." Germany had also been discussed as a post.[38]

"One of the world's richest women will be hostess of the United States Embassy in Communist Russia," reported a New York newspaper in December 1936.[39] Post explained to family biographer Nettie Major that with Hitler in power in Germany and war on the horizon, she understood the U.S. position to be that communism was less of a concern to American interests than the situation in Western Europe. Post's job as ambassadress was to assist with diplomatic relations with the Soviet Union, including hosting dinners and other events at Spaso House, the U.S. embassy in Moscow.[40]

"We were advised by President Roosevelt not to take silver services or gold. He wanted us to take crystal, so the tables were set out entirely in crystal," explained Post. "[For events especially], the whole diplomatic corps shopped together every week [in Warsaw or Helsinki] and a whole carload of food would come into the different embassies and ministries."[41] The American press appeared to enjoy reporting on the food brought into the embassy from the United States. Noting the ambassadress's "precautionary shipments of frozen cream and rock salt," one story included a comment by a Soviet official who said, "Contrary to popular belief, there are cows in Russia."[42] Post later addressed the food situation as she saw it, explaining, "We weren't caught short as many of the embassies were.... Sometimes [we would] go to dinner, and it would be cabbage and carrots and potatoes, and that would be all because the car didn't reach there, didn't come back in time.... We had a lot of frosted food in the cellar in something like twelve enormous storage boxes that were shipped in with American food ... a great comfort for us."[43] In regard to the banquet room, she recalled, "We used to set two huge tables, maybe one of 24 and another of 18 or 24."[44] Life in Moscow wasn't all formal dinners, however. In 1937 the Davies hosted three hundred guests—Soviet officials, members of the diplomatic corps, and press correspondents—for a Fourth of July garden party.[45]

Outside the day-to-day at the U.S. embassy, Davies observed a trial in January 1937. Seventeen people admitted to committing high treason, receiving sentences of ten years in prison or death. Newspapers in the United States followed the proceedings. A Midwestern paper printed that the confessors were "victims of Stalin's attempt to eradicate the last traces of Trotskyism."[46] "We arrived during the second purge trials, and it was

Joseph Davies and Marjorie Post outside St. Basil's Cathedral, Moscow, 1937

certainly a very grim time in Russia," recounted Post. "Night after night [from the embassy you could hear from the nearby buildings] the screams of individuals and their friends and their families.... Off they would go to jail and probably death.... No one could ever find out anything about what had happened to the individual."[47] American papers also reported that "Stalin's eyes and ears" stretched far and wide in the form of the Narkomvnutdel (NKVD), the secret-yet-sometimes-very-visible secret police. They stayed conspicuously close during Davies's tour of the Ukraine in 1937.[48]

In May 1938, Davies and Post toured southern Russia for three weeks. The *New York Times* reported that, with the couple visiting various types of facilities, the trip should provide "exceptional first-hand knowledge of Soviet industry and economy." The ambassador's dispatches on Soviet industrial capacities included communications on the Port of Odessa, a bread-baking factory, an agricultural experiment station, a tea factory, and an oil refinery.[49] Other messages detailed conferences with Soviet officials, treason trials, the anti-religious movement, departures from basic communist principles, European peace, collective farms, and visits to adjacent countries.[50]

Following Davies's last meeting with Premier Vyacheslav Molotov in June 1938, he wrote in a telegram to President Roosevelt and Secretary of State Hull that, to his surprise, "[Stalin] unexpectedly dropped in and we all joined in a friendly and informal talk which lasted over two hours."[51] Davies recorded that they discussed general world political events, battleships, and debts, but cautioned, "It would be very difficult to report by cable or dispatch some of the delicate situations."[52]

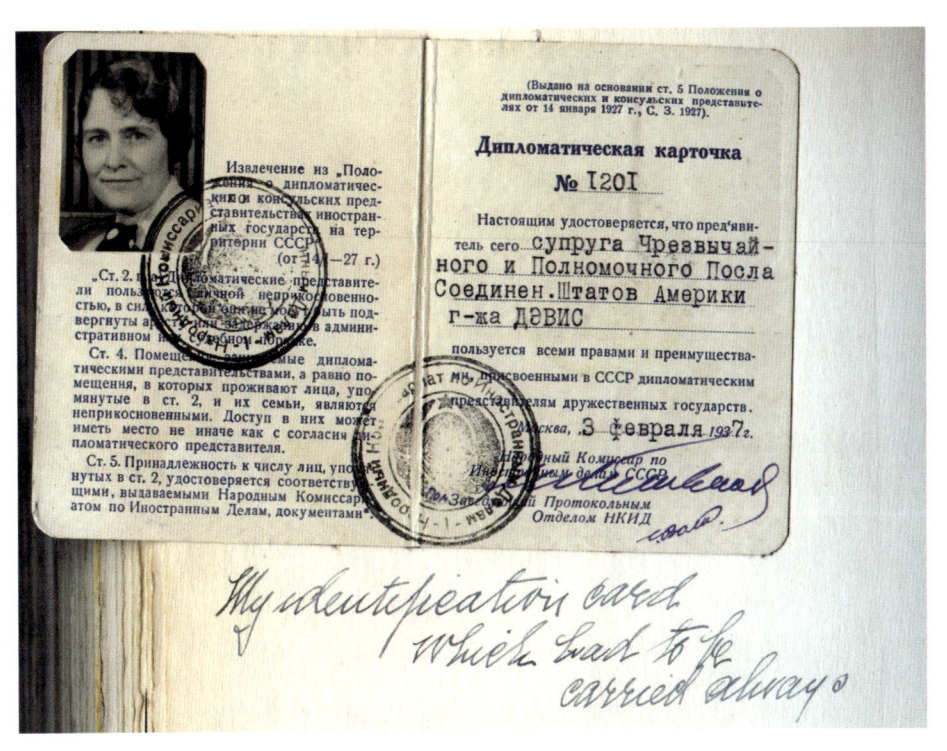

Marjorie Post's identification card while *en poste* in Moscow

The ambassadress also received a surprise—a gift "as a kind remembrance of your sojourn in the Soviet Union," the accompanying typed note card stated.[53] Post recounted selecting one pair of vases: "I was taken to the huge and beautiful ballroom where I found four magnificent pairs of Imperial porcelain vases…. [Then after taking a short tour to think it over], I finally decided on my beautiful blue vases, and they were accordingly delivered the next day at the embassy."[54] The month before, she had presented the Soviet government with American glassware and porcelain, including several pieces made by the Sandwich Glass Company in Massachusetts.[55]

A press report declared that Ambassador Davies fostered "unusually good relations with Soviet officials, [which] has been a direct index of the United States government's anxiety over the political situation in western Europe."[56] Reflecting on working in Moscow from January 1937 to June 1938, Post said, "I must say when it finally came time for us to leave Russia, strangely enough, we rather hated to leave because it was such a challenging place. There were so many things happening there that would be historical, so much to learn."[57]

Marjorie Merriweather Post

Москва, 9 июня 1938 г.

Глубокоуважаемая Мадам ДЭВИС,

Прошу Вас принять две вазы на добрую память о Вашем пребывании в Советском Союзе.

Искренне Ваша

П. Жемчужина

Moscow, June 9, 1938.

Dear Madame Davies,

Please accept two vases as a kind remembrance of your sojourn in the Soviet Union.

Sincerely yours

(signed)   P. ZHEMCHUZHINA.

Note accompanying a gift of two Imperial Porcelain Factory vases to ambassadress Marjorie Post

Service

One of two Imperial Porcelain Factory vases given to Marjorie Post; both vases displayed at Hillwood, Washington, D.C., 1960s

89

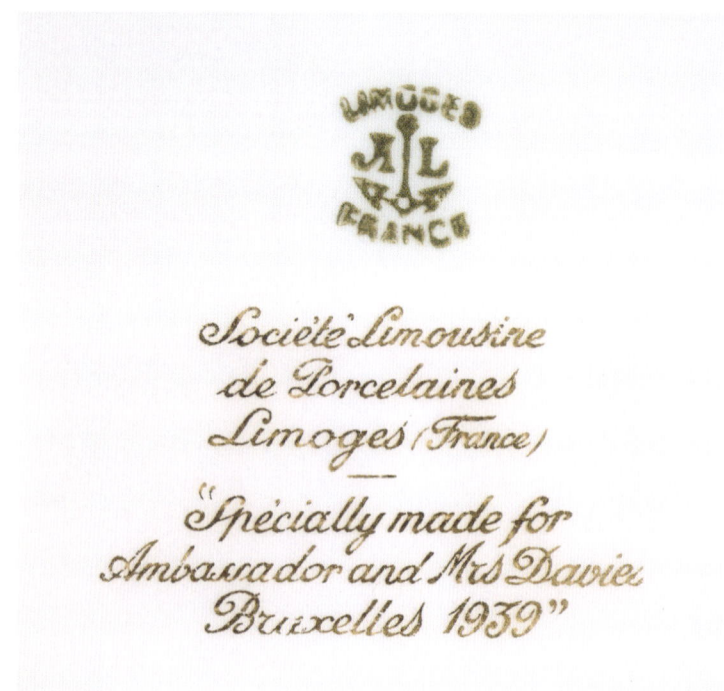

Limoges service made for Joseph Davies and Marjorie Post, 1939

Detail, Limoges service, 1939

Scrapbook page, Joseph Davies's transportation to present credentials to King Leopold III of Belgium, 1938

This is the King's Coach which came to take Joy to the Palace.

Complete with red-cert of gold lively & powdered wigs

Marjorie Merriweather Post

Simon and Schuster published edited versions of Davies's dispatches as *Mission to Moscow* in 1941. The book made it onto bestseller lists. "Is Communism a Menace to Us?" asked the *New York Times Magazine* in April 1942. That same month, the *Daily PM* proclaimed, "Aiding Russia Does Not Make America Red ... Aiding Russia Can Insure the Future of Liberty."[58] *Mission to Moscow*, promoted to readers of popular books, made lists in the *Book of the Month Club* and *Reader's Digest*.[59] In 1943 Warner Brothers, having made note of interest in the book, turned it into a feature film, with Walter Huston playing Joseph Davies and Ann Harding playing the ambassadress.[60]

"Then we went to Belgium," Post recounted. "The contrast in being in that new and raw society, the Soviet Union, and then to go into a monarchy, it was quite a fascinating change."[61] Davies was to present his credentials to King Leopold III on July 20, 1938, and Leopold sent transportation. "The King's coach [pulled by two horses] came to take Joe to the palace," wrote Post in her scrapbook, "[the coachmen] complete with livery and powdered wigs."[62]

"Belgium seemed to be quite a proposition as far as the embassy was concerned [in July 1938]," Post said, reflecting on her assignment, "so when we finally got the place in some kind of shape [by November 1938], it was the most beautiful thing you can think of."[63] Furthermore, she explained, "[Preparing] that embassy was something unbelievable because it was an embassy where you were going to entertain a great deal, much more than you did in Russia.... There was no equipment ... with a big N [nothing] for the table, and the answer from the [State] Department was to bring [it] all."[64] Post brought her own dining wares, and put together beautiful tables, which became noted for Post's penchant for precious porcelain and orchids, as well as her use of color, such as pairing yellow linen and yellow orchids.[65]

In September 1939, with the drums of war beating in Europe, Davies, also minister to Luxembourg, visited the Germany-Luxembourg border where fire was already being exchanged. By November, Belgium had adopted wartime protocols, with regular reports of unknown aircraft flying over the country and fear of Nazi attacks.[66] Davies was recalled to Washington. Not being allowed to return to Belgium, Post sent packers to retrieve her art, jewelry, and other belongings at the embassy in Brussels. As a precaution,

U.S. Embassy, Malachite room, Brussels, Belgium, 1938

"I had it shipped on several different ships so I wouldn't lose it all in case they were torpedoed," explained Post.[67] Fortunately, crews and possessions all returned safely.

Post's luxurious yacht, the *Sea Cloud*, went into service with the U.S. Navy in January 1942.[68] "The *Sea Cloud*'s gone, but I wouldn't have my yacht [be anything] other than patriotic," commented Post.[69] Post had previously offered the vessel to the U.S. government, but the offer was declined due to the cost of conversion. By 1942, however, the magnificent vessel was needed, so it joined the ranks of other great private yachts enlisted for service, among them W.K. Vanderbilt's *Alva* and Vincent Astor's *Nourmahal*. The government chartered the *Sea Cloud* for $1 a year. The checks were never cashed. Post framed them.[70]

Converting a luxury yacht into an armed vessel was an undertaking the Navy could not, and of course did not, take lightly. Removing every item from the *Sea Cloud* was a lavish operation in itself. The job resulted in a thirty-two-page inventory of what amounted to more than six hundred containers of items. Finger bowls, bouillon cups, bon-bon dishes, crystal candlesticks, grape scissors, porcelain miniatures, shell ornaments, marine-themed paintings, chintz coat hangers, golf clubs, a mounted marlin, and a baby grand Steinway piano had to be removed, along with marquetry furniture, large beds, monogrammed linens, cooking equipment, and marble bathroom sinks—all of it entirely functional, but not quite fit for the Navy. Last but not least, about 990 bottles of liquor, champagne, and wine—acquired from ports around the world—departed the *Sea Cloud* before the start of its wartime service.[71]

Replacing the spirits, demitasse saucers, and other accoutrements for Post's luxe voyages aboard the *Sea Cloud* were such necessities as a chemical warfare locker, an armory, 210 gas masks, decontamination gear, scabbards, bayonets, a bulletproof lookout stand, a code room, and 20-mm gun platforms with searchlights. The most dramatic change was the removal of the fore, mizzen, and jigger masts, with the main shortened by a third.[72]

Sailing a customized vessel, as opposed to a standard-issue military ship, officers found themselves "faced with many baffling problems and strange peculiarities."[73] A departing group of seamen sympathetically decided to compile "all the pertinent facts concerning the *Sea Cloud* in one folder so that the new officer may rapidly discover those things that have taken his predecessors months of diligent search to discover."[74] These pertinent facts included variations that worked when going to generator power; fire hydrant locations; the emergency cutoff for fuel supply; ladders and hatches that sometimes led to storage but other times to escape routes; locations of first aid kits; and where to find fresh air supply vents and the semaphore flags. Also left as written instructions was what to do in case of fire in the engine room: "pull control handle marked 'Cylinder Control No. 1' then open the valve 'Engine Room Flooding.'"[75] Where to find a potato peeler, a large coffee urn, and the Coca-Cola machine were also dutifully recorded.[76]

The *Sea Cloud* served as the USS *Sea Cloud* IX 99, a weather patrol ship in the U.S. Coast Guard based in Boston and later in Argentia, Newfoundland. The ship ran a weather station, staying within 50 miles of Atlantic winter storms, and transmitted radio reports. "This meant operating in the roughest seas and weather," explained Commander Carlton Skinner, who was assigned to command in 1943.[77]

After Skinner arrived, one crew and officer rotation in Boston involved the USS *Sea Cloud* receiving "12 Negro apprentice seamen [while] we detached [sic] 12 white seamen." Because of experiences Skinner had had beginning in 1941, he had begun reflecting on naval manpower. He saw that blacks, by regulation, were "only accepted in the Steward's Branch.... This struck me as both unfair and inefficient." Skinner recorded, "Negroes with skills or developable skills in gunnery, radar, sonar, electricity, etc would be assigned to cooking, cleaning officer's [sic] rooms."[78]

Disquieted by all this, Skinner formulated a proposal for an integrated ship, knowing that training into higher ranks was a matter of apprenticing, for "black and white at all levels."[79] He realized, however, that an integrated crew could never receive special treatment or attract attention in the press.[80] When Skinner submitted formal proposals for an integrated ship, he was either denied approval or met with silence, so when he was unexpectedly sent a group of Negro apprentices, he realized he was being told to implement his proposal.[81] From December 1943 to November 1944, the USS *Sea Cloud* IX 99 not only served as a weather ship, but also as a test of integration. This was more than a decade before the Supreme Court ruling in *Brown v. Board of Education* (1954), stating that separate-but-equal facilities had "no place" in American education, ushering in the integration of schools.[82]

Needlework honoring the *Sea Cloud*'s World War II service as the USS *Sea Cloud* IX 99

Among the seamen sent to Skinner was artist Jacob Lawrence. He described, "My whole background, Negro family, Negro community."[83] Lawrence is known for his *Migration of the Negro* series (1941), acquired by the Museum of Modern Art in New York and the Phillips Collection in Washington, D.C., as well as other works.[84] When duty called in 1943, Lawrence's first assignment was on board the USS *Sea Cloud*. With his public relations rating, rather than steward mate, as typically assigned for blacks in the Navy and Coast Guard, "[That] enabled me to paint," Lawrence explained.[85]

Lawrence completed seventeen paintings while in the service. In 1944 the Museum of Modern Art exhibited sixty works from the *Migration of the*

World War II
navigator's
jacket, USS
Sea Cloud IX 99

Jacob Lawrence, *Captain Skinner* (1944), Smithsonian American Art Museum, Gift of Carlton Skinner. Lawrence served on the USS *Sea Cloud*.

Negro and included eight paintings from his time in the Coast Guard.[86] In promoting the exhibition, the museum interpreted: "In Lawrence's Coast Guard pictures, both races face the same fundamental problem—the war."[87] The Coast Guard later sent wartime pieces around the nation on a tour. Unfortunately, most of them would be lost in the postwar demobilization, as the military dispersed and discharged property and personnel in large numbers.[88]

Although firmly committed to the *Sea Cloud*'s enlistment, Post remarked, "I must say that once you have built a ship you feel like its mother, [and] I want to tell you that during the time the *Sea Cloud* was doing her war work, I used to lie awake nights wondering where on earth that ship was and how she was, and saying prayers for her."[89] While moving between Newfoundland and Greenland, Commander Skinner was alerted that a ship was headed straight for the USS *Sea Cloud*. When the radar readings seemed off, the crew realized it was not a ship, but a skyscraper-size iceberg.[90] With some tense maneuvering, a collision was avoided. Later that

Commander Carlton Skinner, the Naval Reserve Yacht Owners Distinguishing Pennant ceremony, 1948

year, 1944, the USS *Sea Cloud*'s sonar operator reported contact with an enemy submarine. While the crew traced the submarine, a destroyer team with air support found the enemy vessel. The USS *Sea Cloud* received an "assist" credit in Navy records.[91]

By autumn 1944, the USS *Sea Cloud* had been decommissioned, as replacement parts proved to be expensive, and other vessels had become available.[92] Before Jacob Lawrence departed for his next assignment, he created a gouache on paper titled *Decommissioning the Sea Cloud*. On December 29, 1944, the Secretary of the Navy wrote to the ship's owners, "The *Sea Cloud* has now been returned to you.... In recognition of the war service ... you are authorized to [display] five chevrons, or one for each six months of service with the Navy."[93] Fittingly, on the Fourth of July, 1946, Post and Davies hosted the press on a restored *Sea Cloud*, still showing bits of wartime wear and tear, including holes left from the sailors playing darts.[94] Later, in 1948, the

Marjorie Merriweather Post

Sea Cloud in service as the USS *Sea Cloud* IX 99

Jacob Lawrence, *Decommissioning the Sea Cloud* (1944), Santa Barbara Museum of Art, Gift of Mr. and Mrs. Burton Tremaine, Jr.

owners were authorized to fly the Naval Reserve Yacht Owners Distinguishing pennant. The Secretary of the Navy and Commander Skinner were among the small group of guests who attended the ceremony.[95]

Post extended additional kindnesses before the war's end. In July 1940, at her Hillwood estate in Roslyn, Long Island, she received, as the press put it, "royal refugees"—Princess Alix, Princess Marie Gabrielle, Prince Charles, and Princess Marie Adelaide—after German troops invaded their homeland of Luxembourg.[96] In November 1944, Post was listed as the sponsor at the launch of the Liberty ship SS *C.W. Post*, a supply ship for troops in the Pacific that called at Pearl Harbor, Iwo Jima, and Okinawa.[97]

In April 1945, to offer respite for those serving at Walter Reed Army Hospital in Washington, D.C., Post hosted a garden party, during which she circulated among the soldiers, serving cookies on a tray.[98] The garden party tradition carried on into the Vietnam War era and included the wounded from Bethesda Naval Hospital.[99] To boost morale, Post opened up Camp Topridge, her Adirondack home, as a place where enlisted personnel could come to recharge. Men and women from the Greater Lake Placid area on military leave could take in movies on Mondays, Wednesdays, and Saturdays at her rustic retreat.[100]

Post also offered prominent public servants access to Camp Topridge as a quiet place to get away from it all. Army generals, White House secretaries (of the Treasury and Navy), ambassadors, congressmen, and senators stayed at the camp for long weekends in the summer. "Camp Topridge is waiting to welcome you!" Post wrote in invitations to her private resort, offering gorgeous views, the tranquility of nature, and ample outdoor recreation, as well as rest, depending on one's preference.[101] The main requirement was to be present at the seated lunch, dinner, and evening group activity, which could mean a movie or square dancing.[102] Among the notable officials who enjoyed the fresh air at Camp Topridge were George Marshall, Paul V. McNutt, Anthony McAuliffe, Wade H. Haislip, Joseph Tydings, Braj Kumar Nehru, Liz Carpenter, Maxwell D. Taylor, Ryuji Takeuchi, Henry H. Fowler, and Wiley T. Buchanan Jr.[103]

Between 1939 and 1958, Post was decorated by the foreign governments of Luxembourg, Belgium, the Dominican Republic, France, and Brazil, and on April 20, 1960, she made it into the *Congressional Record* for "her great selflessness." In 1962 she received the Brotherhood Award from the National

Legion of Honor medal and miniatures, 1957

Conference of Christians and Jews.[104] She also soldiered on with the Red Cross, exchanging bandage rolling for a tiara and gown, becoming a founder of the International Gala for the Red Cross in Palm Beach.[105]

Looking back on her days of knitting and public service, Post acknowledged at least one regret. In that instance, she had been knitting a pair of socks for a godchild. They were olive, because they had to go with Army officer trousers. "One day," Post explained, "[Dwight] Eisenhower was lunching at the house with Mr. Davies and he saw me working…. He said, 'Oh come on, make me a pair like that.'" Post admitted, "Well I never got around to do it and I've always been sorry."[106]

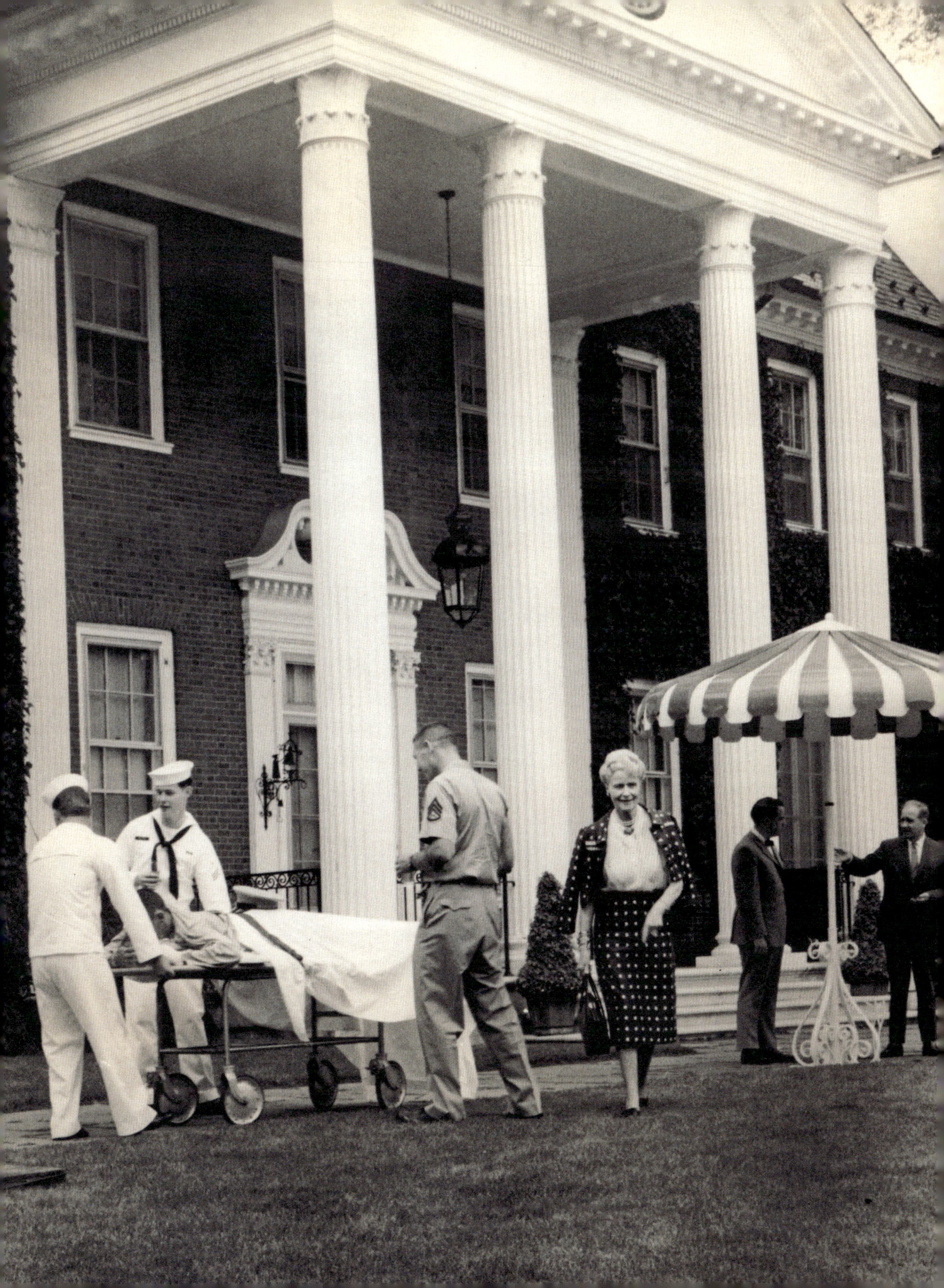

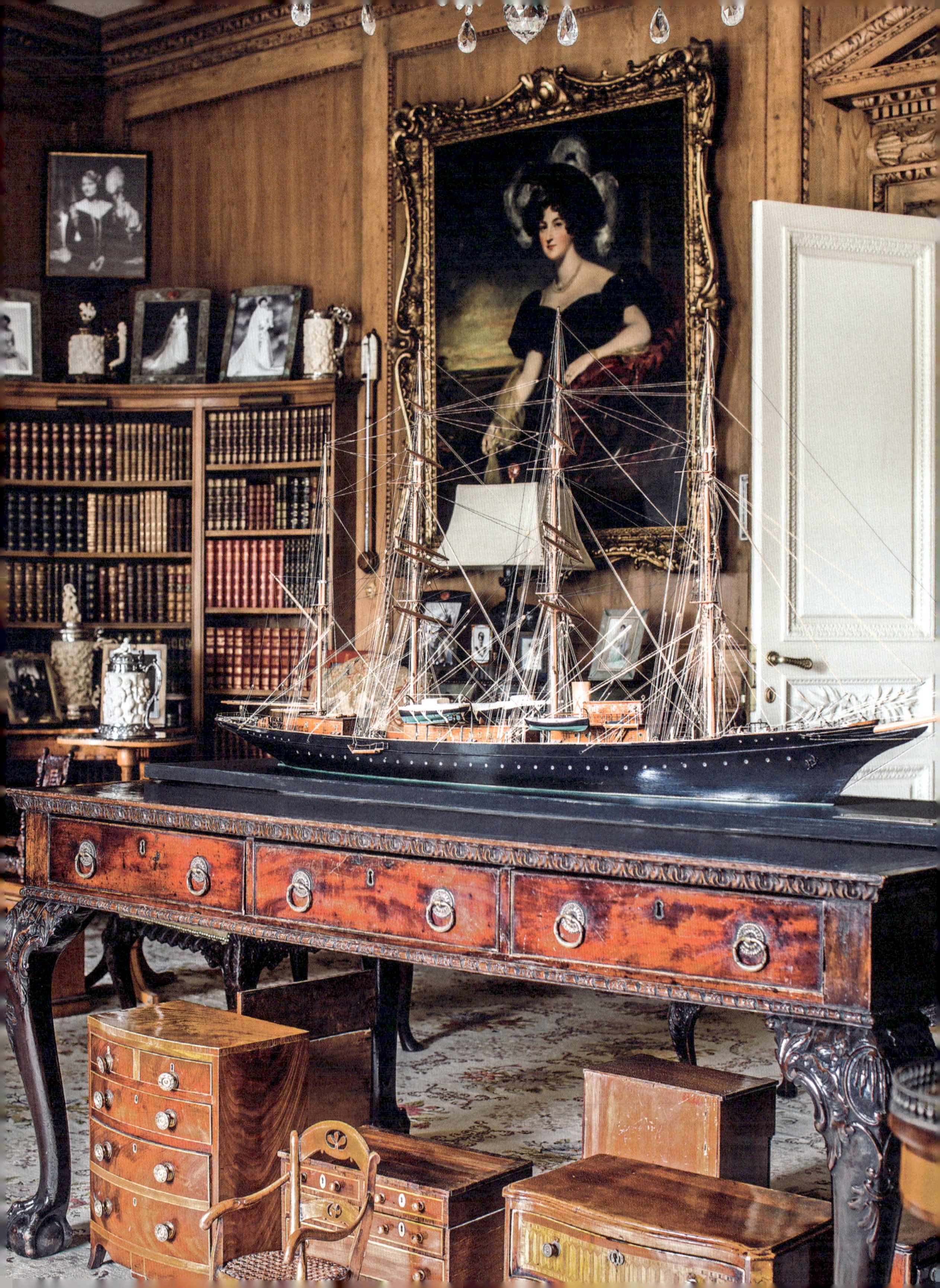

Travel Luxe

Among the passengers aboard the SS *Minnetonka* en route to London in 1904 were a General Harries, a Reverend Howell, one Mr. C.W. Post, and a Miss Marjorie Post "and [her] maid," noted the ship's manifest. Whether for business or pleasure, Marjorie Post always traveled in style. She accompanied her father on numerous business trips and journeyed to Europe for the first time at the age of thirteen. She saw the coastline of foreign lands from the decks of her yachts, ships so lovely they could be called floating mansions. She oversaw the minute details of her expeditions, from the selection of fresh vegetables to the placement of mosquito netting.[1]

Ella Merriweather Post also toured.[2] In the scrapbook "Ella Merriweather Post's Trip to China and Japan," Marjorie Post preserved photographs of her mother, in proper high-necked dresses and carrying a parasol, interacting with kimono-wearing locals and splashing barefoot on the beach in Asia.[3]

Reminiscing about an adventure organized by C.W. Post in 1904, Marjorie Post said, "The automobile was almost in … so he dreamed up the idea of engaging a coach with four horses, driver, [and a] footman … for two weeks of stage coaching down through the south of England."[4] While this journey was inspired by a fading mode of travel, it was not entirely a replication of earlier stagecoach sojourns on bad roads with unpredictable accommodation.[5] The 246-mile tour made by the Post party was recounted in the *Road* magazine. The horses trotted through the counties of Middlesex, Buckinghamshire, Berkshire, Wiltshire, Somerset, and Devon. Post and company declared the "roads in excellent condition." Still, in keeping with the essence of an old-world mode of travel, the stagecoach encountered steep hills that tested the horses' capacity and roads so narrow that the hedges scraped the sides of the coach. The members of the party visited caves, cathedrals, museums, and the seaside. They stopped for tea and enjoyed "splendid accommodation." Other American gentlemen are booking "with the purpose of doing the Old Country," it was reported.[6]

Model of the *Hussar V*, later the *Sea Cloud*, in the first-floor library at Hillwood

Ella Merriweather Post, during a trip to Japan

This adventure by steed was memorable for Post. She recalled, "We'd make about 25 miles per day, and it was all down through that beautiful part of England, to Stonehenge.... As we would approach a village or town, of course, the boys with the horns would announce our coming so that traffic would give way to the stagecoach."[7] Post filled a scrapbook with pictures of Salisbury City Cross, Stonehenge, Bath Abbey, and Exeter Clock Tower, along with personal photographs of the traveling party's antics and her own point of view from the stagecoach—the back of the horse's ears with the charming English landscape ahead.[8]

C.W. Post was a "marvelous arranger for traveling," even in setting the mood, Marjorie Post said.[9] Near the end of another journey, he announced to the group, "Now I want to be endowed with the Iron Cross. We haven't lost a piece of luggage, and we haven't been late for anything."[10] Along with a good-natured approach to being away from home, the Posts also took adventuresome attitudes with them on a visit to Yosemite National Park. Pasted into Marjorie Post's "Travel Snapshots" scrapbook for 1903–5 are photographs with the hand-written caption "Yosemite Indians," alongside images of the park's natural wonders, the majestic Half Dome and Yosemite Falls.[11]

Adventures in Yosemite, from Marjorie Post's album, 1903–5

When "adventuring" to eastern retreats in the United States, Post used a private railcar. Around 1903 she saved a menu from the Pullman Company dining car, likely from her travels with her father.[12] The Pullman Company published booklets about private car service, showing floor plans and pictures of the interior decoration. They also noted, "Rates given include the services of a cook and attendants."[13] For example, the seventy-foot-long Glen Eyre offered "two commodious private rooms, four sections and two folding beds," and the "parlor and observation rooms are finished in vermillion."[14] The Post family's business benefited from the service provided on railcars, as in the case of Post Grape-Nuts cereal being offered for breakfast aboard Union Pacific trains for 30 cents.[15] Later, Post and her first husband, Edward Bennett Close, would belong to the Special Car Club of the New York, New Haven and Hartford Railroad Company.[16] Post and her second husband, E.F. Hutton, took travel to another level with a private railcar of their own.

Marjorie Merriweather Post

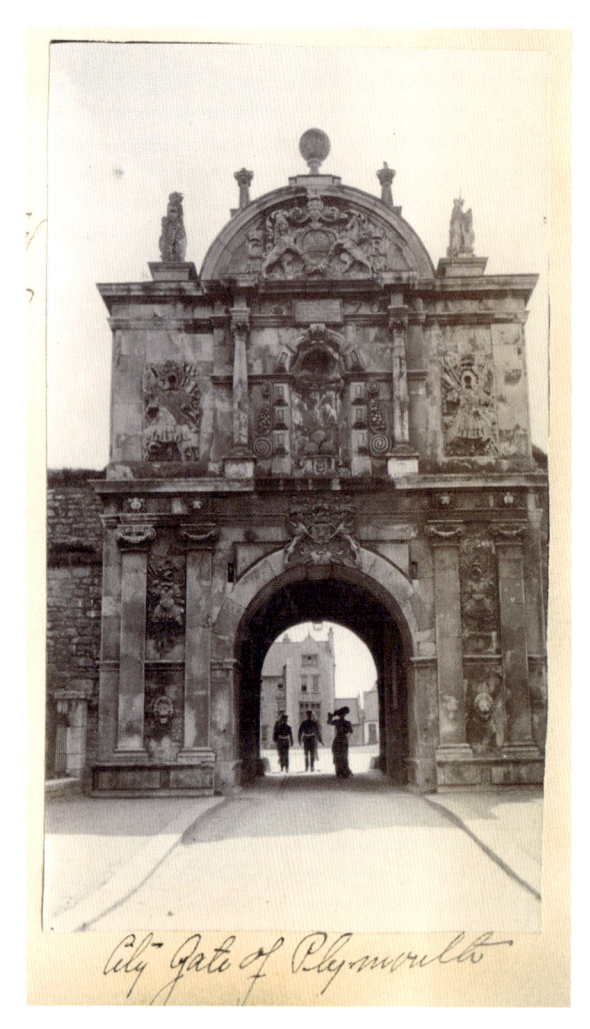

City Gate of Plymouth, England, from Marjorie Post's album "Abroad 1904"

Travel by horse in England, "near Bushey," as noted in Post's 1904 scrapbook

Scrapbook page of the coach-and-four trip through the south of England, 1904

"I remember when I was a little boy, I would go to the station with my father to pick up passengers," recalled Ed Russell Jr., whose father was the superintendent of Camp Topridge, Post's home in the Adirondacks, near Lake Placid, New York. "[The private railcar] was fancy ... something like kings and queens would have."[17] The steel car, completed in 1922 by the American Car and Foundry Company, was not only used for travel to Post's Adirondack estate, but also to Palm Beach, Florida.[18]

By 1928 newspapers had taken notice of this style of train travel, calling a private car "an indication of exclusiveness and membership in high social sets."[19] One article, "Real Palaces on Wheels," described Post's car as "a miniature substitution for a Park Avenue apartment ... [with separate] quarters for servants and luggage."[20] In 1923 the *New York Times* made note of Post, Hutton, and their guests departing Palm Beach for New York in their private car, the Hussar.

Post was a conscientious hostess, especially when traveling with young children by train. Genie Chester, a young guest who had joined Post's daughters Adelaide and Eleanor for a trip, recalled what happened as the train approached a rough crossing. "Mrs. Post rushed to our berths and pushed our feet to the floor, so we would not be jolted."[21]

Hussar, private train car

In Post's eyes, her train car had "no particular decorations, just the standard private car … more or less like the regular ones that one could charter, or rent, from the Pullman company."[22] Although Post felt that her car did not stand out among the available railcars for private hire, it offered the top comforts and amenities of the day. The car's exterior prominently displayed its name, Hussar, on the sides in gold leaf and a subtle clarification with the single word "Private" on the end door. With a frame and roof built of steel, the Hussar's exterior was seemingly simple, but the interior featured two master bedrooms, two bedrooms for guests, a dining room, a lounge, pantry, kitchen, and a staff room with ample bathrooms for all. In short, there was enough space for six passengers and the crew. The dining room seated ten.[23]

The Hussar's interior was finished primarily in mahogany, with one room having an ivory finish with mahogany trim. More than sixty lamps illuminated it. The furnishings included a sofa in brown Spanish leather, mahogany dining room chairs by S. Karpen and Brothers, and seats upholstered in Marshall Field's uncut plush or mohair. Twelve mirrors served as decoration and for personal grooming. Other items included a vacuum cleaner, pressing iron, humidor, five curling iron heaters, and non-striking clocks. The Hussar was fitted with Westinghouse air brakes with emergency reservoirs.[24] Later, as Post explained, "A baggage car was added to this which trailed along behind us and carried trunks, anything extra we might want in the way of an automobile, and so forth."[25]

E.F. Hutton had had the Hussar custom built for his wife. "This was given to me very shortly after I married him," Post said. "[My room] was

Hussar, three-mast auxiliary schooner designed by Cox & Stevens, 1923

quite big, and there was a shower, toilet and basin."[26] Hutton also had his own room, connected to hers. During Post's travels with her father, she had had a favorite Pullman porter named McKay. Hutton and Post offered to equal his pension to secure his employment for their car. They were also able to arrange for their favorite Pullman chef, Brice, to accompany them if they gave the company ample notice. Post recalled that Brice was "the most marvelous cook."[27] The porters and largely African American Pullman staff were known for their excellent work.[28] To book the Hussar to go on a journey was a matter of contacting the railroad coordinator by telegram or telephone and supplying the date, stations, and times, which were according to the existing railroad schedule.[29]

While the Hussar was equipped with vapor heat and eleven three-speed fans, it being 1922, the train car did not have air conditioning. One end had an open platform, allowing passengers to sit outside in cooler air, when the train moved at slow speeds and in mild wind conditions.[30] The Hussar suited Post's needs until 1936, after which she sold it to the Chesapeake and Ohio Railway.[31]

In the matter of traveling by sea, swiftly and in luxury, Marjorie Post mused about her and E.F. Hutton's floating conveyances in an interview: "Then there was always the boat situation which started with the *Lady Baltimore*, a perfectly beautiful little power boat which looked like a baby destroyer with two funnels…. That was succeeded by a very much larger motor boat, which was called *Hussar III* … and then came the schooner which we built, a three mast, a beautiful ship [*Hussar IV*]…. In the meantime, we were working on the plans for the square rigger [*Hussar V*, later *Sea Cloud*], these plans were in the works for five years...."[32] The numbers of the various Hussars—train car and sea vessels—were often mixed up or omitted in news accounts. In record books maintained by Post's estate staff, the vessels were sometimes misspelled *Huzzar*.

Cox & Stevens designed the three-mast auxiliary schooner *Hussar*, and Burmeister & Wain supervised its construction in Copenhagen in 1923. By definition, a schooner consists of at least two masts, the main and a shorter one at the fore. The *Hussar* had three masts, with two 600-horsepower auxiliary diesel engines for use in difficult weather conditions.[33] The schooner was more than 204 feet long. As Burmeister & Wain neared completion of the vessel, they received notice that the king of Denmark wanted to see it. The company wrote to E.F. Hutton, "In order that His Majesty can get the right impression of the yacht we intend to arrange the visit to take place shortly before the vessel is completed.... The visit of his Majesty must be kept secret, until it has taken place."[34]

The finished yacht met Hutton's requirement that the vessel "handle well under sail or under power, would not be unduly expensive to construct or operate, and would provide excellent quarters for the officers and crew."[35] It blended technology with formal interiors by the design firm William Baumgarten & Company, including decorative nautical elements.[36] While ample in overall size, the interiors of the schooner *Hussar* still included space-saving measures, such as built-in cabinets and under-the-bed pullout drawers, along with furnishings of a smaller than usual scale.[37]

The living room featured an electrical fireplace, and the dining room had a skylight with hidden electrical lighting for evening illumination that was "diffused and gives a very beautiful effect."[38] A master control in the wireless room controlled the clocks, while the curtains were made of a rubberized silk to withstand sea conditions.[39] The bridge was positioned with the intent that the captain be able to navigate "without in any way being interfered by, or interfering with, the comfort of the owner and guests."[40] With its two diesel engines and fuel storage, the schooner could travel 9,000 miles, which in land travel terms was roughly three cross-country trips, from Maine to California.[41]

The *Hussar* had two staterooms, each equipped with a bathroom. Near the owners' rooms were accommodations for a maid. The schooner also

Interior of the *Hussar*, by William Baumgarten & Company, 1923

Hussar, Marjorie Post's bedroom, 1923

had four guest rooms. The dining room measured 16 by 21 feet. The pantry was nearby, along with the staff quarters. The living room was decorated in the late Georgian period and the master bedroom in Louis XVI. Nautical elements, such as a ceiling fixture of rope design, portraits of American admirals, panels of marine scenes, and a color glass panel of the *Santa Maria*, accented the interior.[42] The *Hussar* had a Duo-Art Reproducing Piano capable of performing classical favorites as well as popular songs of the day.[43]

The *New York Times* announced the schooner's arrival at New London, Connecticut, in July 1923, having made the ocean crossing in just fourteen days. After being turned over to the owner, the *Hussar* would be kept at

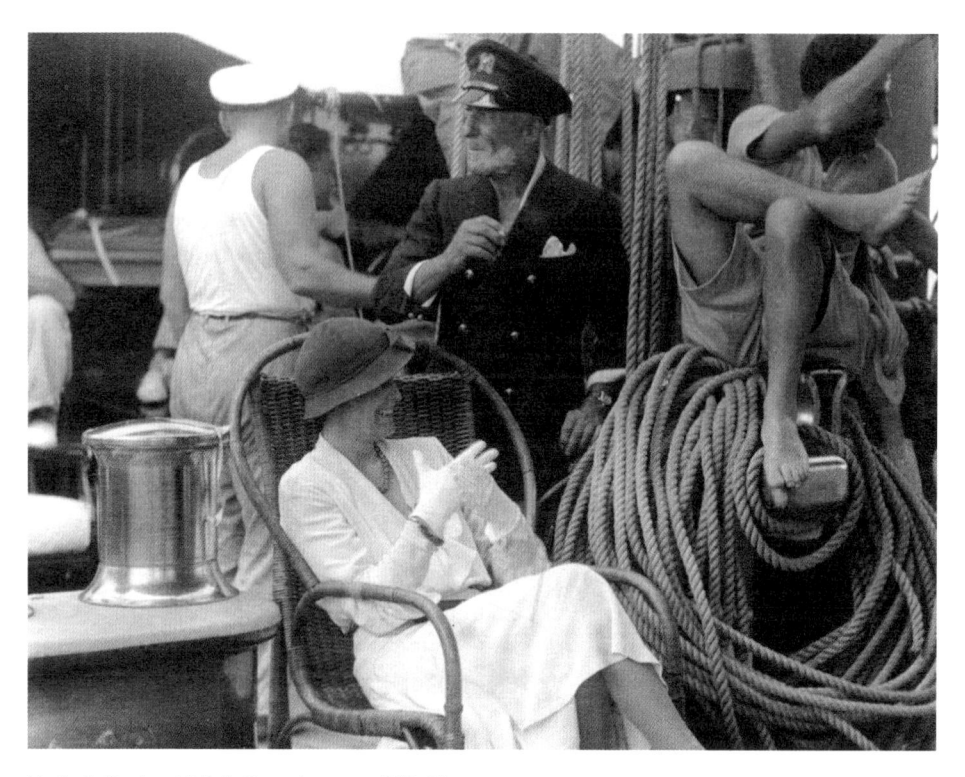

Marjorie Post and E.F. Hutton at sea, ca. 1932–33

the New York Yacht Club.[44] The steel masts, 183 feet tall, had to be lowered to clear the Brooklyn Bridge.[45] In 1927, after a Mediterranean cruise, Post and E.F. Hutton dropped off guests in New Haven to catch a Yale-Georgia football game. The *Hussar*, "with her towering steel masts, [and] a massive eagle for a figurehead, drew the attention and admiration of yachtsmen," commented the *New Haven Register*.[46] By 1932 Post and Hutton had upgraded to the four-masted *Hussar V* and sold their three-masted vessel to George Vettlesen, who rechristened it *Vema*.

The couple announced the construction of the auxiliary barque—with four masts and square principle sails—in 1928.[47] Dina Merrill, Hutton and Post's only child together, summarized the process as a great marital collaboration: "Dad worked with the ship's architect on the overall layout and the sailing part [while] mother designed the interior."[48] The fun on E.F. Hutton's part, according to Norman Skene in *Elements of Yacht Design* (1904),

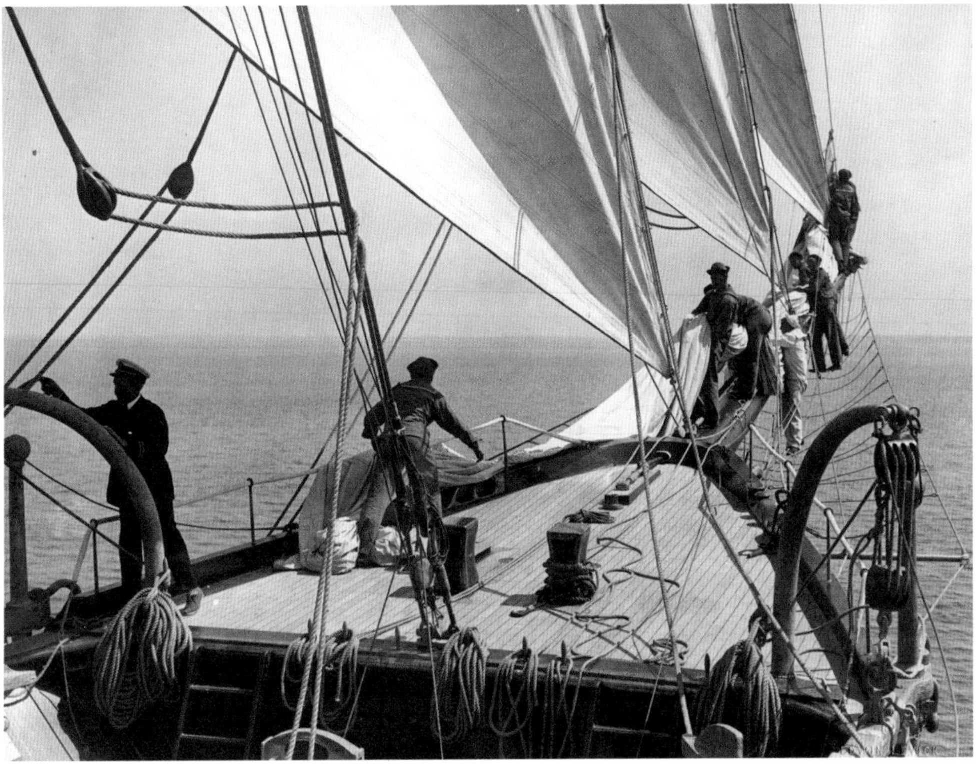

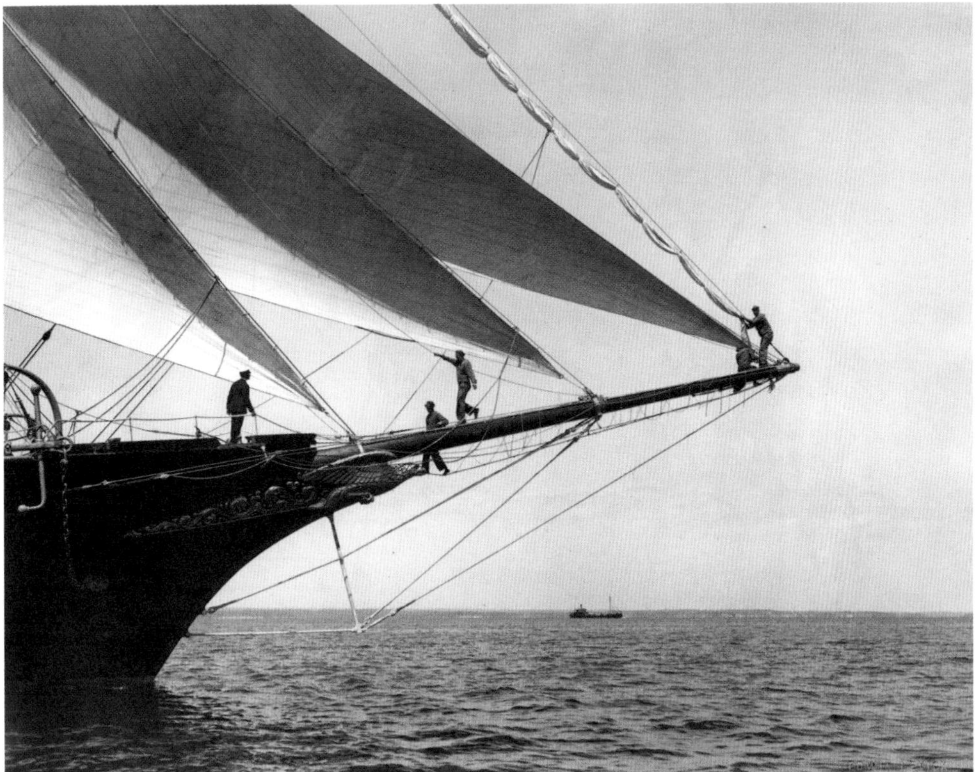

Interiors of the *Hussar V*

might have been solving "the problem of providing the perfect yacht for a given set of conditions."[49] Judging by newspaper accounts, as well as letters from admirers reminiscing about the experience of witnessing the *Hussar V* firsthand, the couple designed a vessel of beauty, which was not a simple task. As Skene remarked about yacht design, "Knowledge of what makes for beauty is largely intuitive."[50]

Registered data for the *Hussar V* detail its magnificent specifications. It could cruise 20,000 miles, which in land terms is close to a round-trip journey between Anchorage and Panama City. Measuring 356 feet, including the figurehead and bowsprit, the 2,323-ton vessel could store 35 tons of refrigerated or frozen food, 22 tons of dry goods, and 116,000 gallons of

The *Hussar V/Sea Cloud* with majestic black hull, and then in white after March 1939

fresh water. As for the rigging, *Hussar V* utilized up to twenty-nine sails, comprising 34,000 square feet, and eight miles of hemp rope. In addition to a chart room for navigation, there was radar and a master gyro with eight repeater compasses. Long- and short-wave radio systems enabled international communications, while a ship-to-shore telephone system kept the *Hussar V* in touch while at sea. Propulsion and auxiliary power entailed two propulsion motors at 3,200 horsepower, with main and emergency generators. For medical emergencies at sea, the yacht housed hospital and operating equipment. For maintaining the vessel, the crew had complete carpentry and machine shops and a sail shop with sewing machines. There were accommodations for 72 officers and crew members, and staterooms for sixteen guests, and there was space to entertain 400. Two onboard projectors screened feature films.[51]

"*Hussar* was the most understated and elegant of Mother's creations," reminisced daughter Dina Merrill. "She took all the dimensions of every room, [then] rented an entire warehouse in New York where she laid out the whole thing, planning what would go where."[52] Post wrote to the interior designer Fred Vogel on June 11, 1930, "I would like to get my part under way…. In making your designs, please bear in mind that this boat is going to be furnished with not quite such a swank feeling as the present [schooner] *Hussar* [IV] so in doing your walls keep them quite restrained."[53] She then instructed him to prepare wall elevations in Venetian, American, "simplified" Louis XVI, Adam, French, and "Modernistic" styles for the owners' rooms, guest spaces, living

Scrapbook page showing E.F. Hutton and Nedenia Hutton (Dina Merrill) fishing on the *Hussar V*

to her – He loved having his neck scratched & here is Mother spoiling him –

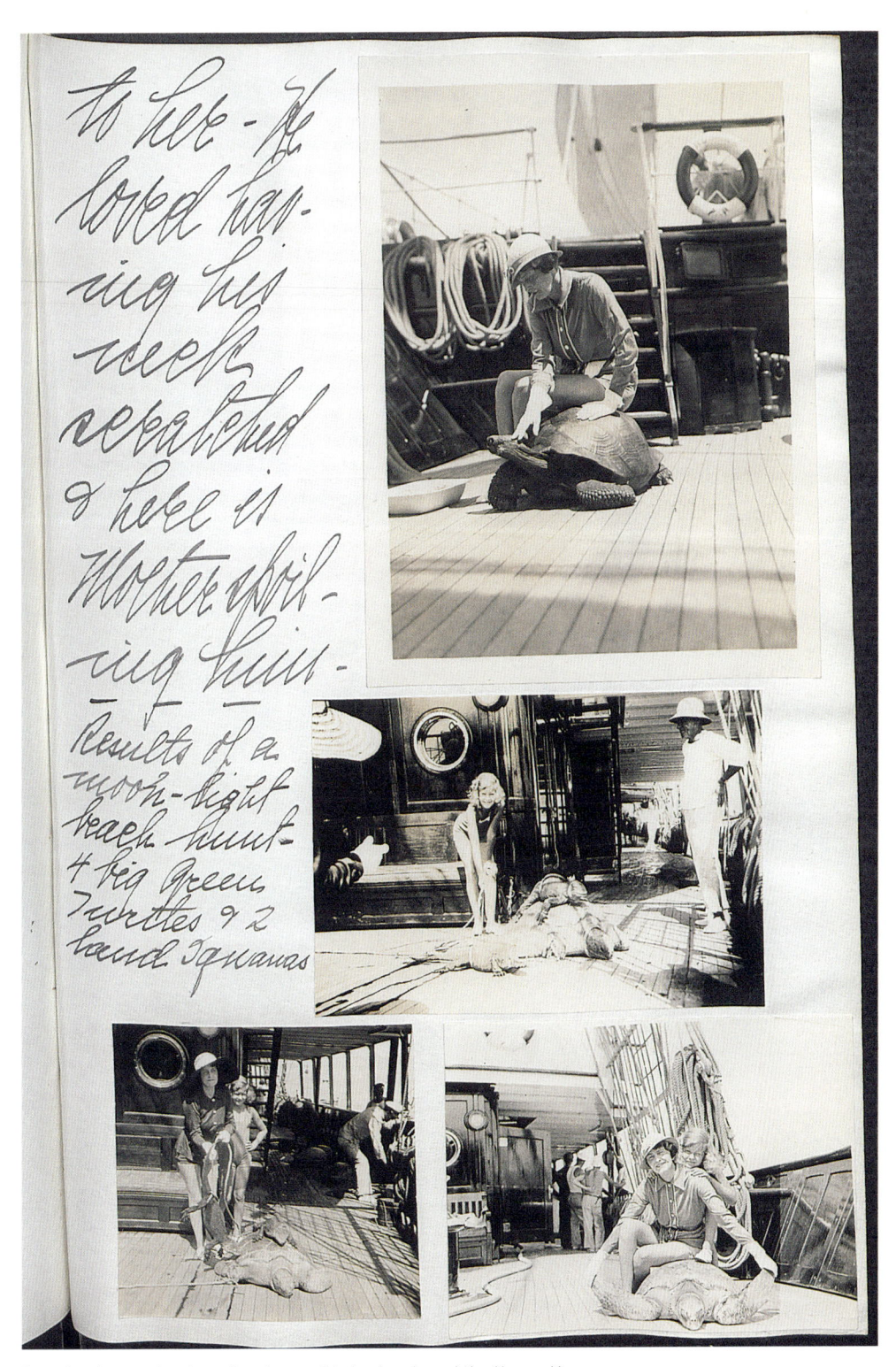

Results of a moonlight beach hunt – 4 big Green Turtles & 2 Land Iguanas

Scrapbook page showing adventures with Jumbo aboard the *Hussar V*

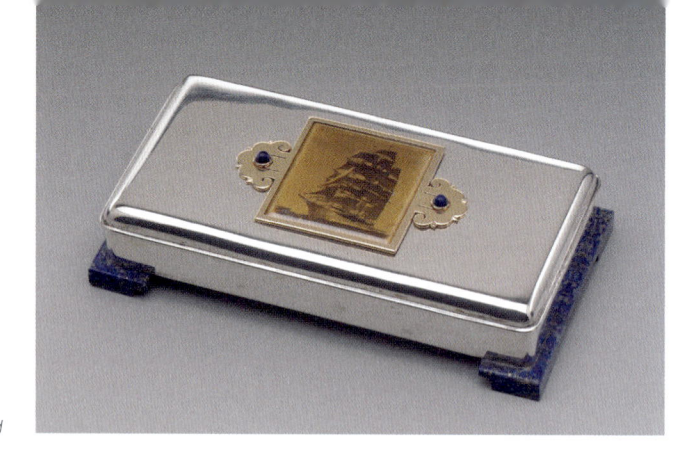

Cartier box with a photograph of the *Sea Cloud*

room, and smoking room. "I am returning on Monday the 16th and the next day will want to see the preliminary sketches of all these rooms because the designs must shortly be handed in to the architect [for cost estimates]," she wrote. "It will be at least a year of building, so there is plenty of time for all the other decorations except the design of the walls."[54]

By September 1930, Post had prepared a list of articles for Vogel to remove from the schooner *Hussar* and move to the new yacht. Nine pages long, the list specified dining room linens, dining room silverware, bed linens, and miscellaneous pieces, such as "16 hat stands." The list also included 535 hand towels, 264 face towels, and 186 bath towels for the crew. Post ordered porcelain and linens with the burgee (triangular flag) of the New York Yacht Club overlaid with Hutton's private signal of a white "H" on a red background.[55] When the boat was completed, Post had the rented warehouse packed up, and then spent ten days arranging the furnishings on the vessel.[56]

The *Hussar V*'s maiden voyage, from Kiel, Germany, to Bermuda, took place in December 1932.[57] Spectators gawked at the ship along its way, and it made headlines, among them "Hutton's Huge Yacht in Port" and "Hussar Is Here! Morgan's Corsair Just a Rowboat." One paper noted, "The floating palace is equipped with every luxury and convenience known to seafaring men."[58] *Hussar V*'s builders wrote to its owners, "Permit us to add the expression of our hopes that the new *Hussar* will always be a source of real pleasure and a place of recreation for your good-selves."[59]

"I loved all our travels. We had the best time," said Dina Merrill. "Dad would look at a chart, point to someplace we hadn't been, and say, 'That looks like a good island. Let's go there.'"[60] Using a fisher boat alongside *Hussar V*, father and daughter would put their reels to water. "I had so much fun with him," she shared.[61] "One of the things that Daddy used to do when we were at sea, he'd get the fire hose out and make the [crew] guys run it.… We didn't swim when we were underway, so he'd get the fire hose out and we'd have a nice hosing down.… Oh we had a lot of fun on the ship."[62]

The fun only started, however, after school lessons taught by the onboard nanny. "We told the school I was going to be gone a certain amount of time.… They'd give us [study materials]," Merrill explained. "So I used to work in the mornings." Sometimes the journeys lasted three months or more.[63] When back at school, the young Dina Merrill had to pay a penalty, as she called it. "I had to give a talk to the assembly with a map telling what I'd done in each place," she recalled.[64]

The *Hussar V* crew exceeded seventy people. "They had more than they needed," said one of Post's property managers.[65] Dina Merrill pointed out that counting engineers, stewards, and the deck watch, "That's twenty-four right there for the sails."[66] There was also a masseur for Post, as well as a personal maid and social secretary. The latter two also worked at Post's homes that did not float.[67] Most of the *Hussar* staff were assigned only to the vessel, including a general practitioner and a surgeon.[68]

Post hosted movies, with her daughter and the occasional other children sitting on pillows, while the crew watched along with any guests. "I think I got to know every word of *Naughty Marietta* because Mother loved it," said Dina Merrill. "She loved Jeanette MacDonald, and we played it over and over and over.… I knew all the songs."[69] "Ship Ahoy," from *Naughty Marietta*, certainly suited the setting and helped the evenings clip along aboard *Hussar V*.

"This trip to the Galapagos [in the 1930s] was one of the high points of my life," said Dina Merrill. "To see all those animals and the blue-footed booby birds … [with] these bright blue feet, they were absolutely entrancing." She also noted, "The animals weren't afraid [of people].… They didn't bite, they didn't scratch."[70] When Post asked the crew to bring a turtle shell to the ship, "They brought back this land tortoise which is not a turtle shell at all," said Merrill. She adored this tortoise, whom she adopted and called Jumbo. "When it was hot, we'd turn on the fire hose and get him all wet.… He'd stretch out his neck and twist his head all around."[71] He ate lettuce, cabbage, and hamburgers, and would stretch his neck out especially long when the vessel was about two days away from land.[72] "We kept Jumbo all the way to Hawaii and put him in a zoo there."[73] All in all, Dina Merrill concluded, "I really grew up on that ship. I adored her. I used to kiss the

Marjorie Merriweather Post

Sea Cloud shoes, by Bob, Inc.

mast good-bye when I had to go back to school."[74] Knowing her affection for the *Hussar*, "[Captain] Lawson built me this beautiful model of her," she said. "I love it."[75]

Post and Hutton divorced in September 1935. Two months later, a newspaper announced, "*Sea Cloud*, Formerly *Hussar*, Preparing to Unfurl Its Canvas." The article stated that a court had awarded the vessel to Post. "It is reported that [Post] is to marry a distinguished Washington attorney and diplomat and that the cruise is to follow the marriage."[76] Regarding the square rigger *Hussar V*, Post explained, "After the divorce, when I took it into my hands, I renamed it the *Sea Cloud* because the *Hussar* name was very definitely connected with Hutton, and I felt that if he was going to have another boat and so forth, he'd want the name."[77]

Post married Joseph Davies on December 15, 1935, and set out on an extended Caribbean voyage aboard the *Sea Cloud* for their honeymoon.[78] They departed the Bahamas in early January and arrived in Miami at the end of April 1936.[79] In between, the newlyweds sailed and auxiliary-powered to the Dominican Republic, Haiti, Honduras, Puerto Rico, Virgin Islands, Trinidad, Venezuela, Curacao, St. Vincent, Barbados, Grenada, St. Lucia, Martinique, Saint Christopher, Saba, Jamaica, and Cuba, before winding up the honeymoon in Miami.[80] In "Marjoe Cruise," Post's honeymoon scrapbook, she left an undated handwritten note on a loose piece of paper. It

Joseph Davies and Marjorie Post, page from the scrapbook "Marjoe Cruise," 1935–36

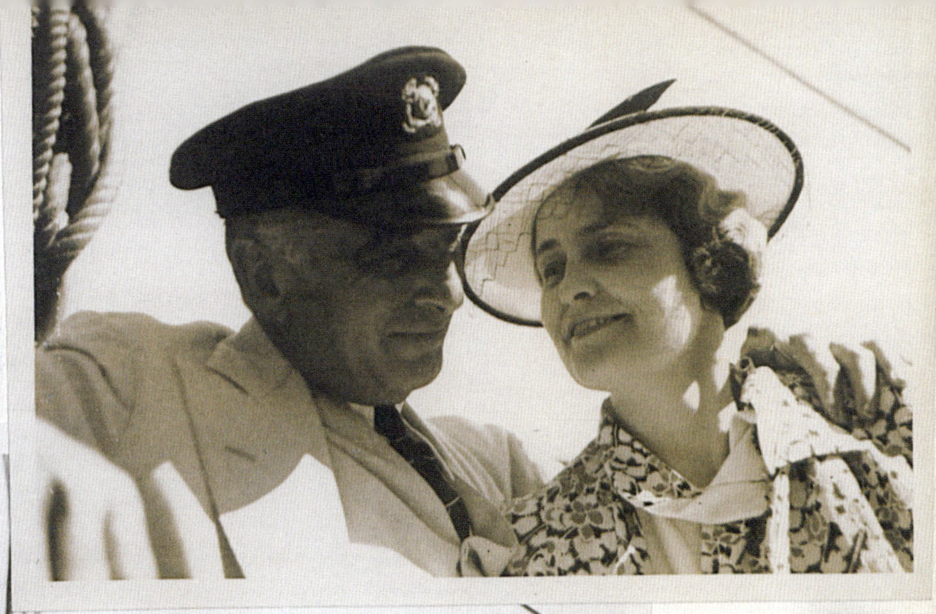

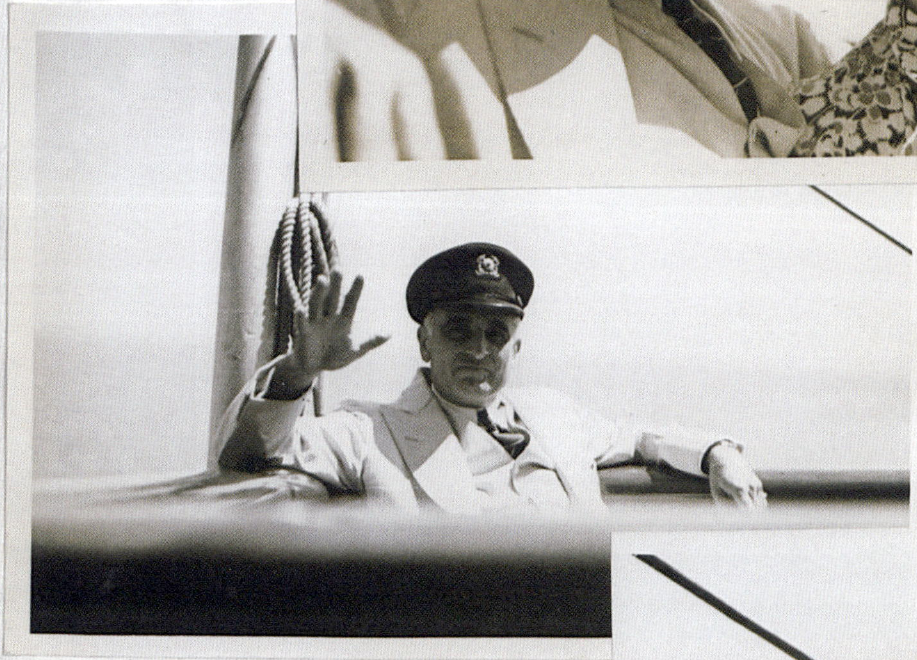

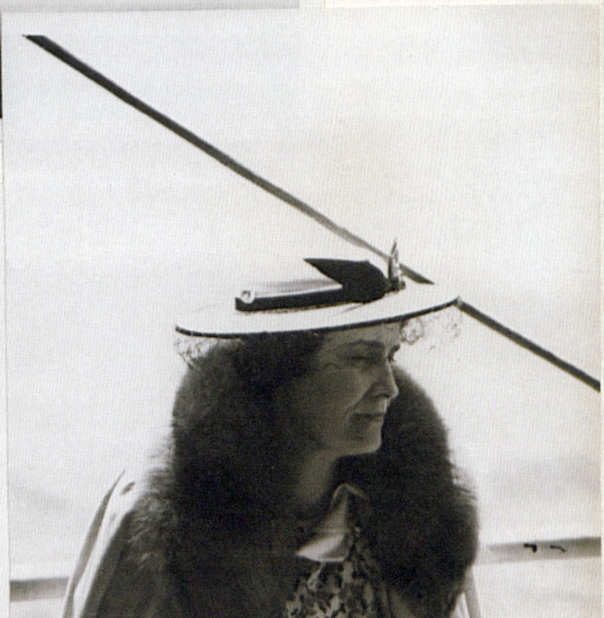

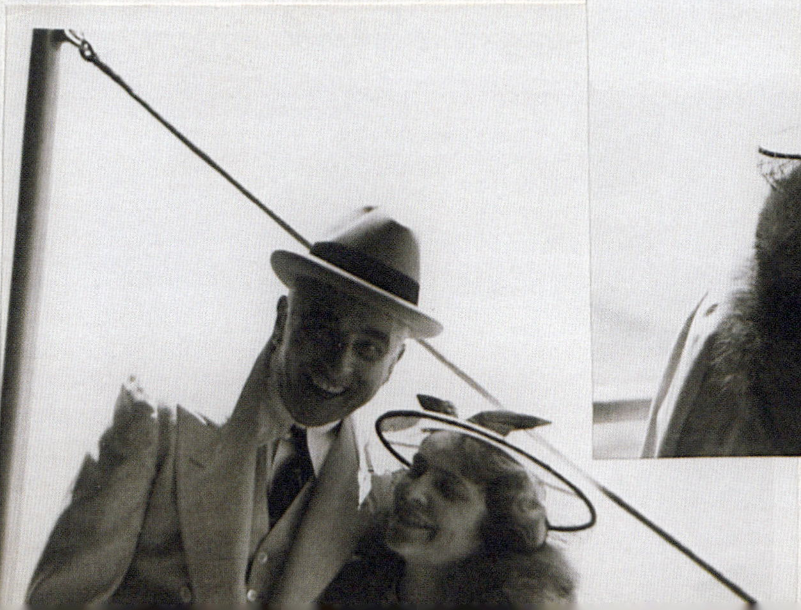

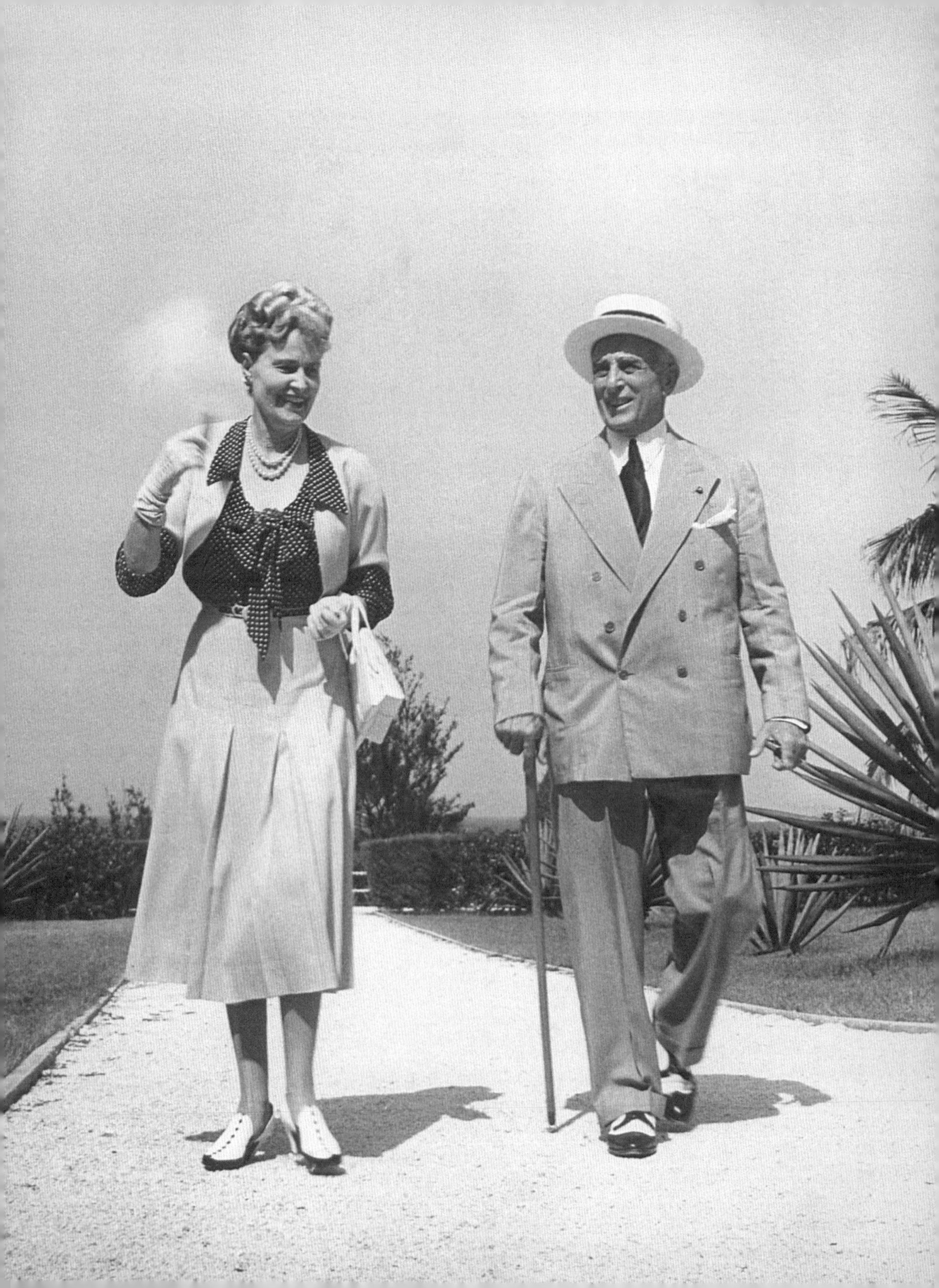

Travel Luxe

opposite
Marjorie Post and Joseph Davies, ca. 1948

The Duke and Duchess of Windsor, guests of Marjorie Post and Joseph Davies at sea

Sea Cloud table linens

read, "What a year it's been—the heights and the depths—but now we are in the peaceful waters—all my dreams come true."[81]

The *Hussar V* became the *Sea Cloud* in late 1935, keeping its majestic black hull. Then in March 1939, in addition to overhauled diesel engines, the *Sea Cloud* debuted its new "spring dress of white and gold."[82] An inspired reporter with Jacksonville's *Florida Times-Union* encouraged readers to view "what is generally considered one of the most palatial pleasure craft afloat."[83] When Post saw it in May 1939, she wrote, "What a beautiful sight she is—all is anew—White Dress—(can't wait to have Joe see her)."[84]

The Duke and Duchess of Windsor (the former Edward VIII and Wallis Simpson) enjoyed a series of events aboard the *Sea Cloud* as guests of Post and Davies in 1948. When asked to make a statement about their arrival in Cuba, the duke replied in Spanish, describing his trip as a personal one.[85] In Havana on April 3, the Windsors dined with the Davies, the American ambassador, and the British minister to Cuba.[86] The next day, a luncheon and sail were in order. On April 8, the travelers and others enjoyed tea and cocktails from 6:30 to 8:00 p.m. aboard the *Sea Cloud*. Among the seventy guests were the Cuban prime minister, the Belgian minister to Cuba, and the Canadian minister to Cuba, along with their wives. In a thank you letter, the duke wrote, "The Duchess and I could not have enjoyed the cruise more, whether at sea and especially under sail…. It was an ideal combination of rest and quiet, and then the interest and excitement of visiting the historic and picturesque capital of Cuba for the first time."[87] The Windsors planned to reciprocate the hospitality by hosting the Davies for a weekend at Severn, Long Island, that May.

Post sold the *Sea Cloud* in August 1955 to the Gibbs Corporation, and fourteen years later she received an unprompted letter. "I am taking the

Glassware for the *Sea Cloud*, 1935

liberty of writing because I know you were once the owner of one of the most beautiful objects in the world—the *Sea Cloud*," wrote a fan. "[I spent] hours just looking at your beautiful yacht." The letter concluded with a request for a professional photograph of the *Sea Cloud*: "If you have one you could spare I would cherish it." Other letters made their way to Post from people who felt moved by just a glimpse of the vessel. "This romantic and mysterious lady of the sea was enough to capture any young boy's imagination," one person wrote.[88]

Post also traveled by land and air in custom-designed vehicles. In January 1948, she wrote to the manager of the Chrysler Automobile Salon on Lexington Avenue, "There are certain features I want to work out, namely, that the seat be far enough ahead to permit a circulation of air without the miserable draft which comes when the seat is too far back."[89] She revealed, "These streamlined things built in the form of a duck, I do not care for at all."[90] Post ultimately submitted a deposit on a 1948 custom Derham Crown Chrysler limousine with the Derham Custom Body Company in Rosemont, Pennsylvania.[91] According to the agreed specifications, the car was to be maroon with black trim and the interior was to include black hand-buffed landau leather, woodwork in burl walnut, and a curtain for the rear window. Because of Post's impeccable posture, the upholstery for her seat was to be "shaped for erect sitting rather than for lounging, but of course to be soft."[92] In developing the seat, Derham stated, "[We] will take into consideration your height, which we believe you stated as five foot seven inches."[93]

Post knew that she wanted her car to have "a long chassis for comfortable riding."[94] She had arrived at this conclusion based on previous experience. Records show that in 1928 she had purchased a Coupe de Ville, body number 6926, from Hooper and Company Coachbuilders of London. The interior consisted of framing and panels of English ash, suede upholstery, an ebony cabinet for two bottles, the Rolls-Royce mascot, and a dictograph for communicating with the chauffeur. The body sat on a 20-horsepower Rolls-Royce chassis, model GUJ-57. In 1935, she ordered a Packard Twelve chassis for the Rolls-Royce body, and later she would replace that with a 1939 Packard Twelve chassis, at which time the upholstery was also refreshed.[95]

By the late 1950s, Post had thirty-four vehicles to move her staff, guests, and belongings between her three residences: Hillwood, in Washington D.C., Camp Topridge, near Lake Placid, New York, and Mar-A-Lago, in Palm Beach, Florida. The fleet included station wagons, limousines, and luxury sedans by Plymouth, Pontiac, Chrysler, and Oldsmobile.[96] She also had a series of Cadillacs. "They had a 1959 first. She never complained about it," recalled Frank Del Monte, one of Post's chauffeurs. "We got a 1962. She never complained about it…. We got the 1964, she starts complaining [that] her hat is hitting [the roof]."[97] Post's drivers then worked with Hess and Eisenhardt in Ohio to find a custom solution—raising the roof of her 1964 Cadillac Series 75 limousine by five inches over her seat.[98] The Cadillac also had an amperage issue, needing more power than just one battery to start, but the chauffeurs resolved this by rigging the vehicle with two batteries hooked together.[99]

On February 4, 1959, Post registered a Vickers Viscount model 786 airplane.[100] Post's grandson Stanley Rumbough said, "We used to kid my mother [Dina Merrill] that there was some royalty in the family"— "the Viscount Merriweather."[101] One reporter, Dorothy McCardle, wrote that travel via Post's private aircraft, the *Merriweather*, was a royal luxury, "the last word in sky comfort."[102] The plane once had forty-four seats but was transformed into a spacious lounge for seventeen passengers. For the interior, Post selected apricot and gray swivel chairs, Dixie cup holders, throw pillows for the curved lounge seating area, and Formica cabinets in shades of champagne and cocoa. She was also selective about the seat belts and service trays, requesting "the new type of seat belt which has a flat fastening, so that you don't have something sticking out on your stomach [interfering] with your lap comfort…. We would like, if possible, to have the service trays and all the dishes in a salmon-colored plastic to match the tiny narrow line stripe in the curtains."[103]

Merriweather, a Vickers
Viscount model
786 airplane

In flight on the *Merriweather*, 1969

Along with a captain, co-pilot, mechanic, and steward, Post's staff created an itinerary for flights hopping from Pittsburgh to Calgary, then to Banff and Lake Louise, then to Anchorage, cities in the Pacific Northwest, a stop in Springfield, Illinois—followed by lunch in Battle Creek, Michigan—then back to Pittsburgh all in one month. Another schedule showed flights from Iceland to Greenland, then France, Belgium, England, Italy, and Austria, returning by way of Newfoundland.[104] The *Merriweather* also ferried guests, potted plants, and enormous beauty salon hairstyling equipment between Post's homes.[105]

In addition to tending to meals, navigation, and in-flight safety, Post's staff saw to key maintenance details, such as securing a spare Rolls-Royce Dart 510 engine after they were no longer in production, and the use of airport facilities.[106] Post kept the private aircraft until she died, in 1973. Nettie Major, the family biographer, remarked of her, "[She] has spanned the age of transportation from horse and buggy ... all types of automobiles, private sailing vessels ... to her own private airplane—a cycle accomplished by very few."[107]

It is likely that only a limited number of people in their lifetime have booked a daily session with the entire dance team of a cruise ship. Among such people would be Post, and in her case, it happened on the *Gripsholm*, owned by Swedish American Line. No longer in possession of the *Sea Cloud*, Post booked twelve cabins for a cruise. Three of the rooms were

Travel Luxe

Merriweather napkins

Merriweather, Marjorie Post's private plane

to accommodate her two maids and her social secretary, and another was for clothing.[108] The cruise took place shortly after Post's wedding to fourth husband Herbert May in June 1958. The entourage of eight guests, three staff, and the newlyweds departed New York for Antwerp on June 28. Three cabins were for the newlyweds, with one serving as a sitting room, therefore that room's two beds and dressing table were removed. The ship's crew adjusted curtains to cover holes in the walls.[109] Post brought along her own 57-inch bed and mattress with all the necessary linens. Other details required changing the chest of drawers, dressing table, reading lamps, and night stands.[110] The travel manager coordinated other arrangements in advance for the Post party, such as a twice-weekly 9:30 a.m. massage for Post, a daily 4:00 p.m. session with the dance team, deck chair reservations on the veranda, and a safe deposit box. A list of fresh vegetables available while at sea was also provided.[111]

Post, who had supervised more than seventy crew members on the *Sea Cloud*, took the time to appreciate the staff and amenities on other vessels. In 1961 she wrote a thank you note to the head of the *United States* cruise liner, remarking, "The ship is superb in every way and the service could not have been better.... Everyone was so attentive and courteous.... My warm thanks to you."[112]

Another thoughtful gesture by Post was to ask the Duke of Sutherland, "Are there any American 'gadgets' you would like us to bring to you?" She was making arrangements in 1956 for the use of the duke's estate, Sutton Place, after a delightful stay there two years earlier.[113] The estate, in Surrey, England, offered a car—a 1955 Mark VII Jaguar—for her household employees. Staying at the property for a few weeks, Post added an extra footman and laundress, dined on the duke's crested porcelain, and requested mosquito nets for her bedroom. When asked if she would like two ponies, her short handwritten notation was simply, "Not needed."[114] Everything was in order.

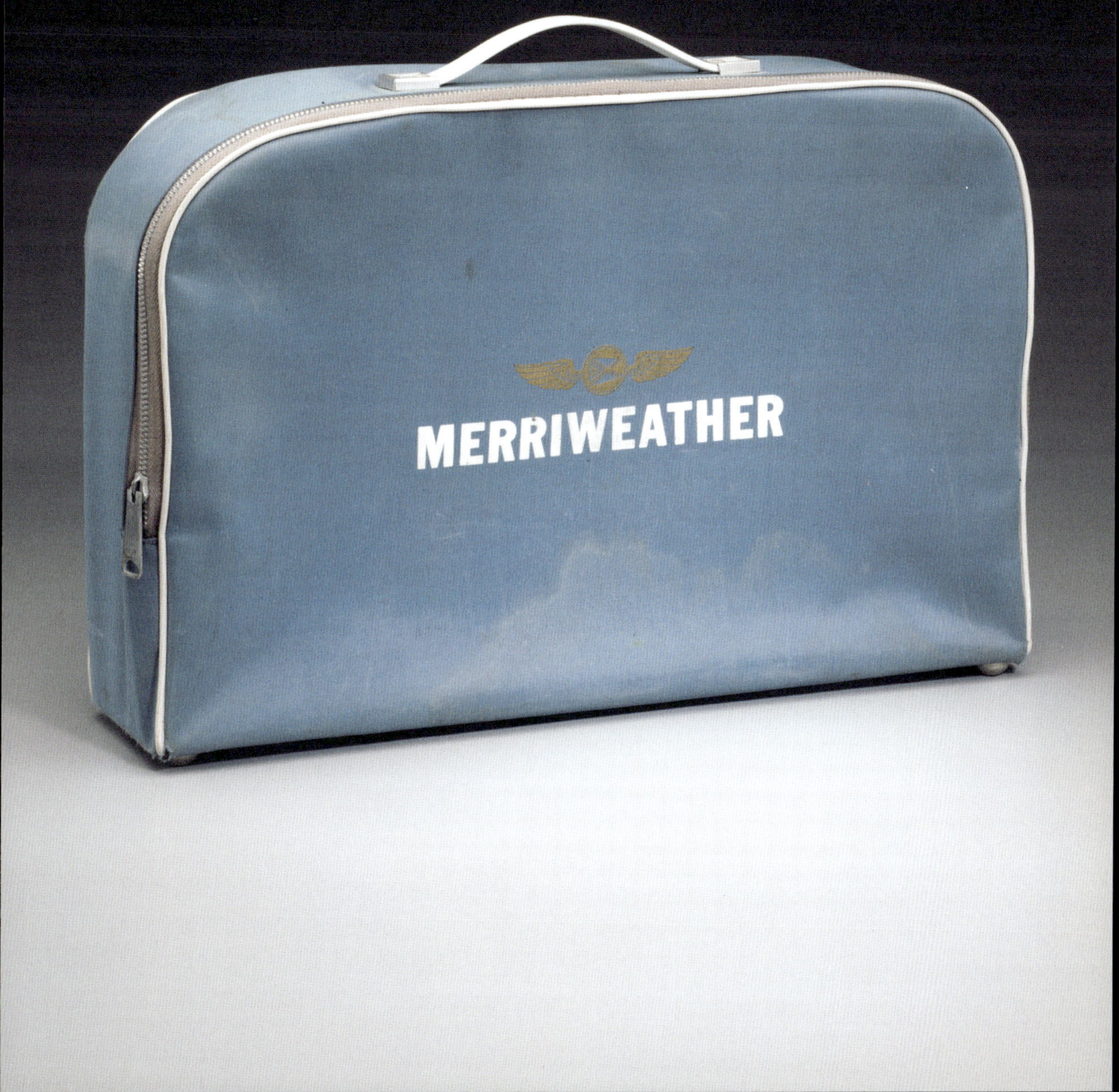
MERRIWEATHER

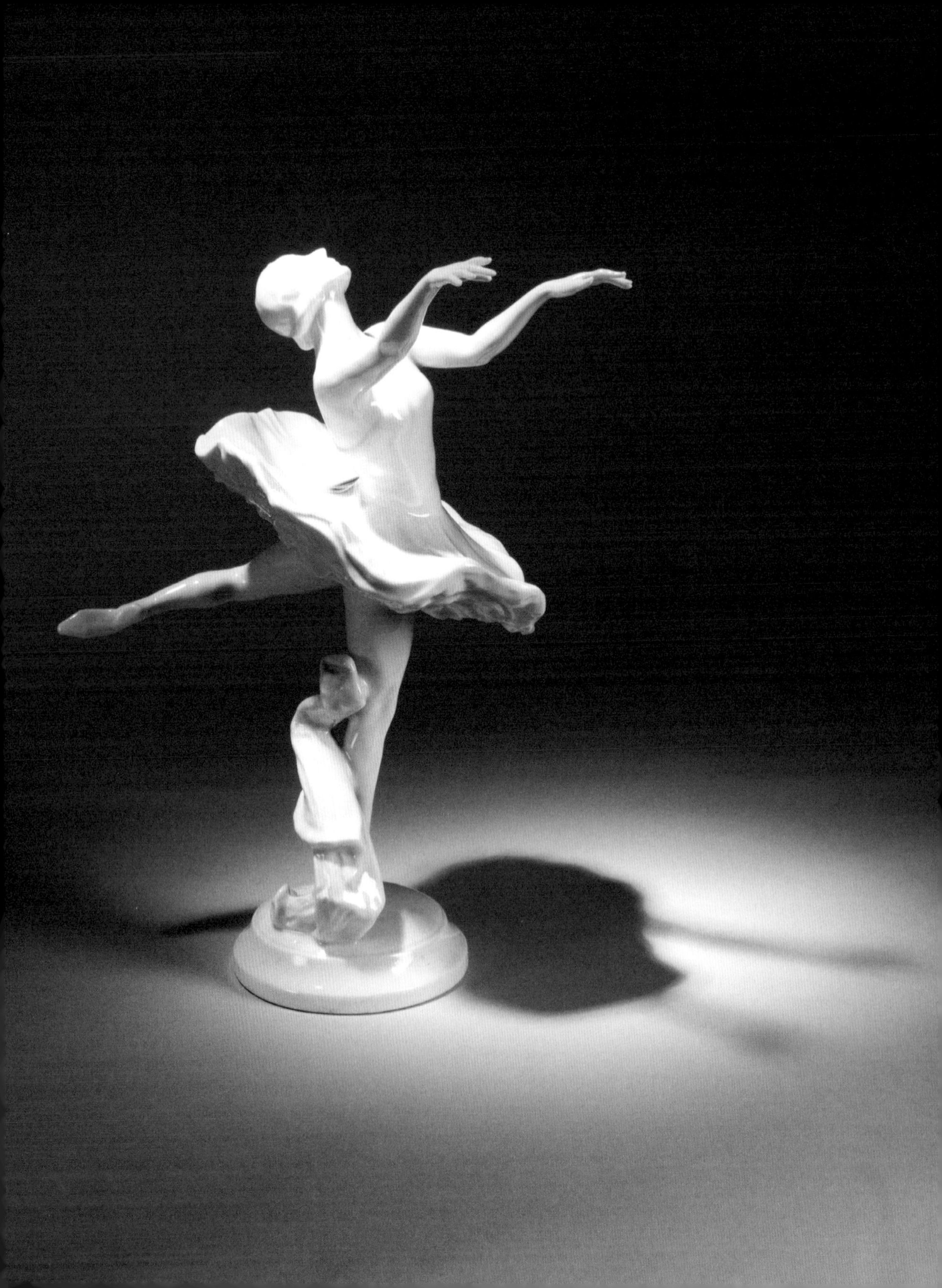

Giving

"Your generous gift has also created a lake," read a thank you letter to Marjorie Post from 1967.[1] Post lent her business acumen and substantial financial support to a variety of cultural, artistic, and educational institutions, especially programs for young people. Her gift for giving often included delightful and thoughtful surprises, such as the use of a DC7 airplane, fine linens, a beauty salon, and even fresh kumquats. While she was generous to many groups and communities, sometimes privately so, there were long-standing efforts that went on record, leaving enduring marks on the arts and education. It was her pleasure to give.

Post's granddaughter Ellen Charles said, "I was aware of her philanthropy…. She believed very strongly in it … because she felt that you ought to share what you have and try and improve someone else's life."[2] Donald Handelman, who, with his father, Meyer, handled taxes, investments, and other business matters for Post, remarked, "[She] was a generous person, but she didn't just hand it out…. There always had to be a reason. If there wasn't a reason, she wouldn't do it."[3] Post's financial secretary Betty Cannella sketched out part of the process, commenting, "Detailed charitable contributions were recorded by me…. I, in turn, would advise Mrs. Post of the request and tell her of her past [gifts] … then she would let me know what she wanted to do in that particular year, or at that particular time."[4]

"If you are in Washington and feel groovy," suggested a New York newspaper announcement in 1962, "drop in at the Georgetown Inn benefit for the Washington Ballet Guild." The event promised a tango performance by none other than Marjorie Post.[5] When the day came, Post, age seventy-five, danced the tango on stage, smiling ear to ear, partnered with a former professional dancer turned realtor. With each step, her multi-layered skirt floated upwards.[6] Every move she made was to benefit the ballet, as was a more understated tea she hosted at Hillwood. "Tea cup talk was on its toes with plans for the season's opening performance," reported a District publication in 1957. Members of the Ballet Guild, to which Post belonged, had agreed to sponsor that season's performances.[7]

Figurine of prima ballerina Anna Pavlova

Marjorie Post performing the tango, 1962

"She was just a lovely, lovely, lovely person and I loved her very much," reminisced Mary Day, director of the Washington School of Ballet. "She did many nice things for the school, and for the dance company then, the Washington Ballet we called it." In those days, Day was developing the ballet's college preparatory school. "[It combined the] curriculum of dance and academics, and [Post] was very interested in that because that was the way they trained in Russia," Day explained.[8] The new ballet school blended "footwork [and] brainwork," reported the *National Observer*, describing

New Year's Greetings to Mrs. May from the Students of the Washington School of Ballet

Greetings to Marjorie Post from the students of the Washington School of Ballet

the daily mix of schoolbooks and leotards.[9] As a board officer, Post cut the ribbon on the ballet's building in 1963 and also unveiled a plaque that read, "Dedicated to ballet and the academic arts, this institution is the first in the United States to offer these studies in one curriculum."[10] Graduation included performances of ballet, character dances, and modern dance, followed by the customary commencement exercise with the presentation of diplomas.[11]

The Washington Ballet's profile also got a boost from the nation's first lady. Jacqueline Kennedy held the honorary chairmanship of the foundation in 1962, as its organizational structure transitioned from a guild to a board. The foundation purposefully set out to open a non-segregated school and to provide scholarships "to be awarded without regard to race."[12] Post's husband Herbert May served as honorary foundation president, and Post filled the role of honorary vice president.[13] May and Post hosted a post-performance reception for Kennedy at Anderson House, taking great care

National Society of Arts and Letters awards, 1956

Marjorie Post at Lake Merriweather with Boy Scout members, Virginia

that the wildly popular first lady would not be overrun by well-heeled admirers, as was known to happen.[14] The couple also hosted a luncheon at Hillwood for the American Ballet Theater and the principal dancers of the Washington Ballet in 1963.[15] In addition, in 1961 Post hosted a luncheon at Hillwood for the entire Kirov ballet company during a stop in Washington.[16]

Post financed a visit to Pittsburgh by the Washington Ballet to benefit Health Center Hospitals. Society columnist Betty Beale proclaimed, "There are few … [who can] transport an entire ballet company to another city…. [Marjorie Post] did it last night."[17] With the costs covered by Post, all the proceeds from the sold-out performance could go to the Health Center Hospitals.[18]

By damming a river in Virginia, a two-and-a-half-mile manmade lake was created near the Goshen Pass in the Blue Ridge Mountains of Virginia and served as a waterfront for several Boy Scout camps.[19] Post wrote, "I do want you all to know how thrilled [I am that the lake] is to be called 'Lake Merriweather' for me."[20] A press release from the National Capital Area Council of the Boy Scouts of America shared that Post's "activities on behalf of scouting ranged from Texas to New York to Washington, D.C."[21] In a 1959 letter, Post remarked that she knew Mortimer Schiff, a key figure in early scouting, and over the years she observed "the wonderful time that the youngsters have and how much they learn during those summer [scout] trips."[22]

Plaque of thanks to Marjorie Post from the South Plains Council of the Boy Scouts of America, July 1957

While Post generously supported scouting facilities, from lakes to camps to office space, she did not expect to be consulted on the details. "I feel I should tell you do not count on me for this," she replied to an offer to review plans for the Merriweather Post Dining Hall at Camp Bedford in New York, near the Adirondacks. "I am sure it will all work out splendidly, and I thank you for your courtesy of thinking of me."[23] Post did, however, participate in lending a decorative hand in two instances: upon request she provided pictures of her father, mother, and herself for the headquarters of Camp Post in Texas. Also, for the headquarters of the National Capital Area Council in Washington, she donated a mounted twelve-point elk head, which would not have been out of place in her Camp Topridge estate in the Adirondacks.[24] More typical was a thank you note from recipients of Post's generosity and an update to her on how projects she contributed to were developing. Sometimes they would ask her for feedback, and a representative reply from her might be, "Letter received; Am delighted with idea so go ahead; Am thrilled about it all."[25]

Pennsylvania Republica

Marjorie Merriweather Post May

Giving

Massage room, which Marjorie Post also used for hairdressing, filled with pictures and tokens of appreciation, Hillwood

141

Silver Fawn, an international award given to one woman a year by the Boy Scouts

In 1955 Post was delighted to help make possible the capital area Boy Scouts' move to new headquarters at 1742 Connecticut Avenue NW, complete with a scout trading post for supplies, registration information office, and council administration space for a staff of forty-five.[26] Thirteen years later, the council wrote to Post, "Today we made final payment on the mortgage you helped us obtain.... Thought you might like to share our joy."[27] She went on to be a strong supporter of a large scout service center as the National Capital Area Council grew. On Lake Merriweather, the Boy Scouts established a new Camp Post, one among seven other camps, and the Post Lodge provided cooking and dining facilities for two hundred.[28]

In an update to Post, the capital area scouts reported that they were the "largest single scout council in the country ... a significant breakthrough in reaching both inner-city and rural areas."[29] In hindsight, this meant that the capital area scouts were active in an inner city–rural program to markedly "make the benefits of scouting readily available to all boys regardless of race."[30] After all the camps at Goshen got into full swing, Post received an inspired thank you note: "It is a stirring sight to see several hundred [scouts] in boats and canoes and swimming in beautiful Lake Merriweather."[31]

In 1959 Post wrote, "Some years ago our Texas properties were deeded over to the Boy Scouts of Texas, quite a sizable property near Post City."[32]

Marjorie Post's activities on behalf of scouting ranged from Texas to New York to Washington, D.C.

The South Plains Council of Texas reported in 1972, "As you probably know, Camp Post is the most widely used grounds year-round in West Texas." It further noted that, while most of the scouts had full family support for their activities, there was "[another] group of boys who without outside help could not enjoy a week at camp." This group—some from large families where the father worked two jobs to keep food on the table—learned first aid, basic swimming, plant and wildlife identification, and tried their hand at archery.[33]

At a ceremony at Hillwood in 1972, scouts aged 10–15, from Cub Scouts to Eagle Scouts, bestowed upon Post the Silver Fawn, an international honor awarded to one woman each year.[34] On the occasion, the National Capital Area Council declared Post the "First Lady of Scouting."[35] Other tokens of appreciation for Post's good works over the years included a plaque for

```
VALENTINE'S DAY ♥ GREETINGS
                    by western union

SY SKA013 GTG PD .=SARANAC LAKE NY 14 923A EST.=
MRS MARJORIE MERRIWEATHER POST.=
   1100 SO OCEAN BLVD PALMBEACH FLO.=

THINKING OF YOU ON THIS VALENTINES DAY. OVER 3000 KISSES
FROM THE BOY SCOUTS AND LEADERS OF THE ADIRONDACK COUNCIL
BOY SCOUTS. BEST WISHES.=
        BOB F BAUER NATL COUNCIL 2 PARK AVE    NYC.=
```

More than 3,000 scout kisses to Marjorie Post, 1968

her garden, a heart-shaped pin, red roses, and a Valentine's Day telegram delivering "over 3000 [scout] kisses" from the Adirondacks.[36] It also made the news that Post was the first American woman to be pinned by the Boy Scouts. Post's published response to this singular award was, "I didn't believe it, but now I am terribly proud."[37]

When Post's alma mater, Mount Vernon Seminary and Junior College, in Washington, D.C., closed its seminary so it could focus on the college, she told the New York Club of the school, "It is a wise decision."[38] She further remarked in 1965, "If we do not bend with the times, we will break."[39] Post had graduated from Mount Vernon Seminary in the class of 1904. The school catered to women "who feel the necessity of further education to fit them for their position in life."[40] She later joined the school's board as the first alumna trustee, serving from 1933 to 1943.[41]

One of her notable contributions to the school was during the Great Depression, when she covered faculty salaries and other financial obligations to keep it in operation.[42] Amid World War II, she stepped down from the board over discussions about the Navy taking over the campus. In her letter of resignation, she expressed her desire to "conserve the property

Giving

Marjorie Post around the time of her studies at Mount Vernon Seminary, ca. 1902–3

Plaquette with a view of Marjorie Post's alma mater, Mount Vernon

of the school," while also acknowledging, "We are now facing conditions which none of us could foresee."[43]

Despite leaving the board, she remained involved, funding Post Hall and Library, named for her parents, as well as the Merriweather House. Other projects she supported included installing additional power lines and a portico to protect visitors from inclement weather.[44] Cash contributions and gifts of General Foods or International Business Machines stock—all to benefit the institution—were familiar.[45]

In 1957 Post accepted the distinction of being named honorary chairman of the board at Mount Vernon.[46] At the dedication ceremony for Post Hall in November 1956, the school had placed historical documents from Mount Vernon's history into the cornerstone of the new facility, including a biography of Post.[47] The profile noted her leaving Battle Creek at the age of fourteen for Mount Vernon to study with school founder Elizabeth Somers, noting the founder's "conviction of the important role women play in the building of the greater America."[48] In a speech to those in attendance, trustee Elmer Louis Kayser said Mount Vernon students and staff had "an added obligation ... to see that advantages are transformed into realized opportunities."[49]

Beyond Post literally providing foundations for buildings, she was also appreciated as the "heart of Mount Vernon," symbolized by a simple, heart-shaped pendant given to her by admiring alumni. Her involvement with Mount Vernon had a personal and knowing touch, perhaps inspired by her memories as a student of the class of 1904.[50] At one point, Post found herself thinking about the school's reception area in the middle of the night and soon after sent a note inquiring about the space, "where young gentleman callers could be received ... something very important in many of the girls' minds, as you well know."[51]

Post frequently sent furnishings and decorative objects to Mount Vernon for common areas used by students and staff, even instructing decorators Mitchell Samuels of French & Company and Fred Vogel Interior Decorations to send a particular light fixture or a selection of linens.[52] Leonard Carmichael, secretary of the Smithsonian, credited Post for not only providing Mount Vernon with buildings, but also with "outstanding collections of objects to embellish them ... [giving] a character unmatched in most other educational institutions."[53]

Marjorie Post and daughters unveiling C.W. Post's portrait at the Long Island University campus dedicated in his name, 1954

Post also sent small delights, such as fresh kumquats, which home economics classes turned into preserves, and through her connections in government, inauguration medallions that enthralled the faculty.[54] The interaction was a source of gratification for Post, who wrote to the student body president in 1953, "The joyous youth ... of all you girls and your high purpose and fine character [give] me quite a kick."[55] Likewise for Post, the sisters of the Sigma Alpha Theta sorority at C.W. Post College–Long Island University were a "grand group of girls."[56] She also took great pleasure in receiving letters addressed to her as "Mother Marjorie" and "Aunt Marjorie" from the Sigma Alpha Epsilon fraternity, when she served as their honorary housemother.[57]

Marking the centennial of Post's father's birth, the Brookville, Long Island campus was rededicated to C.W. Post in 1954. On the occasion, Marjorie Post unveiled her father's portrait in the institution's Great Hall.[58]

Medal from Mount Vernon to Marjorie Post for distinguished service to her alma mater, 1937

Her 123-acre estate, Hillwood, in Brookville village near Roslyn, New York, had been sold to Long Island University for its campus.[59] The school's first class, arriving in September 1955, consisted of 19 women and 102 men, and by 1965 the university hosted over 5,000 students in a range of programs.[60] Sorority sister Lisa Smith explained, "For some of us, we might have been the first woman or first person in our families to go to college."[61] Marjorie Post May Hall, a women's residence, was completed in 1963, providing not only housing for more than 250 students and faculty, but a beauty salon as well.[62] Post became pen pals with the presidents of the fraternity and sorority, responding to their letters and taking time to acknowledge their achievements.[63]

Post planned and funded educational trips to Washington, D.C., for the brothers and sisters with the highest scores and best financial practices, the latter meaning that their sorority or fraternity dues and accounts were paid in full.[64] While in the capital, they would naturally visit key historical and cultural sites, as well as Hillwood. Post had also delighted in

Laying the cornerstone for Post Hall, Mount Vernon Junior College, 1956

extending this educational indulgence to twenty-four Battle Creek High School teens, chartering a DC7 for the occasion, as her own private turboprop only seated seventeen. She joined them on the bus she chartered as they toured the nation's capital.[65]

She also gave generously to the world of music. "Although I have had something to do with the ballet," said Post, "it is nothing compared to my activity with the symphony."[66] Post served on the board of directors for the National Symphony Orchestra for more than three decades, from 1942 to 1973.[67] In 1962 Lloyd Symington, president of the board, wrote to Post, "[Just received] the marvelous news of your two contributions to the sustaining fund which sets a new record in individual giving."[68]

Post's fellow board members, recognizing the energy she brought to her

Token of heart-felt appreciation to Marjorie Post from the New York Club alumni of Mount Vernon, ca. 1960

duties, thanked Post in the 1954 gala program "for [her] continuing devotion, moral, and financial assistance."[69] A 1954 article in *Life* magazine, "Resplendent Ball," reported that a substantial sum of money had been raised for the symphony.[70] The gala committee, with Post as honorary chair, organized a formal gathering with guests waltzing to music provided by symphony musicians. The assistant secretary of state won the waltz contest. A brand new Studebaker was auctioned off—by an auctioneer brought in by Post—and perfume and pedigree poodles were given away as prizes. President Dwight Eisenhower, Vice President Richard Nixon, and thirty-three ambassadors made donations as patrons. The ball was the largest fundraiser to date for the orchestra.[71]

The journalist Selwa Roosevelt called it "a night for white tie and tails for men, and mink, ermine and white fox, velvets, satins and sequins for the women."[72] Post wore a gray dress with an ostrich feather stole. While columnists enjoyed covering such events light-heartedly (the columnist Betty Beale joked, "Now [that] the National Symphony Ball is over, Washingtonians can rest their eyes that were blinded by all that jewelry") or wordsmithing clever photo captions (to wit, "The social note is music"), the actual high note for the committee was funding the orchestra's financial needs for that year. That meant taking advantage of nearly every fundraising enticement available, from dance contests to puppy prizes and ending with the crescendo of a chance to win a new car.[73]

In 1955, thirteen years into Post's tenure as an orchestra board member, conductor Howard Mitchell discussed with the board his hope to someday lengthen the orchestra's season by performing for high school groups visiting the nation's capital. With the idea being of interest to the board, the discussion turned to how to fund the program. Post excused herself from the room and telephoned her financial consultant. Returning to the meeting, she announced that she would fund the project.[74]

Mitchell's idea was the perfect combination of his passion for the art form and the philanthropist's interest in young people. According to Mitchell, "Youngsters sop up other forms of culture, [although] never hearing so much as an oboe."[75] For Post the philanthropist, funding five weeks of concerts fulfilled her "fondest wish that the thousands of young people who attend the concerts will return to their homes throughout the country with a desire to hear more of the world's fine music, and that the series will

Marjorie Post hosting
students from C.W. Post
College at Hillwood,
Washington, D.C.

Marjorie Post giving a tour of her home and art collection, Hillwood

Pull-out drawers with information for visitors about Marjorie Post's art collection, Hillwood

serve to promote the cause of symphony orchestras in hundreds of small communities all over the United States."[76] In the end, 61,266 children from forty-three states enjoyed the Music for Young America concerts during its first season, in 1956. For the majority of them, it was the first time they had heard a live orchestra.[77]

About the Music for Young America series, Post remarked, "Well, it's been a thrill to watch these youngsters, to hear their comments, to get their letters." Young people wrote to Post about their experience of seeing and hearing live performances of works by Brahms, Mozart, Ravel, Wagner, Beethoven, Barber, Gershwin, Debussy, Rimsky-Korsakov, and Stravinsky.[78] A student from Linesville, Pennsylvania, wrote, "I am the only child of an average family that always considered 'long-hair' music [i.e., by classical

Kornilov Brothers Factory porcelain in Marjorie Post's collection

Imperial Porcelain Factory plate

Members of Sigma Alpha Epsilon at C.W. Post College present a gift to their honorary housemother, Marjorie Post, 1965

composers] dizzy stuff.... I sat on the edge of my seat the whole time and I hoped that the concert would never end."[79] A group from Hazlehurst, Georgia, wrote in appreciation, "None of the group had ever had the experience of hearing such an orchestra."[80]

In 1967 a Music for Young America concert was held and recorded on the White House lawn. First lady, Lady Bird Johnson, delivered remarks, with President Lyndon Johnson at her side. The event was to be broadcast over the eastern educational network of public television. Edmund Campbell, the president of broadcasting station WETA, wrote to Post, "The nation's capital needs broader interpretation across the nation—interpretation which includes not just the politics of Washington but the cultural aspects as well."[81] Sixty-two years after the first Music for Young America concert, the National Symphony Orchestra still includes offerings for young audiences in its program.[82]

One of the symphony's publications described Post as "one of the [philanthropic] angels of the NSO." Her thirty-one years with the orchestra,

Members of Sigma Alpha Epsilon from C.W. Post College in the Japanese-style garden at Hillwood

however, were not always grand balls and adorable hand-written thank you letters from children.[83] The symphony faced real challenges in keeping the music playing over those three decades, and, as a board member, Post was aware of them and stayed on. She not only contributed substantial financial assistance, but also offered gentle-but-clear advice about matters of governance at the board level. She was prompt to clarify her intentions for gift giving, and encouraged and offered friendly tips to the management staff, but without telling them how to run the day-to-day operations of the symphony or how to do their jobs.

The staff, for its part, deserved credit for this heavenly relationship with Post the philanthropist. They proposed suitable and engaging projects to her, shared their hopes for the orchestra, disclosed problems, asked for financial support in a business-like manner, and promptly provided additional details when asked. They also sent Post regular thank you notes acknowledging her wide-ranging participation as a board member, made suitable gestures, and found gifts to give her as a small token of their gratitude.[84] "A life-saving transfusion" is how Mitchell expressed his gratitude to Post at one point in a thank you note.[85] Numerous plaques, concerts played in honor of Post, and even gifts for her garden were sent her way in thanks.[86]

In addition, Post bought bulk tickets and season subscriptions that she shared or gifted to others, so they too could enjoy the performances. She

Battle Creek High School students on a tour of Washington, D.C., and Hillwood, May 1963

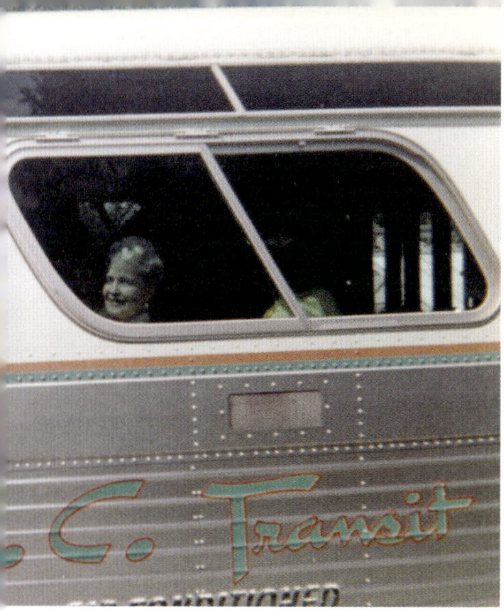
C. Transit
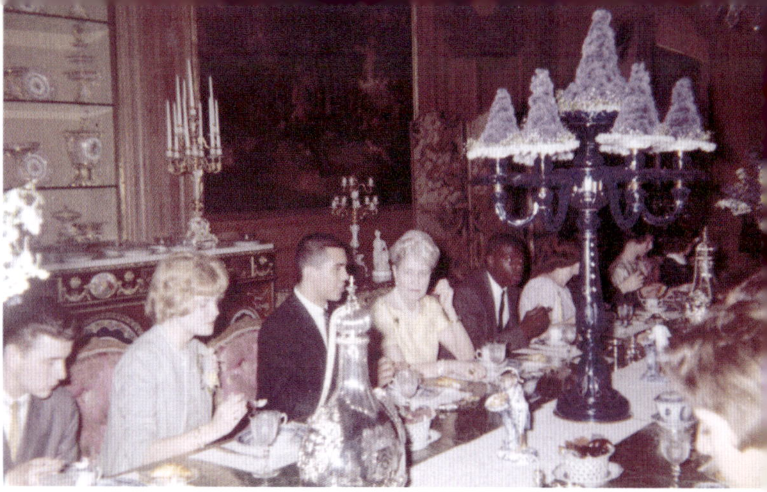
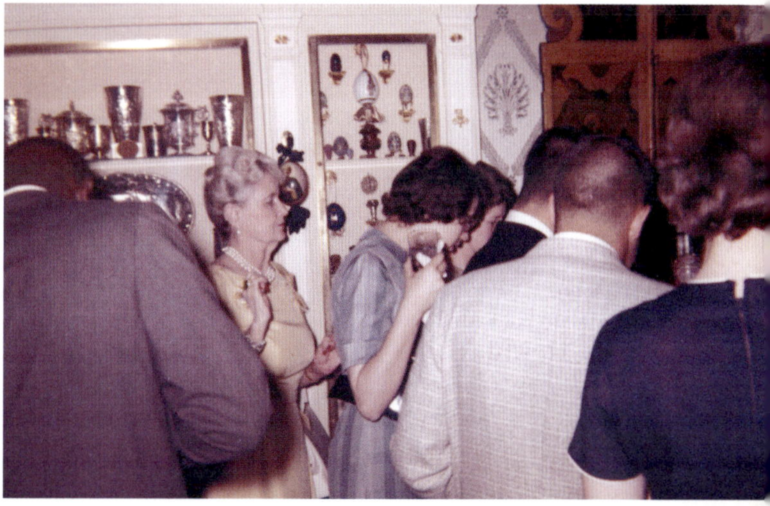
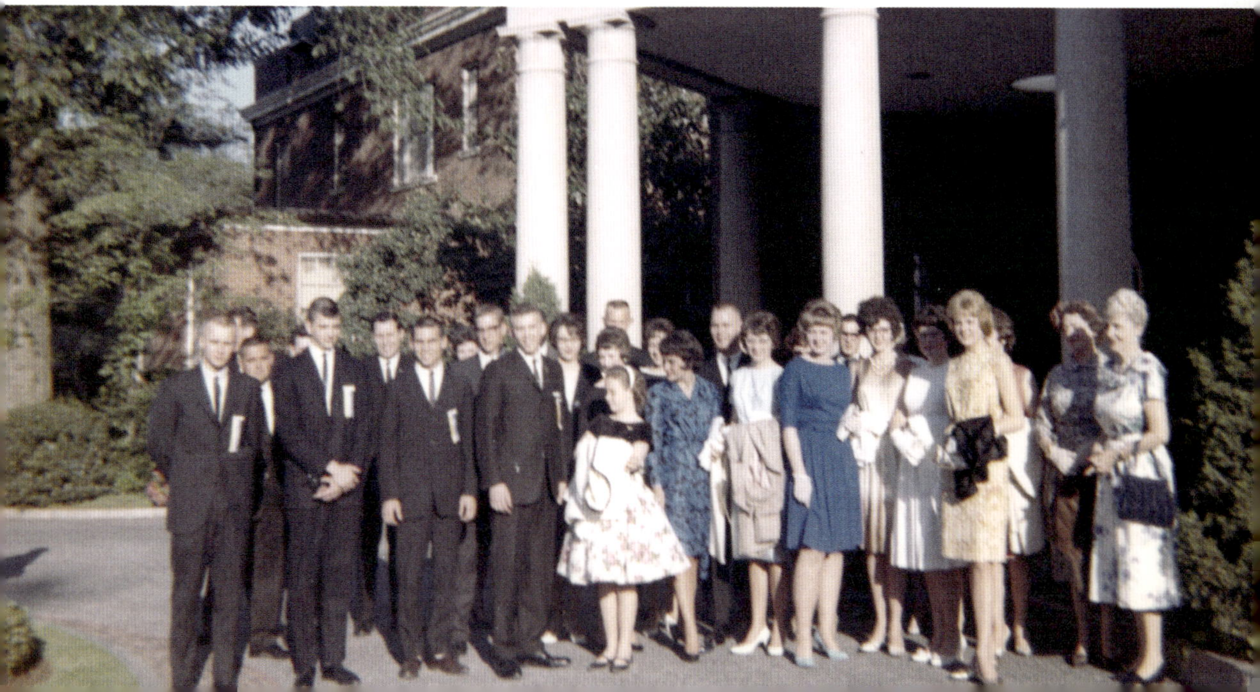

French porcelain room, Hillwood

sometimes paid the fee for a big-name soloist to perform with the orchestra and put forth matching funds to encourage others to give to cover badly needed funding.[87] Post read up on the status and straits of other major orchestras to stay informed.[88] To extend the professional musicians' season of employment, she guaranteed five weeks of Music for Young America over the length of the musicians' three-year contract, which the musicians' union greatly appreciated. When a newspaper critic opined that the symphony "simply isn't tops" in a review, Post wrote in support to the orchestra's

Sèvres potpourri vases in Marjorie Post's collection

Draped vases by Sèvres

NATIONAL SYMPHONY ORCHESTRA
OF WASHINGTON, D. C.

HOWARD MITCHELL, Music Director

in conjunction with

"Music for Young America"

Announces with **Pride** *the*

MERRIWEATHER POST CONTEST
open to high school students
FOR THE
MERRIWEATHER POST MUSIC AWARD

ELIGIBILITY

1. Contest is open to all pianists, violinists and cellists attending a public, private or parochial high school. Student shall not have graduated by March 1, 1957 (closing date for applications to be submitted).
2. Contestant must be able to play from memory a complete concerto from standard symphony repertoire.
3. Contestant must be recommended by his or her music teacher, school principal or a conductor.

WINNER OF THE MERRIWEATHER POST AWARD WILL RECEIVE—

1. A guest appearance with the National Symphony Orchestra.
2. $2,000.00 cash award.

FINALISTS WILL RECEIVE—

1. Guest appearance with the National Symphony Orchestra.
2. $100.00 cash award.

Mrs. Merriweather Post

This contest is in tribute to Mrs. Merriweather Post, 1st Vice President and one of the founders of the National Symphony Orchestra. The Merriweather Post Contest is being held in conjunction with the MUSIC FOR YOUNG AMERICA series of Free concerts which Mrs. Post is sponsoring. These concerts will be given every evening from April 17th through May 21st, 1957, and all high school students visiting Washington, D. C. during this 5 week period are cordially invited to attend. Free tickets for these concerts, and further information about the contest, may be obtained by writing:

RALPH BLACK, Manager
National Symphony Orchestra
1779 Massachusetts Avenue, N.W.
Washington 6, D. C.

RALPH BLACK, Manager   FRITZ MAILE, Assistant Manager
EDITH MORGAN, Coordinator "Music for Young America"

Merriweather Post Music Award

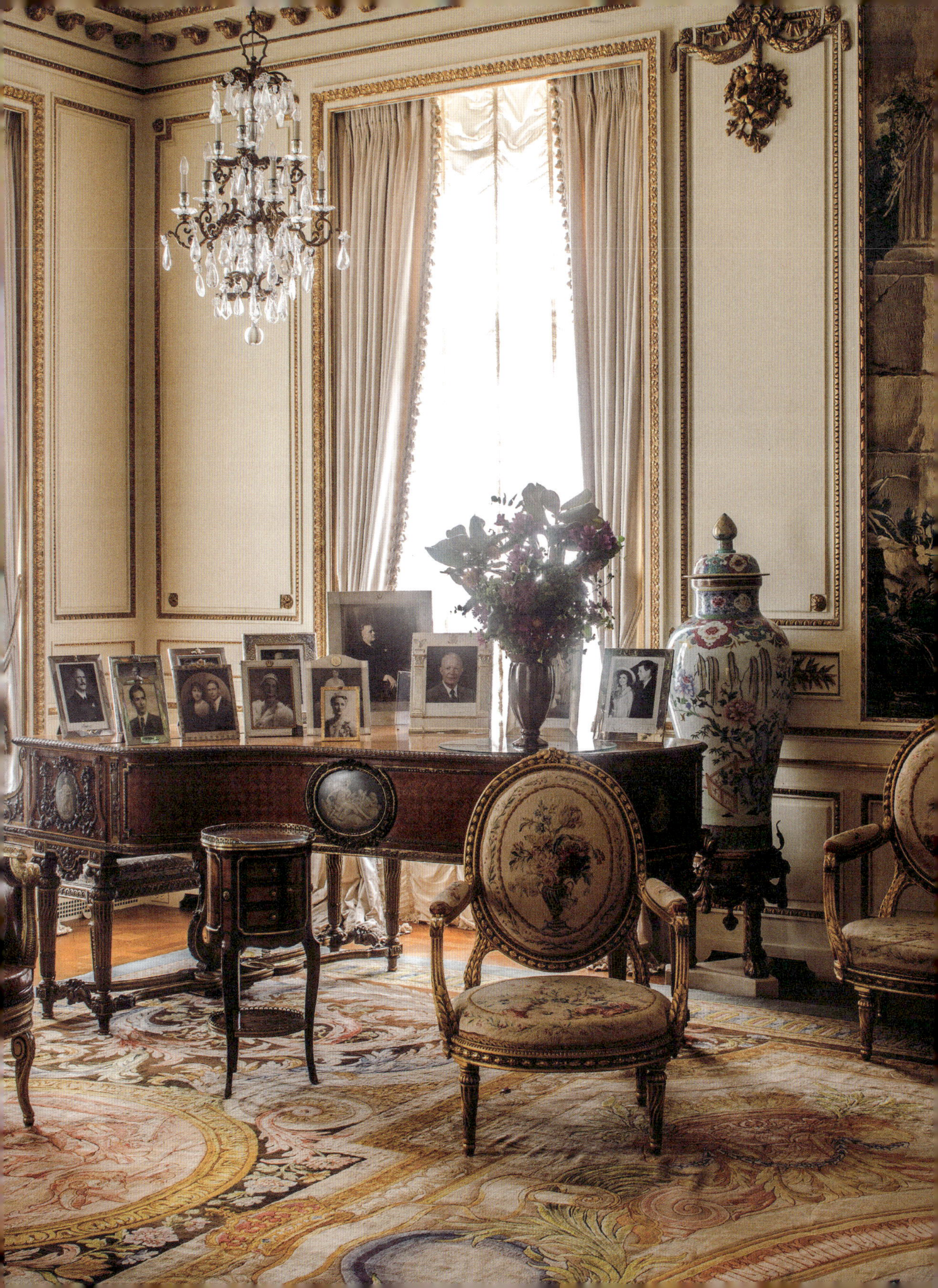

manager, who had shared the article with her, "[The critic] is indeed quite a menace," and encouraged him to "simply ignore the whole situation."[89]

In another act of generosity, and indicative of Post's love of music, the Merriweather Post Contest was launched in 1956. Open to high school students hoping to make a career in music, the competition offered the winner a cash award, a scholarship toward attending the Juilliard School of Music, and a soloist performance with the National Symphony Orchestra.[90] Post had good fun, following the competition winners as they went on to music conservatory training and university, to such events as the International Tchaikovsky Competition, and to soloing with other orchestras.[91]

Accepting one of twelve places on the National Cultural Center's Washington Advisory Committee on the Arts, Post prepared a statement as the first vice president of the National Symphony Orchestra and vice president of the Washington Ballet Guild. She asserted, "Congress has an opportunity to [provide] … a site where music, dance, drama and other performing arts can be presented," adding with caution not to delay with hopes of securing a different or better site. In 1963, she very publicly donated $100,000 to the project, pointedly stating that the gift should be understood in the spirit of "[encouraging] other people to contribute gifts of any size to help make the Center a reality."[92] In May 1971 she gave a dinner party and attended the first official preview for the facility, the John F. Kennedy Center for the Performing Arts, still then under construction.

Another music venue, located in Columbia, Maryland, bears Post's own name. In July 1966, Robert Rogers, the manager of the symphony, wrote to her, suggesting how it would be fitting "to recognize what you have done and are continuing to do by naming the amphitheater the Merriweather Post Pavilion of Music." Rogers continued, regarding the summer venue for the orchestra, "I hope you agree, and that the proposal is acceptable to you." Post replied, "Yes indeed."[93]

Opening of the Merriweather Post Pavilion of Music, Columbia, Maryland, 1967

1967 opening

MERRIWEATHER POST PAVILION OF MUSIC

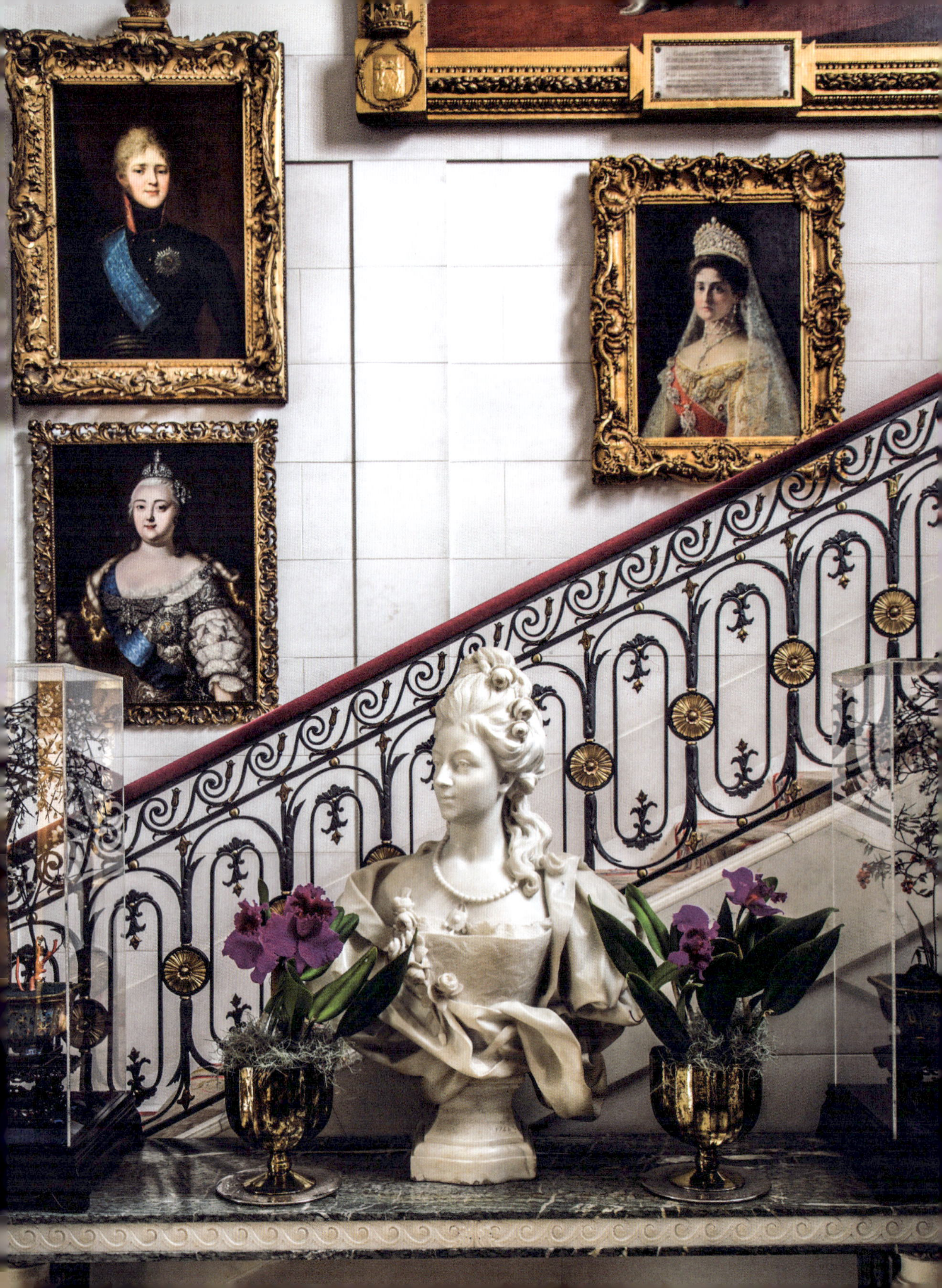

Legacy

"A home you could live in, and a home where you could enjoy works of art…. I think she became really caught up in it all," said financial manager Donald Handelman, describing Marjorie Post's Hillwood estate.[1] Post handpicked Handelman to project manage the transformation of the property. "I want to put you in charge of the grounds and construction that I want done," Post half-asked and half-stated to Handelman.[2] Moreover, she pointedly said to him in 1955, at the age of sixty-eight, "This is going to be my last home."[3] In the end, with renovations from 1955 to 1957, what Post created at Hillwood, according to financial secretary Betty Cannella, was "the place of treasures and the place for the future."[4] There were formal garden rooms, a greenhouse, a mansion, and outbuildings to house a staff to run it all. Post's daughter, the actress Dina Merrill, explained that Hillwood as a museum was "[Mother's] wish to show a certain way of life that was dying, that wouldn't exist again, and to share the collections that she made and loved."[5]

"She wanted the pavilion [with feature film equipment], she also wanted certain rooms to display art. This was her lifestyle," recalled Handelman, who indeed agreed to work as project manager for the renovations. "I think that the idea and concept of a museum began to grow on her as she saw how the house was evolving."[6] Post decisively stated that for Hillwood to function as her home, it first required a curved driveway and then outbuildings as housing and facilities for the staff. She also provided a mere two-page executive summary outlining her initial intentions for the mansion. Post had remained anonymous during the real-estate transaction to acquire the estate. The work to be done to make it her residence was quietly outlined in January 1955.[7] Two months later, in March, she and Joseph Davies divorced.[8]

Post bought the mansion, designed by the architect John Deibert and built in 1926, from the Erwin family, who called it Arbremont.[9] Incidentally, the architect had also created a similar, "sibling" house of sorts elsewhere in the city, but with a different roof plan, that Mrs. Erwin's sister occupied.[10] To transform the Erwins' Arbremont into Post's vision of the future Hillwood, the first-floor living room became a library. "Please locate a Georgian Pine

Entry hall, Hillwood, Washington, D.C.

Marjorie Post's collection in the context of Hillwood; French drawing room

168

French drawing room, Hillwood

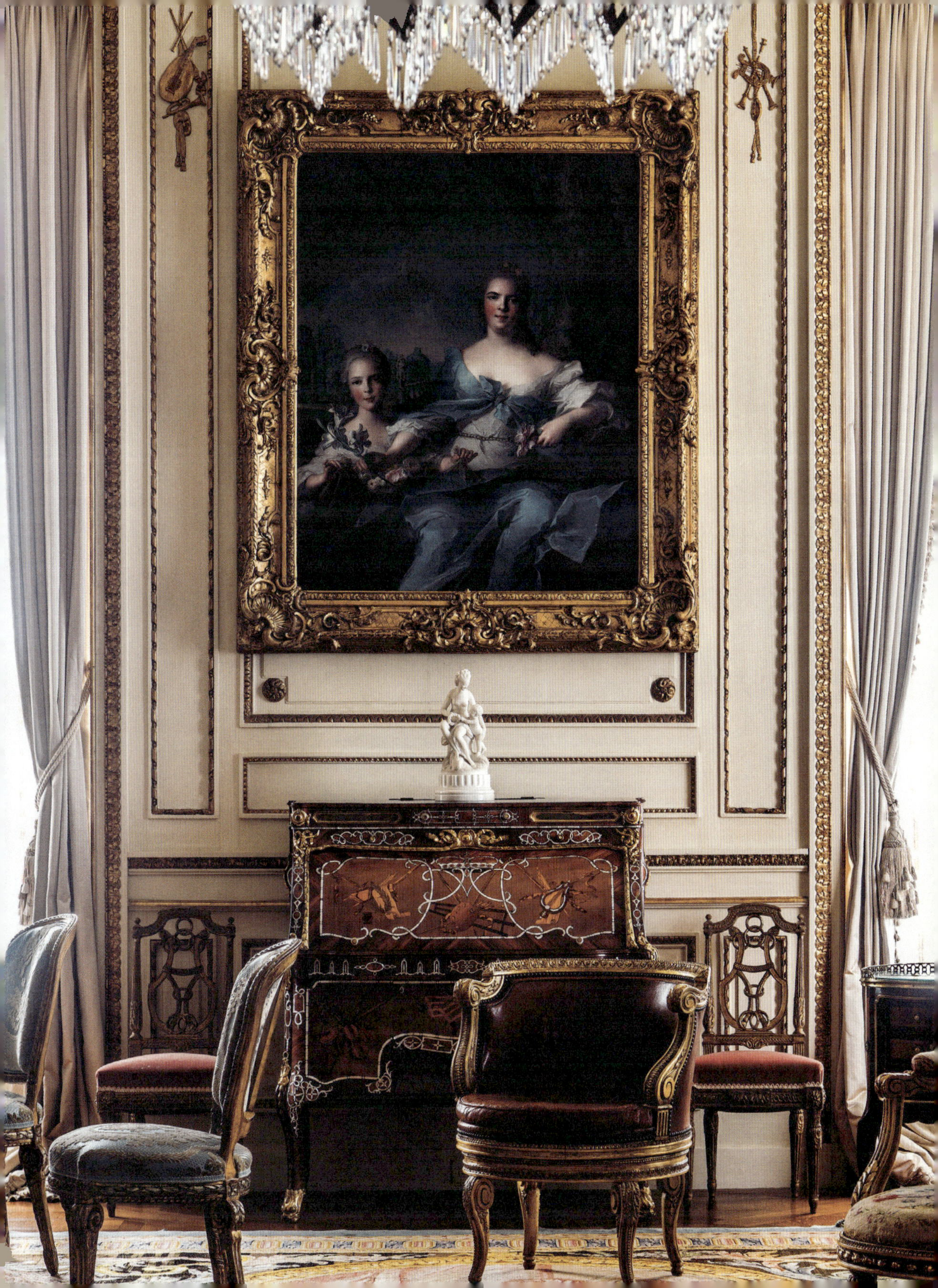

Room, an old one which would convert [the paneling] to this size," Post instructed. For the entry hall she said, "There must be a beautiful, typically French stairway."[11] The swimming pool was filled in, additional land purchased to accommodate entrance gates to the estate, air conditioning installed, the electrical system replaced, display rooms for Post's porcelain and icon collections designated, the ceiling above the dining room demolished and heightened, and the roof raised two feet, among other changes.[12] In all, the transformation took about two and half years, passing a District of Columbia inspection by October 1957.[13]

In envisioning Hillwood as a future museum, Post spoke with the National Trust for Historic Preservation and other institutions knowledgeable about such matters. Meanwhile, she hired a private curator, Marvin Ross, to work with her collections. He certainly recommended new acquisitions, but his duties also involved detailed inventories for insurance coverage and preparations for the professional management of Post's vast holdings, knowing that the collection would someday be part of a public museum.[14] Ross also handled tours of the mansion and gardens, lectured, conducted research, and published parts of Post's collection.[15] "Marvin used to talk to various people around [Washington] about this, and he was trying very hard to make it into a museum even before it was open to the public," recalled Alan Fern, a fellow culture and museum professional who interacted with Ross during that era.[16]

The shift in Post's thinking about transforming a private collection into one to share with the public was clear in 1965. At that time she admitted, "In those [early] days, I was not collecting for a museum the way I am now."[17] As Cannella recalled, "The 1960s were very busy because we were getting into a more detailed inventory [of the art collection]." Her duties grew to include, among other things, working with Ross on catalogues of the collection. Cannella also prepared numbers on the cost of running Hillwood, as if budgeting for a museum.[18] There was a leak to the press in 1962, announcing Post's gift of Hillwood to the Smithsonian Institution, but the actual agreement would not be official until December 1968, five years before her death.[19]

On September 12, 1973, Post's three daughters telegrammed former first lady Mamie Eisenhower with the message, "Our beloved mother passed away peacefully in her sleep this morning, we thought you would want to

Rose garden during Marjorie Post's lifetime, Hillwood, 1967

know."[20] Syndicated news reports said that Post's health "had been failing rapidly in recent weeks" and called her "one of the nation's top philanthropists."[21] Family and friends, including Mamie Eisenhower, neighbors, and members of Congress, attended her funeral service on September 17, 1973, at the National Presbyterian Church in Washington.[22]

After an organ prelude, followed by readings from the Old and New Testaments, Post's son-in-law Cliff Robertson, the actor, married to Post's daughter Dina Merrill, delivered the eulogy he had written and titled "This Lady."[23] He cited her many admirable traits, including possessing humanitarianism and compassion, coming to the aid of her country "without being called," fostering "artistic nourishment," leading an examined life that "consistently put the material in a subordinate position," and having a "belief in the dignity and rights of all people, of all faiths, color and origin."[24] Later that day, a private Christian Science service was held at Hillwood, and Post's ashes were placed in the rose garden monument. Post's longtime butler Gus Modig remembered, "It was a very rainy evening, and if I may [say] so, I had the honor to carry the urn from the house and put it

Rose garden obelisk, Marjorie Post's final resting place, Hillwood

into the monument."[25] Post's household staff chipped in to purchase a large basket of orchids to pay tribute to their former employer.[26]

In Palm Beach, residents gathered to pay their respects at Bethesda-by-the-Sea Episcopal Church in January 1974. They dedicated the Marjorie Merriweather Post Memorial Causeway in 1975.[27] Meanwhile, in Michigan, a reporter wrote, "[Post's] decisions, together with her father, played a great part in determining what is Battle Creek today," noting that Marjorie Street, the company housing development called Post Addition, and the Post School were still familiar places around town.[28]

In autumn 1977, newspapers in the nation's capital announced Hillwood's opening to the public.[29] It was not, however, operating as part of the Smithsonian Institution. The main culprit for this change in plans? The unforeseen high inflation of the mid-1970s. The economic situation after Post's death made it impossible for the Smithsonian to operate the estate as per the agreement with her, namely, that the estate should reflect the manner in which she had lived. Although the number crunching provided

Legacy

Autumn colors in the Japanese-style garden, Hillwood

by Post and her financial secretary could not stand against the crushing inflation of the decade, another forward-thinking measure made the museum nonetheless possible: A provision of the agreement stated that if the Smithsonian could not operate Hillwood as a nonprofit museum, the property could revert to the Marjorie Merriweather Post Foundation. And so it did, on July 1, 1976. The following year, visitors began enjoying Hillwood, with its remarkable grounds and mansion.[30]

Around the time of Hillwood's public opening, Post's daughter Dina Merrill shared, "Mother was not afraid of hard work.... She believed in being prepared for any kind of life.... She always felt that no matter what happened, she could be an excellent hairdresser and manicurist if she had to … and she would have done it too, without a qualm."[31] In reality, however,

French parterre, Hillwood

Post's lot in life—bolstered by her education, skills, and desires—was to be a twentieth-century business executive (as a director of General Foods) and a philanthropist, neither of which were typical expectations for a woman born in 1887, nor even typical for a man.

    Shortly after Post died, Senator Jennings Randolph of West Virginia remarked in the *Congressional Record*, "Her brilliant mind, vision, organizing ability and decisiveness were respected and her counsel was sought by many." The senator continued, "[With her passing] ends an era of elegance and excellence, possibly never to be matched."[32] Post's lifestyle, collection, mansion, and gardens remain on view and open to visitors to experience at Hillwood in Washington, D.C.

Hillwood's remarkable grounds and celebrated mansion are open to the public

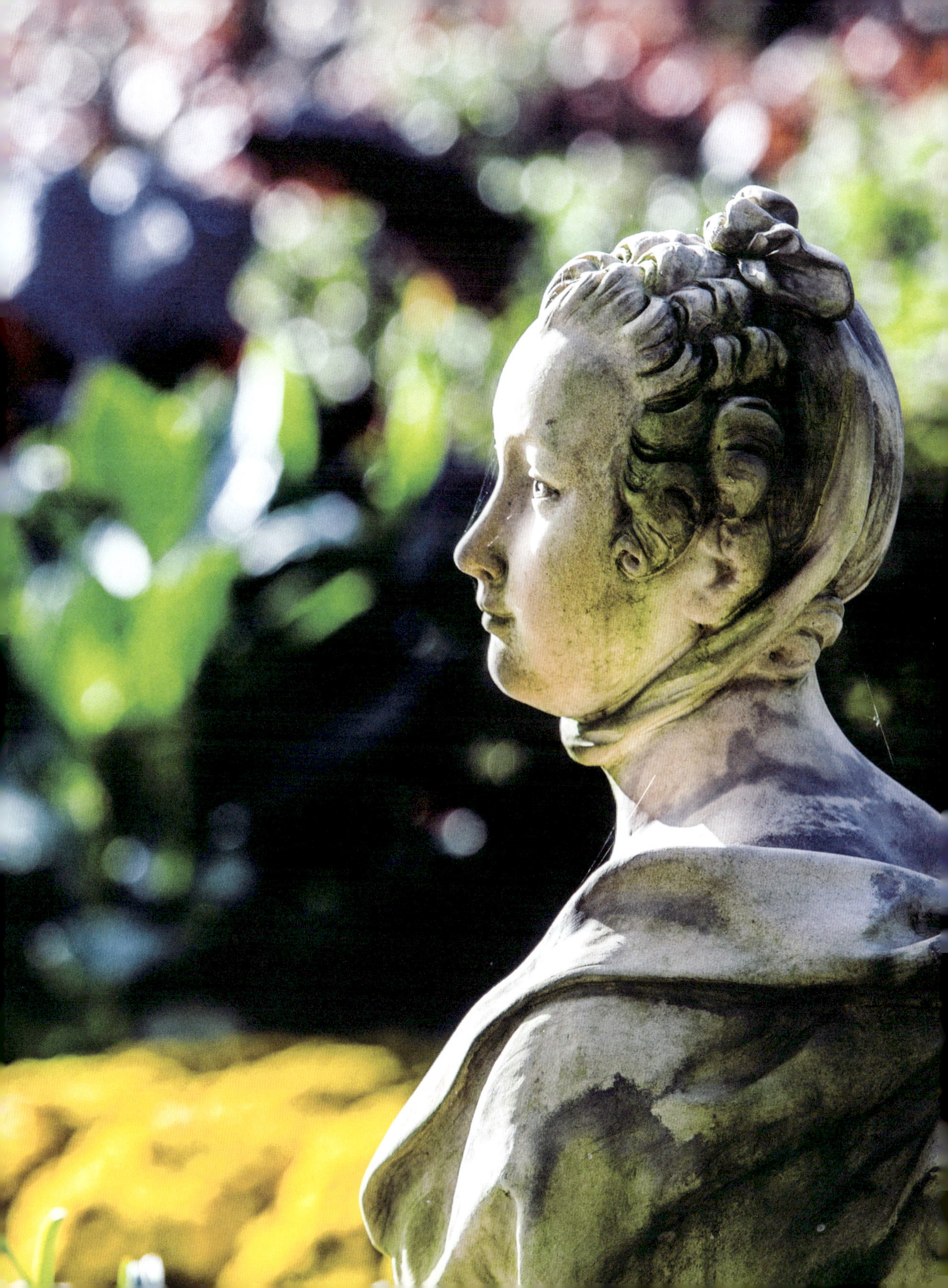

Notes

Introduction

1. Betty Cannella, oral history interview by Nancy Harris, November 1998.
2. Chung, *Living Artfully*, 17.
3. "Mother's Hillwood Home," in *PS10*, n.d., clippings, Hillwood Archives.
4. Post to Dietrich, September 28, 1964, Marjorie Post Papers, Bentley Historical Library.
5. Chung, *Living Artfully*, 75–76, 92.
6. Marjorie Post, interview by Nettie Major, February 1962.
7. Major, *C.W. Post*, 30–31, 293.
8. Marjorie Post, interview by Nettie Major, December 1960.
9. Marjorie Post, interview by Nettie Major, December 1964.
10. Ibid.
11. Marjorie Post, interview by Nettie Major, December 1960.
12. Major, *C.W. Post*, 20–30.
13. Ellen Charles, oral history interview by Stephanie Brown, November 2003; Walter Beach, oral history interview by Stephanie Brown, November 2003; Rose Dickens, oral history interview by Stephanie Brown, May 2004; Michael Tucci, oral history interview by Estella Chung, November 2011; Marjorie Post, interview by David Zeitlin, August 1964; Christian Science letters in James Griffin file [17–25], Marjorie Post Papers, Bentley Historical Library; Chung, *Living Artfully*, 33–36; Hillwood menus, Hillwood Archives.
14. Marjorie Post, interview by Nettie Major, December 1964.
15. Ibid.
16. Marjorie Merriweather Post Papers, Special Collections Research Center, George Washington University, B1-F1.
17. Mikhalevsky, *Dear Daughters*, 19–20.
18. Gordon Hoxie, "Mount Vernon's Magnificent Opportunity," November 1966, in an album made for the convocation honoring Post, Mount Vernon Seminary and Junior College, George Washington University.
19. Marjorie Post, interview by David Zeitlin, August 1964.
20. Address at Battle Creek, December 31, 1904, C.W. Post Papers [4-4], Bentley Historical Library.
21. Major, *C.W. Post*, 161, 293; Rubin, *American Empress*, 62.
22. Marjorie Post, interview by Nettie Major, December 1960.
23. Chung, *Living Artfully*, 13; Marjorie Post, interview by David Zeitlin, August 1964.
24. C.W. Post to Marjorie Post, April 1, 1908, C.W. Post Papers [4-17; 4-18], Bentley Historical Library.
25. C.W. Post to Marjorie Post, April 17, 1909, C.W. Post Papers [4-17; 4-18], Bentley Historical Library.
26. "American Women and Marriage," *Vogue*, March 16, 1905.
27. Peggy Brown, oral history interview by Stephanie Brown, February 2005.
28. "How Some Society Leaders Have Married and Remarried," clipping, scrapbook 1919–23, Marjorie Post Papers, Bentley Historical Library.
29. Betty Beale, oral history interview by Stephanie Brown, January 2004.
30. Ellen Charles, oral history interview by Stephanie Brown, November 2003.
31. Marjorie Post, interview by Nettie Major, December 1964.
32. Marjorie Post, interview by Nettie Major, January 1965.
33. Marjorie Post, interview by Nettie Major, December 1964.
34. Major, *C.W. Post*, 169–71, 294–97.
35. Ibid., 171–77, 297–98.
36. E.F. Hutton to Marjorie Post Hutton, n.d., scrapbook, 1919–23, Marjorie Post Papers, Bentley Historical Library.
37. Rubin, *American Empress*, 193–95.
38. Dina Merrill, oral history interview by Stephanie Brown, February 2004.
39. Marjorie Post Papers [12-9], Bentley Historical Library.
40. Dina Merrill, oral history interview by Stephanie Brown, February 2004.
41. Marjorie Post, interview by Nettie Major, December 1964.
42. Marjorie Post Davies to George Lloyd, March 6, 1955. Marjorie Merriweather Post Papers, Special Collections Research Center, George Washington University, B1-F1.
43. On May's career, see "Herbert May Dies on Cruise," *Washington Post*, March 13, 1966.
44. Rubin, *American Empress*, 350–53; Dina Merrill, oral history interview by Stephanie Brown, February 2004.
45. Dina Merrill, 2007.
46. Peggy Brown, oral history interview by Kathi Ann Brown, 1997.
47. Ellen Charles, oral history interview by Stephanie Brown, November 2003.
48. Ibid.
49. "Foundation Chief Adelaide Riggs Dies," *Washington Post*, January 8, 1999; "Adelaide Close Riggs, 90, Supported Horse Racing Industry," *Baltimore Sun*, January 8, 1999.
50. Eleanor Close Barzin, interview by Nettie Major, June 1965; Major, *C.W. Post*, 171–77, 297–98.
51. Major, *C.W. Post*, 171–77, 297–98; Dina Merrill, oral history interview by Estella Chung, September 2010; "Dina Merrill, Actress and

Philanthropist, Dies at 93," *New York Times*, May 22, 2017; "Notice: Eleanor Close Barzin," *Washington Post*, March 25, 2007.
52. Marjorie Post, interview by Nettie Major, December 1964.
53. Dina Merrill, oral history interview by Stephanie Brown, February 2004; *Sea Cloud* data authentication and registration by Lloyds of London and the United States Coast Guard Marine Inspection Service, Marjorie Post Papers [31], Bentley Historical Library.
54. Dina Merrill, 2007.
55. Ellen Charles, Memories of Camp Topridge Member Program, Hillwood, 2010.
56. Nina Rumbough, oral history interview by Estella Chung, September 2010.
57. Ellen Charles, oral history interview by Stephanie Brown, November 2003.
58. Ibid.
59. Donald Handelman, oral history interview by Kathi Ann Brown, June 1998.
60. Ibid.
61. "Mar-a-Lago, 1100 South Ocean Boulevard, Palm Beach, Palm Beach County, FL," Historic American Buildings Survey, FLA-195, 1967.
62. Chung, *Living Artfully*, 15, 52–70.
63. Wright, *Heiress*, 258.
64. Ibid., 240.
65. Major, *C.W. Post*, 171, 177–98; Rubin, *American Empress*, 95, 128–30, 261, 338.
66. Dina Merrill, oral history interview by Stephanie Brown, February 2004.
67. Marjorie Post, "Foreword," in Ross, *The Art of Karl Fabergé*.
68. Arend, "Furnishing Hillwood"; Odom, *Hillwood: Thirty Years of Collecting*, 9; Fisher et al., *Post's Art Collector's Personal Museum*, 16–17.
69. Ellen Charles, oral history interview by Stephanie Brown, November 2003.
70. Odom and Salmond, *Treasures into Tractors*, 267.
71. Ibid., 268.
72. Fisher et al., *Post's Art Collector's Personal Museum*, 18–20.
73. Odom and Salmond, *Treasures into Tractors*, 270.
74. Marjorie Merriweather Post, "Foreword," in Ross, *Russian Porcelains*, ix.
75. Marjorie Merriweather Post, in *Notes on Hillwood*; Kettering, *Russian Glass at Hillwood*, 6.
76. Donald Handelman, oral history interview by Kathi Ann Brown, June 1998.
77. Betty Beale, oral history interview by Stephanie Brown, January 2004; Beale, *Power at Play*, 331–32; Chung, *Living Artfully*, 24–70.
78. Chung, *Living Artfully*, 26–27.
79. Clem Conger, oral history interview by Kathi Ann Brown, 1997.
80. Ibid.
81. Ellen Charles, oral history interview by Stephanie Brown, November 2003.
82. Clem Conger, oral history interview by Kathi Ann Brown, 1997.
83. Chung, *Living Artfully*, 45, 114.
84. Marjorie Post Papers, Bentley Historical Library.
85. Chung, *Living Artfully*, 42–44.
86. *Congressional Record*, September 20, 1973, Marjorie Post Papers [35], Bentley Historical Library.
87. Ellen Charles, oral history interview by Stephanie Brown, November 2003.

Business

1. Marjorie Post, interview by Nettie Major, December 1960.
2. Ibid.
3. Marjorie Post, oral history interview, 1964, Columbia University.
4. Marjorie Post, interview by Nettie Major, February 1962.
5. Major, *C.W. Post*, 28–35.
6. Marjorie Post, interview by David Zeitlin, August 1964.
7. Major, *C.W. Post*, 28–34.
8. Marjorie Post, interview by Nettie Major, December 1960.
9. Major, *C.W. Post*, 41.
10. Marjorie Post, interview by Nettie Major, December 1960.
11. Marjorie Post, interview by David Zeitlin, August 1964.
12. Major, *C.W. Post*, 117–23.
13. Marjorie Post, interview by Nettie Major, December 1960.
14. Pamphlet, "50 Years at Post Products," Marjorie Post Papers, Bentley Historical Library; Postum Cereal Company Ltd., *There's a Reason*, Battle Creek, Michigan: Postum Cereal Company Ltd., n.d., Hillwood Special Collections Library; Major, *C.W. Post*, 123.
15. Postum Cereal Company Ltd., *There's a Reason*, Battle Creek, Michigan: Postum Cereal Company Ltd., n.d., Hillwood Special Collections Library.
16. C.W. Post, address to employees, December 1906, C.W. Post Papers [3-10], Bentley Historical Library.
17. Clipping, June 8, 1914, Marjorie Post Papers [13-20], Bentley Historical Library.
18. C.W. Post to the Cabinet, September 14, 1909, C.W. Post Papers [4-21], Bentley Historical Library.

19. Ibid.
20. Major, *C.W. Post*, 88.
21. Marjorie Post, oral history interview, 1964, Columbia University.
22. C.W. Post Papers [4-35; 3-5], Bentley Historical Library.
23. C.W. Post Papers [1-32], Bentley Historical Library.
24. C.W. Post Papers [4-4; 3-10], Bentley Historical Library.
25. C.W. Post Papers [3-10], Bentley Historical Library.
26. Marjorie Post Papers [13-26], Bentley Historical Library.
27. Clippings, C.W. Post Papers [3], Bentley Historical Library.
28. Major, *C.W. Post*, 145–46.
29. Clippings, C.W. Post Papers [3], Bentley Historical Library.
30. Clippings, C.W. Post Papers [9], Bentley Historical Library.
31. Clippings, C.W. Post Papers [3], Bentley Historical Library.
32. Marjorie Post, interview by David Zeitlin, August 1964.
33. Marjorie Post Papers [13-26], Bentley Historical Library.
34. Marjorie Post Papers [13-24], Bentley Historical Library.
35. Clippings, C.W. Post Papers [9], Bentley Historical Library.
36. Photographs, C.W. Post Papers [9], Bentley Historical Library.
37. Photographs and clippings, C.W. Post Papers [9], Bentley Historical Library.
38. Clippings, C.W. Post Papers [9], Bentley Historical Library.
39. "Brother Rollin and Sister Carrie" to K. Post, May 1914, C.W. Post Papers [9], Bentley Historical Library.
40. *New York Herald*, May 26, 1914, C.W. Post Papers [2-38], Bentley Historical Library.
41. Copy of C.W. Post's will from November 1913, C.W. Post Papers [2-38], Bentley Historical Library.
42. Clippings, Marjorie Post scrapbook no. 8, 1915, Bentley Historical Library.
43. Unmarked clipping, and *Grand Rapids Herald*, December 1, 1915, Marjorie Post scrapbook no. 8, 1915, Bentley Historical Library.
44. *Grand Rapids Herald*, December 1, 1915, Marjorie Post scrapbook no. 8, 1915, Bentley Historical Library.
45. "Widow Loses as Result of His Oath in Bankruptcy Case," *Detroit Free Press*, Marjorie Post scrapbook no. 8, 1915, Bentley Historical Library.
46. Major, *C.W. Post*, 31.
47. Clippings, Marjorie Post scrapbook no. 8, 1915, Bentley Historical Library.
48. "Post's Heirs Agree: No Suit Over Will," *New York Times*, December 9, 1915, Marjorie Post scrapbook no. 8, 1915, Bentley Historical Library.
49. Clippings, Marjorie Post scrapbook no. 8, 1915, Bentley Historical Library.
50. Marjorie Post, oral history interview, 1964, Columbia University.
51. Major, *C.W. Post*, 171; Marjorie Post, oral history interview, 1964, Columbia University.
52. Marjorie Post, oral history interview, 1964, Columbia University.
53. Major, *C.W. Post*, 171.
54. Marjorie Post, interview by Nettie Major, February 1962.
55. Ibid.
56. Major, *C.W. Post*, 169, 171.
57. Draft article for comment, *Fortune*, 1955, Marjorie Post Papers [General Foods], Bentley Historical Library.
58. Major, *C.W. Post*, 171.
59. Ibid., 173.
60. Marjorie Post, oral history interview, 1964, Columbia University.
61. Major, *C.W. Post*, 169.
62. Ibid., 173.
63. Baker, *Directors and Their Functions*; "Postum Cereal Company, Cumulative Preferred Stock, February 1922," Marjorie Post Papers [45], Bentley Historical Library.
64. Marjorie Post, interview by Nettie Major, December 1960.
65. "Postum Cereal Company, Cumulative Preferred Stock, February 1922," Marjorie Post Papers [45], Bentley Historical Library.
66. Major, *C.W. Post*, 173.
67. Marjorie Post, oral history interview, 1964, Columbia University.
68. Ibid.
69. Baker, *Directors and Their Functions*.
70. Dina Merrill, oral history interview by Stephanie Brown, February 2004.
71. Baker, *Directors and Their Functions*.
72. Major, *C.W. Post*, 173–74.
73. Marjorie Post, interview by Nettie Major, December 1960.
74. Ibid.
75. Kurlansky, *Birdseye: Adventures of a Curious Man*, 166–74.
76. Ibid., 167.
77. Ibid., 166–68.
78. Ibid., 168.
79. Ibid., 171.
80. Major, *C.W. Post*, 173.
81. Baker, *Directors and Their Functions*.
82. "Acceptance of Birds Eye Frosted Foods," *Barron's*, March 30, 1936.
83. Chung, *Living Artfully*, 90.

84. "Mrs. Davies Elected to General Foods Board," news clipping, Marjorie Post Papers, Bentley Historical Library.
85. Ibid.
86. "General Foods Names Woman to the Board," news clipping, Marjorie Post Papers, Bentley Historical Library.
87. "General Foods Names Woman to the Board," and "Corporation Job for Marjorie Post," April 9, 1936, clippings, Marjorie Post Papers, Bentley Historical Library.
88. "Mrs. Davies is Director of General Foods," scrapbook SB03, Hillwood Archives.
89. "Investing in Industrial Leadership," *Barron's*, October 28, 1940.
90. Charles Mortimer, interview by Nettie Major, August 1965.
91. "The Beginnings Are Notes Here: Post Products Celebration Last Night of 11 Held Throughout Nation," *Battle Creek Enquirer and News*, December 24, 1941.
92. Baker, *Directors and Their Functions*.
93. Charles Mortimer, interview by Nettie Major, August 1965.
94. General Foods Corporation to Marjorie Post Davies, February 17, 1949, Marjorie Post Papers [General Foods], Bentley Historical Library.
95. Memo/Statement, February 22, 1949, Marjorie Post Papers [General Foods], Bentley Historical Library.
96. Marjorie Post Davies to General Foods, March 28, 1949, Marjorie Post Papers [General Foods], Bentley Historical Library.
97. General Foods, "Miracles with Minute Tapioca," 1948, Hillwood Special Collections Library.
98. General Foods, "Cake Making at High Altitudes," 1949, Schlesinger Library, Harvard University.
99. General Foods, "Bakers Favorite Chocolate Recipes," 1952, Schlesinger Library, Harvard University.
100. Marjorie Post Davies to General Foods, draft letter, October 17, 1953.
101. Marjorie Post to General Foods, November 27, 1957, Marjorie Post Papers [General Foods], Bentley Historical Library.
102. Ibid.
103. Chung, *Living Artfully*, 80.
104. Ibid.
105. Marjorie Post May to General Foods, November 23, 1959, reel 14, Marjorie Post Papers, Bentley Historical Library.
106. Maxwell House Division of General Foods to Marjorie Post May, December 9, 1959, reel 14, Marjorie Post Papers, Bentley Historical Library.
107. Chung, *Living Artfully*, 81.
108. Ibid.
109. Marjorie Post to General Foods, June 5, 1958, Marjorie Post Papers [General Foods], Bentley Historical Library.
110. Marjorie Post Papers [General Foods], Bentley Historical Library.
111. Dorothy McCardle, "Her Fortune Has Smiled on Many Others," *Washington Post*, March 12, 1967, Marjorie Post scrapbook, 1967, Bentley Historical Library.

Service

1. Major, *C.W. Post*, 188.
2. Clippings, Marjorie Post Papers, oversize vol. no. 7, 1916, Bentley Historical Library.
3. Lettie Gavin, *American Women in World War I: They Also Served* (Boulder: University Press of Colorado, 2006), 180.
4. Cholly Knickerbocker, "Greenwich Women and Red Cross," August 1917, Marjorie Post Papers, oversize vol. no. 7, 1916, Bentley Historical Library.
5. Ibid.
6. "The Woman's Share of the War," *Vogue*, July 1, 1917.
7. Ibid.
8. Marian Moser Jones, *The American Red Cross from Clara Barton to the New Deal* (Baltimore, MD: Johns Hopkins University Press, 2013), 157–58.
9. Ford, *Medical Department of the United States Army in the World War*, 635–36.
10. "Accepts Honorary Chairmanship," *Washington Times-Herald*, September 14, 1941; Major, *C.W. Post*, 171.
11. Major, *C.W. Post*, 171; "Suffragists Had $420,405," *New York Times*, April 16, 1918, Marjorie Post Papers, scrapbook 1917, Bentley Historical Library.
12. Clippings and speech notes, Marjorie Post Papers, scrapbook 1932, Bentley Historical Library.
13. "Mrs. Hutton to Receive Flag Honor at White House Today," *Washington Star*, December 12, 1933, clippings, Marjorie Post Papers, oversize vol. no. 12, Bentley Historical Library; scrapbook SB07, Hillwood Archives.
14. Clippings, Marjorie Post Papers, oversize vol. no. 12, Bentley Historical Library; scrapbook SB07, Hillwood Archives.
15. "Woman at Capital Starts Crusade to Abolish Crime," *Camden New Jersey Courier-Post*, January 12, 1934, Marjorie Post Papers, oversize vol. no. 12, Bentley Historical Library.

16. "Millions Can't Set Her Free," clipping, Marjorie Post Papers, oversize vol. no. 12, Bentley Historical Library.
17. "NY Society Leaders Direct Energies to Welfare Work," *Sioux City Journal*, December 12, 1932, scrapbook SB07, Hillwood Archives.
18. "Millions Can't Set Her Free," clipping, Marjorie Post Papers, oversize vol. no. 12, Bentley Historical Library.
19. "Mrs. Hutton Talks to Women Relief Workers," clipping, December 1932, Marjorie Post Papers, oversize vol. no. 12, Bentley Historical Library.
20. Dina Merrill, oral history interview by Stephanie Brown, February 2004.
21. The Salvation Army, *Report of Unemployment Relief Work in Greater New York, October to September 30, 1931*, Salvation Army Archives, Alexandria, Virginia.
22. "Meals for 700 Supplied Daily by Mrs. Hutton," *New York Herald Tribune*, December 4, 1932, clipping, Marjorie Post Papers, oversize vol. no. 12, Bentley Historical Library.
23. Ibid.
24. Scrapbook SB07, Hillwood Archives.
25. The Salvation Army, *Report of Unemployment Relief Work in Greater New York*.
26. Ibid.
27. "Meals for 700 Supplied Daily by Mrs. Hutton," *New York Herald Tribune*, December 4, 1932, clipping, Marjorie Post Papers, oversize vol. no. 12, Bentley Historical Library.
28. Post Family Collection, oversize vol. no. 12, Bentley Historical Library.
29. The Salvation Army, *Report on the Operation of the Marjorie Post Hutton Food Station from November 19, 1931 to May 1, 1932*, Marjorie Post Papers [16-9], Bentley Historical Library.
30. Ibid.
31. Ibid.
32. Ibid.
33. The Salvation Army, *The Marjorie Post Davies Food Station Oct 1935–Oct 1936*, Marjorie Post Papers [22-27], Bentley Historical Library.
34. Major, *C.W. Post*, 185.
35. "Davies Takes Envoy's Oath in Festive Rite," *Louisville Times*, November 24, 1936; "Davies Is Named Envoy to Russia," Marjorie Post Papers, oversize vol. no. 12, Bentley Historical Library.
36. Ibid.
37. Davies, *Mission to Moscow*, 4–5.
38. Marjorie Post, interview by Nettie Major, January 1965.
39. Clipping, Marjorie Post Papers, oversize vol. no. 12, Bentley Historical Library.
40. Major, *C.W. Post*, 185.
41. Marjorie Post, interview by Nettie Major, January 1965.
42. "Envoy to Russia Off to New Post," January 7, 1937, clipping, Marjorie Post Papers, oversize vol. no. 12, Bentley Historical Library.
43. Marjorie Post, interview by Nettie Major, January 1965.
44. Ibid.
45. Joseph Davies Papers, part 2:36, folder 4, Manuscript Division, Library of Congress.
46. "Trial in Moscow," and "Sing and Be Shot," January and February 1937 clippings, scrapbook SB07, Hillwood Archives.
47. Marjorie Post, interview by Nettie Major, September 1964.
48. "Russian Secret Police Are Stalin's Eyes and Ears," *Blackwell Journal*, June 9, 1937, clipping, Marjorie Post Papers, oversize vol. no. 12, Bentley Historical Library.
49. Joseph Davies Papers, part 2:37, folder 1, Manuscript Division, Library of Congress.
50. Joseph Davies Papers, part 2:36, folder 9, Manuscript Division, Library of Congress.
51. Joseph Davies Papers, part 2:37, Manuscript Division, Library of Congress.
52. Ibid.
53. Marjorie Post Papers [38-Russia 1937-38], Bentley Historical Library.
54. Ibid.
55. Ibid.
56. Clippings, scrapbook SB01, Hillwood Archives.
57. Marjorie Post, interview by Nettie Major, January 1965.
58. Clippings, Marjorie Post Papers, oversize vol. no. 25, Bentley Historical Library.
59. Ibid.
60. Ibid.
61. Marjorie Post, interview by Nettie Major, March 1962.
62. Clippings and handwritten notes, scrapbook SB14, Hillwood Archives.
63. Marjorie Post, interview by Nettie Major, January 1965.
64. Ibid.
65. Marjorie Post Papers [38-Belgium vol. 2], Bentley Historical Library.
66. Associated Press, "Joseph Davies Near War Zone," September 1939, and "Netherlands, Belgium Invoke Wartime Rules," *Washington Post*, November 9, 1939, clippings, Marjorie Post Papers, vol. 13, Bentley Historical Library.
67. Marjorie Post, interview by Nettie Major, March 1962.
68. January 18, 1942, clipping, Marjorie Post Papers, scrapbook 26, Bentley Historical Library.

69. "Davies' Party Draws," clipping, Marjorie Post Papers, scrapbook 26, Bentley Historical Library.
70. Clippings, Marjorie Post Papers, scrapbook 26, Bentley Historical Library.
71. Customs memo, April 1942, Marjorie Post Papers [31], Bentley Historical Library.
72. "Instructions and Plans to the Entire Crew," Marjorie Post Papers [31], Bentley Historical Library.
73. Ibid.
74. Ibid.
75. Ibid.
76. Ibid.
77. "USS *Sea Cloud* and Racial Integration in the U.S. Coast Guard, Chief Warrant Officer Professional Development," United States Coast Guard Museum, New London, Connecticut.
78. Ibid.
79. Ibid.
80. Ibid.
81. Ibid.
82. Howard Zinn, *A People's History of the United States* (New York: HarperCollins, 1990), 441.
83. "Oral History Interview with Jacob Lawrence, 1968 October 26," Smithsonian Archives of American Art.
84. Nesbett and DuBois, *Jacob Lawrence Paintings, Drawings, and Murals*, 47; "Oral History Interview with Jacob Lawrence, 1968 October 26," Smithsonian Archives of American Art.
85. "Oral History Interview with Jacob Lawrence, 1968 October 26," Smithsonian Archives of American Art.
86. Press release, "Paintings by Leading Negro Artist," Museum of Modern Art, October 3, 1944.
87. Ibid.
88. Skinner, "The Lost Wartime Paintings of Jacob Lawrence."
89. Marjorie Post, interview by Nettie Major, January 1965.
90. "USS *Sea Cloud* and Racial Integration in the U.S. Coast Guard, Chief Warrant Officer Professional Development," United States Coast Guard Museum, New London, Connecticut.
91. Ibid.
92. Ibid.
93. From Secretary of the Navy, December 1944, scrapbook 15, Hillwood Archives.
94. Clipping, scrapbook 10, Hillwood Archives.
95. Clipping, scrapbook 15, Hillwood Archives.
96. "Davies' Estate on L.I. to be Used by Royalty," *New York Journal-American*, July 23, 1940, clippings, Marjorie Post Papers [Box 38-Russia], Bentley Historical Library.
97. Marjorie Post Papers, oversize vol. 27, Bentley Historical Library.
98. Ibid.
99. Chung, *Living Artfully*, 43–44.
100. "Men in Service Guests at Davies Summer Home," *Herald Tribune*, August 27, 1944, Marjorie Post Papers [25], Bentley Historical Library.
101. Marjorie Post Papers [Camp Topridge], Bentley Historical Library.
102. Chung, *Living Artfully*, 52–71.
103. Marjorie Post Papers [Camp Topridge], Bentley Historical Library.
104. Major, *C.W. Post*, 198, 208.
105. Chung, *Living Artfully*, 122–24.
106. Marjorie Post, interview by Nettie Major, September 1964.

Travel Luxe

1. Marjorie Post Papers [25-alpha/travels], Bentley Historical Library.
2. Marjorie Post Papers, oversize vol. 3, Bentley Historical Library.
3. Marjorie Post Papers [52], Bentley Historical Library.
4. Reminiscences of Marjorie Merriweather Post, oral history, February 13, 1964, 30.
5. Donna R. Braden and Judith E. Endelman, *Americans on Vacation* (Dearborn, MI: Henry Ford Museum and Greenfield Village, 1990), 31–32.
6. "A Successful Coach Tour," *Road*, September 1904, 218–19, C.W. Post Papers, News Clippings no. 5., Bentley Historical Library.
7. Reminiscences of Marjorie Merriweather Post, oral history, February 13, 1964, 30–31.
8. Marjorie Post Papers [52], "Travel Snap Shots," 1903–5, vol. 77.
9. Reminiscences of Marjorie Merriweather Post, oral history, February 13, 1964, 31–32.
10. Ibid.
11. Marjorie Post Papers [52], "Travel Snap Shots," 1903–5, vol. 77.
12. Marjorie Post Papers, oversize vol. no. 3., Bentley Historical Library.
13. Pullman Company, *Private Car and Special Train Service in 1901*.
14. Ibid. For broader histories of Pullman, see Joe Welsh and Bill Howes, *Travel by Pullman: A Century of Service* (St. Paul, MN: MBI Publishing Company, 2004); Joe Welsh, Bill Howes, and Kevin J. Holland, *The Cars of Pullman* (Minneapolis, MN: Voyageur Press, 2010); and Christian Wolmar, *The Great Railroad Revolution: The History of Trains in America* (New York: Perseus Books, 2012), 181–90.

15. Menu, Union Pacific, 1930s, from H. Roger Grant, *Railroads and the American People* (Bloomington: Indiana University Press, 2012), 16.
16. Records of the Special Car Club from Its Organization, April 1888 to April 1915, Historical Society of the Town of Greenwich.
17. Ed Russell Jr., oral history interview by Estella Chung, September 2014.
18. American Car and Foundry Company, Shop Specification for One Steel Private Car, 1922, curator files, Hillwood; Stanley M. Rumbough Jr., oral history interview by Estella Chung, February 2011.
19. "Pullman Rivals Social Register as Guide to Palm Beach Guests," *Columbus Dispatch*, March 8, 1928, Marjorie Post Papers, vol. 10, Bentley Historical Library.
20. Dolena Rutherford, "Real Palaces on Wheels," *Providence Journal*, July 15, 1928, Marjorie Post Papers, vol. 10, Bentley Historical Library.
21. "Hail and Farewell," *The Nutmegger: A Magazine Devoted to Greenwich*, November 1973, Historical Society of the Town of Greenwich.
22. Marjorie Post, interview by Nettie Major, December 1964.
23. American Car and Foundry Company, Shop Specification for One Steel Private Car, 1922, curator files, Hillwood; DeWitt Chapple, oral history interview by Estella Chung, October 2012.
24. American Car and Foundry Company, Shop Specification for One Steel Private Car, 1922, curator files, Hillwood.
25. Marjorie Post, interview by Nettie Major, January 1964.
26. Marjorie Post, interview by Nettie Major, February 1962.
27. Marjorie Post, interview by Nettie Major, January 1964.
28. DeWitt Chapple, oral history interview by Estella Chung, October 2012.
29. Ibid.
30. American Car and Foundry Company, Shop Specification for One Steel Private Car, 1922, curator files, Hillwood; DeWitt Chapple, oral history interview by Estella Chung, October 2012.
31. Wolmar, *The Great Railroad Revolution*, 187. For a broad picture of the treatment of African American Pullman porters, see pp. 186–87.
32. Marjorie Post, interview by Nettie Major, February 1962.
33. *English Oxford Living Dictionary* online; *Encyclopedia Britannica* online; "What's in a Rig – The Schooner," American Sailing Association online, December 9, 2015.
34. Burmeister and Wain to E.F. Hutton, April 23, 1923, Marjorie Post Papers, vol. 9, Bentley Historical Library; DeWitt Chapple, oral history interview by Estella Chung, October 2012.
35. "Auxiliary Schooner Hussar Latest Addition to the New York Yacht Club Fleet," *Yachting*, September 1923, scrapbook 2010_03_S022, Hillwood Archives.
36. Ibid.
37. "Ship's Quarters Made Home-Like: Colonial Room on the Yacht Hussar Owned by Edward F. Hutton of New York," undated, ca. 1924, scrapbook 2010_03_S022, Hillwood Archives.
38. "Auxiliary Schooner Hussar Latest Addition to the New York Yacht Club Fleet," *Yachting*, September 1923, scrapbook 2010_03_S022, Hillwood Archives.
39. Ibid.
40. Ibid.
41. "A Large Three-Masted Steel Auxiliary Yacht," *Spur*, February 15, 1923, scrapbook 2010_03_S022, Hillwood Archives.
42. "Auxiliary Schooner Hussar Latest Addition to the New York Yacht Club Fleet," *Yachting*, September 1923, scrapbook 2010_03_S022, Hillwood Archives.
43. Duo-Art advertisement, *Yachting*, September 1923, 164–65, scrapbook 2010_03_S022, Hillwood Archives.
44. "New Yacht Arrives Here," *New York Times*, July 29, 1923, Marjorie Post Papers, vol. 9, Bentley Historical Library.
45. "Yacht Hussar Brings Party to Game Here," *New Haven Register*, October 10, 1927, Marjorie Post Papers, vol. 10, Bentley Historical Library.
46. Ibid.
47. *New York Evening Post*, September 15, 1928, Marjorie Post Papers [47-3], Bentley Historical Library. For barque design, see Tall Ships America online.
48. Dina Merrill, 2007.
49. Norman L. Skene, *Elements of Yacht Design* (New York: Sheridan House, 2001), 3.
50. Ibid.
51. Yacht Sea Cloud data authenticated and registered by Lloyds of London and the United States Coast Guard Marine Inspection Service, Marjorie Post Papers [31], Bentley Historical Library; Major, *C.W. Post*, 184.
52. Dina Merrill, 2007; see also Jennifer Rahel Conover, "Sea Cloud Then and Now, 1931–94," *Gold Coast*, October 1994.

53. Marjorie Post Hutton to Fred Vogel, June 11, 1930, Marjorie Post Papers [31], Bentley Historical Library.
54. Ibid.
55. Dina Merrill, 2007. For an example of the burgee and signal, see scrapbook 2010_03_S005, Hillwood Archives.
56. Dina Merrill, oral history interview by Stephanie Brown, February 2004; Nettie Major notes on *Hussar*, Marjorie Post Papers [47], Bentley Historical Library.
57. Marjorie Post Papers [31-Maiden Voyage], Bentley Historical Library.
58. "Hutton's Yacht Here after Atlantic Trip," *Miami Herald*, January 2, 1934; "Hutton's Huge Yacht in Port," *Los Angeles Times*, April 24, 1934; "Hussar Is Here! Morgan Corsair Just a Rowboat," *New York Daily News*, July 11, 1934; and "Palatial Yacht Brings Trophies of Long Cruise," *Seattle Washington Times*, May 8, 1934, Marjorie Post Papers [31-Maiden Voyage], Bentley Historical Library.
59. Fried. Krupp to E.F. Hutton, December 29, 1931, Marjorie Post Papers [31], Bentley Historical Library.
60. Dina Merrill, oral history interview by Stephanie Brown, February 2004; Dina Merrill, 2007.
61. Dina Merrill, oral history interview by Stephanie Brown, February 2004.
62. Ibid.
63. Scrapbooks S001, S005, SB07, Hillwood Archives.
64. Dina Merrill, oral history interview by Stephanie Brown, February 2004.
65. James Griffin Jr., oral history interview by Nancy Harris, May 1998.
66. Dina Merrill, oral history interview by Stephanie Brown, February 2004.
67. Dina Merrill, oral history interview by Stephanie Brown, February 2004; James Griffin Jr., oral history interview by Nancy Harris, May 1998.
68. Ibid.
69. Dina Merrill, oral history interview by Stephanie Brown, February 2004.
70. Ibid.
71. Dina Merrill, 2007.
72. Dina Merrill, oral history interview by Stephanie Brown, February 2004.
73. Ibid.
74. Dina Merrill, 2007.
75. Dina Merrill, oral history interview by Stephanie Brown, February 2004.
76. "Hutton Yacht to Sail Again," *Charleston Post*, November 15, 1935, scrapbook SB04, Hillwood Archives.
77. Marjorie Post, interview by Nettie Major, February 1962.
78. Scrapbook SB04, Hillwood Archives.
79. Scrapbooks SB03, SB04, SB07, Hillwood Archives; Marjorie Post Papers, oversize vol. 12, Bentley Historical Library.
80. Scrapbooks SB03, SB04, SB07, Hillwood Archives.
81. Scrapbook SB04, Hillwood Archives.
82. "Yacht Glistens In Spring Dress For Long Voyage," *Florida Times-Union*, March 26, 1939, and Leigh Culley, Marine Reporter, "News of the Port," *Jacksonville Journal*, April 10, 1939, scrapbook SB17, Hillwood Archives.
83. Yacht Glistens In Spring Dress For Long Voyage," *Florida Times-Union*, March 26, 1939, scrapbook SB17, Hillwood Archives.
84. Scrapbook SB17, Hillwood Archives.
85. "Duke and Duchess Arrive Here," *Havana Post*, April 4, 1948, scrapbook SB15, Hillwood Archives.
86. Marjorie Post Papers [25-24], Bentley Historical Library.
87. Duke of Windsor to Joseph Davies, April 12, 1948, scrapbook SB15, Hillwood Archives.
88. Marjorie Post Papers [31], Bentley Historical Library.
89. Marjorie Post (Mrs. Joseph P. Davies) to Chrysler Automobile Salon, January 8, 1948, Marjorie Post Papers [30-automobiles], Bentley Historical Library.
90. Ibid.
91. Marjorie Post (Mrs. Joseph P. Davies) to Derham Custom Body Company, May 6, 1948, Marjorie Post Papers [30-automobiles], Bentley Historical Library.
92. Derham Custom Body Company to Marjorie Post (Mrs. Joseph Davies), April 24, 1948, Marjorie Post Papers [30-automobiles], Bentley Historical Library.
93. Ibid.
94. Marjorie Post (Mrs. Joseph P. Davies) to Chrysler Automobile Salon, January 8, 1948, Marjorie Post Papers [30-automobiles], Bentley Historical Library.
95. Marjorie Post Papers [30-automobiles], Bentley Historical Library.
96. Chung, *Living Artfully*, 17–18.
97. Frank Del Monte, oral history interview by Stephanie Brown, February 2004.
98. Chung, *Living Artfully*, 17–18.
99. Frank Del Monte, oral history interview by Stephanie Brown, February 2004.

100. Marjorie Post Papers [31], Bentley Historical Library.
101. Stanley Rumbough, oral history interview by Estella Chung, September 2011.
102. Dorothy McCardle, "Sky Fever Becoming Epidemic," *Washington Times-Herald*, December 24, 1967.
103. Marjorie Post Papers [30, 31, 50], Bentley Historical Library.
104. Ibid.
105. Chung, *Living Artfully*, 17–18.
106. Marjorie Post Papers [30, 31, 50], Bentley Historical Library.
107. Major, *C.W. Post*, 202.
108. Marjorie Post Papers [25-28], Bentley Historical Library.
109. Ibid.
110. Ibid.
111. Ibid.
112. Ibid.
113. Marjorie Post Papers [25-12], Bentley Historical Library.
114. Ibid.

Giving

1. Burke to Post, September 11, 1967, Marjorie Post Papers [15], Bentley Historical Library.
2. Ellen Charles, oral history interview by Stephanie Brown, November 2003.
3. Donald Handelman, oral history interview by Kathi Ann Brown, June 1998.
4. Betty Cannella, oral history interview by Nancy Harris, November 1998.
5. "If You Are in Washington," *New York Journal-American*, April 23, 1962, Marjorie Post Papers, scrapbook no. 32, Bentley Historical Library.
6. "Two To Tango," *Rochester New York Democrat*, May 27, 1962, Marjorie Post Papers, scrapbook no. 32, Bentley Historical Library.
7. "Tea," *Washington Post Herald*, November 10, 1957, Marjorie Post Papers, scrapbook no. 31, Bentley Historical Library.
8. Mary Day, oral history interview by Stephanie Brown, February 2004.
9. "The European Approach: New Ballet School Blends Footwork, Brainwork," *National Observer*, October 29, 1962, Marjorie Post Papers, scrapbook no. 34, Bentley Historical Library.
10. Marjorie Post Papers, scrapbook no. 35, Bentley Historical Library.
11. Washington School of Ballet graduation program, 1964, Marjorie Post Papers, scrapbook no. 36, Bentley Historical Library.
12. "First Lady to Head National Ballet Foundation," *Washington Post*, April 19, 1962; Ballet program, 1963, Marjorie Post Papers, scrapbook 1963, Bentley Historical Library.
13. Ibid.
14. "Jacqueline Kennedy's Comfort at the Anderson House Reception," clipping, Marjorie Post Papers, scrapbook no. 33, Bentley Historical Library.
15. Photo caption, *Evening Star*, February 11, 1963, clipping, Marjorie Post Papers, scrapbook no. 35, Bentley Historical Library.
16. Clipping, November 1961, Marjorie Post Papers, scrapbook no. 35, Bentley Historical Library.
17. Betty Beale, "Only One Capital Hostess Could Give This Function," *Evening Star*, Marjorie Post Papers, scrapbook no. 33, Bentley Historical Library.
18. Ibid.
19. *Scouter*, September 26, 1966, and Kurtz to Post, June 26, 1968, Marjorie Post Papers [15], Bentley Historical Library.
20. Post to Slosted, March 28, 1966, Marjorie Post Papers [15], Bentley Historical Library.
21. Boy Scouts press release, April 1960, Marjorie Post Papers [15], Bentley Historical Library.
22. Post to Gore, May 7, 1959, Marjorie Post Papers [15], Bentley Historical Library.
23. Post to Chase, June 24, 1969, Marjorie Post Papers [15], Bentley Historical Library.
24. Boy Scout press release, 1961, Marjorie Post Papers [15], Bentley Historical Library.
25. Post to Braverman, January 18, 1968, Marjorie Post Papers [15], Bentley Historical Library.
26. "Given Boy Scout Oscar," clipping, Marjorie Post Papers [15], Bentley Historical Library.
27. Kurtz to Post, May 15, 1969, Marjorie Post Papers [15], Bentley Historical Library.
28. *Scouter*, May 1968.
29. Slosted to Post, April 6, 1968, Marjorie Post Papers [15], Bentley Historical Library.
30. Wills, *Boy Scouts of America*.
31. Kurtz to Post, June 16, 1968, Marjorie Post Papers [15], Bentley Historical Library.
32. Post to Gore, May 7, 1959, Marjorie Post Papers [15], Bentley Historical Library.
33. South Plains Council of Texas, July 1972, Marjorie Post Papers [15], Bentley Historical Library.
34. Ceremony, June 6, 1971, Marjorie Post Papers [15], Bentley Historical Library.
35. Remarks by Douglas Smith, Silver Fawn ceremony, Marjorie Post Papers [15], Bentley Historical Library.

36. Post to Wilson, April 1968; Post to Chase, February 1968; Post to Chase, July 1971; Adirondack Council to Post, February 1968.
37. Marie McNair, "First Woman in U.S.A. Pinned by Boy Scouts of America," clipping, Marjorie Post Papers [15], Bentley Historical Library.
38. Minutes, NY Club of Mount Vernon Seminary and Junior College, November 1965, Marjorie Merriweather Post papers, MVC0017, box 1, Special Collections Research Center, George Washington University.
39. Ibid.
40. Mikhalevsky, *Dear Daughters*, 18.
41. Marjorie Merriweather Post papers, MVC0017, box 1, Special Collections Research Center, George Washington University.
42. Biography placed in cornerstone, Marjorie Merriweather Post papers, MVC0017, box 1, Special Collections Research Center, George Washington University.
43. Letter of resignation, Marjorie Post Davies to MVS Board of Directors, June 8, 1943, Marjorie Merriweather Post papers, MVC0017, box 1, Special Collections Research Center, George Washington University.
44. Post to Talman, January 1957; "Remembering Marjorie Merriweather Post," *MVS Bulletin*, Marjorie Merriweather Post papers, MVC0017, box 1, Special Collections Research Center, George Washington University.
45. Marjorie Merriweather Post papers, MVC0017, box 1, Special Collections Research Center, George Washington University.
46. Letter of acceptance, Post to Talman, January 1957; "Remembering Marjorie Merriweather Post," *MVS Bulletin*, Marjorie Merriweather Post papers, MVC0017, box 1, Special Collections Research Center, George Washington University.
47. "Remembering Marjorie Merriweather Post," *MVS Bulletin*, Marjorie Merriweather Post papers, MVC0017, box 1, Special Collections Research Center, George Washington University.
48. Biography placed in cornerstone, Marjorie Merriweather Post papers, MVC0017, box 1, Special Collections Research Center, George Washington University.
49. "Remembering Marjorie Merriweather Post," *MVS Bulletin*, Marjorie Merriweather Post papers, MVC0017, box 1, Special Collections Research Center, George Washington University.
50. Ibid.
51. Post to Lloyd, January 1956, Marjorie Merriweather Post papers, MVC0017, box 1, Special Collections Research Center, George Washington University.
52. French & Company, March 1953, and Fred Vogel, March 1953, Marjorie Merriweather Post papers, MVC0017, box 1, Special Collections Research Center, George Washington University.
53. Leonard Carmichael, "Marjorie Merriweather Post: An Appreciation," Hillwood Archives, Mount Vernon, no. 18.
54. Thank you note for kumquats, February 13, 1961, Marjorie Merriweather Post papers, MVC0017, box 1, Special Collections Research Center, George Washington University; Marjorie Post Davies letter, January 24, 1941, and Lloyd to Davies, February 17, 1947, Marjorie Merriweather Post papers, MVC0017, box 1, Special Collections Research Center, George Washington University.
55. Post to Razook, May 1953, Marjorie Merriweather Post papers, MVC0017, box 1, Special Collections Research Center, George Washington University.
56. Marjorie Post Papers [24-31; 24-33], Bentley Historical Library.
57. Marjorie Post Papers [15], Bentley Historical Library.
58. C.W. Post College yearbooks and pamphlets, Marjorie Post Papers [39], Bentley Historical Library.
59. Rubin, *American Empress*, 302–4.
60. C.W. Post College yearbooks and pamphlets, Marjorie Post Papers [39], Bentley Historical Library.
61. Lisa Smith, oral history interview by Estella Chung, August 2009; Chung, *Living Artfully*, 48.
62. *Post College News*, 1963, Marjorie Post Papers, scrapbook no. 35, Bentley Historical Library.
63. Ibid.
64. Chung, *Living Artfully*, 45–48, 120–23.
65. Major, *C.W. Post*, 200.
66. Post to Mrs. John McCone, March 12, 1965, Hillwood Archives, symphony no. 38.
67. Libbey, *The National Symphony*, 146–47.
68. Symington to Post, July 9, 1968, Hillwood Archives, symphony no. 36.
69. National Symphony Ball program, 1954, Marjorie Post Papers, scrapbook 1954, Bentley Historical Library.
70. "Resplendent Ball," *Life*, December 13, 1954, Marjorie Post Papers, scrapbook 1954, Bentley Historical Library.
71. Ibid.

72. Selwa Roosevelt, "Dancing With a Purpose," newspaper clipping, Marjorie Post Papers, scrapbook 1954, Bentley Historical Library.
73. Marie McNair, "Setting Still Secret for Symphony Ball," *Washington Post*, October 22, 1955, and Betty Beale, "Symphony Winners Tally Up Profits," *Evening Star*, newspaper clippings, Marjorie Post Papers, scrapbook 1955, Bentley Historical Library.
74. Everett Helm, "Music for Young America," *Musical America*, June 1962, Hillwood Archives, symphony no. 34.
75. Newspaper clipping, Marjorie Post Papers, scrapbook 1956, Bentley Historical Library.
76. Press release, 1956, Hillwood Archives, symphony no. 39; newspaper clipping, Marjorie Post Papers, scrapbook 1956, Bentley Historical Library.
77. Clipping, Marjorie Post Papers, scrapbooks 1955 and 1956, Bentley Historical Library.
78. Chung, *Living Artfully*, 44–45; Hillwood Archives, symphony no. 34; Marjorie Post Papers [21-2], Bentley Historical Library.
79. Music for Young America scrapbook, Marjorie Post Papers [40], Bentley Historical Library.
80. Clippings, Marjorie Post Papers, scrapbook 1956, Bentley Historical Library.
81. Campbell to Post, July 17, 1967, Hillwood Archives, symphony no. 38.
82. National Symphony Orchestra, calendar of programs, 2018.
83. Libbey, *The National Symphony*, 50.
84. Hillwood Archives, Symphony documents; Marjorie Post Papers [National Symphony], Bentley Historical Library.
85. Mitchell to Post, October 22, 1963, Hillwood Archives, symphony no. 37.
86. Hillwood Archives, symphony no. 38.
87. Ibid.
88. Marjorie Post Papers [21-2], Bentley Historical Library.
89. Marjorie Post Papers [40], Bentley Historical Library.
90. Marjorie Post Papers [54], Bentley Historical Library.
91. Hillwood Archives, symphony no. 34.
92. Marjorie Post Papers [19-4; 19-7], Bentley Historical Library.
93. Rogers to Post, July 8, 1966, Hillwood Archives, symphony no. 38; see also Chung, *Living Artfully*, 44–45.

Legacy

1. Donald Handelman, oral history interview by Kathi Ann Brown, June 1998.
2. Chung, *Living Artfully*, 74–75; Donald Handelman, oral history interview by Kathi Ann Brown, June 1998.
3. Donald Handelman, oral history interview by Kathi Ann Brown, June 1998.
4. Betty Cannella, oral history interview by Nancy Harris, November 1998; Hillwood Preservation Plan, 1997, Frederick J. Fisher Papers, Hillwood Archives.
5. Rubin, *American Empress*, 358.
6. Donald Handelman, oral history interview by Kathi Ann Brown, June 1998.
7. Ibid.
8. Rubin, *American Empress*, 318.
9. Hillwood Preservation Plan, 1997, Frederick J. Fisher Papers, Hillwood Archives.
10. Henry Erwin, oral history interview by Estella Chung, August 2014.
11. Hillwood Preservation Plan, 1997, Frederick J. Fisher Papers, Hillwood Archives.
12. Ibid.
13. Ibid.
14. Betty Cannella, oral history interview by Nancy Harris, November 1998; Alan and Lois Fern, oral history interview by Estella Chung, May 2013; Ellen Charles, oral history interview by Stephanie Brown, November 2003.
15. Marvin Ross Papers, Hillwood Archives.
16. Alan and Lois Fern, oral history interview by Estella Chung, May 2013.
17. Marjorie Post, interview by Nettie Major, January 1965.
18. Betty Cannella, oral history interview by Nancy Harris, November 1998.
19. "Mrs. May Gives Treasures to Smithsonian," and Betty Beale, "Palatial Hillwood Estate in Capital to be Museum," clippings, Marjorie Post Papers, scrapbook 1962, Bentley Historical Library.
20. Marjorie Post Papers [35], Bentley Historical Library.
21. Clippings, Marjorie Post Papers [35], Bentley Historical Library.
22. Dorothy McCardle, "Tributes Are Paid to Marjorie Post," *Washington Post*, September 17, 1973.
23. Program, memorial service for Marjorie Merriweather Post, September 17, 1973; Clifford P. Robertson III, "This Lady," Hillwood Archives.
24. Clifford P. Robertson III, "This Lady," Hillwood Archives.
25. Gus Modig, oral history interview no. 3, by Anne Odom and Liana Paredes, February 1999.

26. Earl Loy, oral history interview by Stephanie Brown, May 2004.
27. Press notices, 1974–75, Hillwood Museum Collection, Hillwood Archives.
28. "Mourning Mrs. Post," *Battle Creek Enquirer*, clippings, Marjorie Post Papers, scrapbook 1973, Bentley Historical Library.
29. Press notices, 1977, Hillwood Archives.
30. Hope Ridings Miller, *Antique Monthly*, September 1977, press notices, 1977, Hillwood Archives.
31. Dina Merrill and Sandra McElwaine, "Mother's Hillwood Home," clipping, press notices, 1977, Hillwood Archives.
32. *Congressional Record*, September 20, 1973, Marjorie Post Papers [35], Bentley Historical Library.

Selected Bibliography

Archival Sources

Archives of American Art, Smithsonian Institution, Washington, D.C.
    Oral history interview with Jacob Lawrence, October 26, 1968.

The Arthur and Elizabeth Schlesinger Library on the History of Women in America, Radcliffe Institute for Advanced Study, Harvard University, Cambridge, MA
    Culinary Pamphlets and Reference Collections

Bentley Historical Library, University of Michigan, Ann Arbor, MI
    Post Family Papers
        Barzin, Eleanor Close. Interview by Nettie Major, June 1965.
        Mortimer, Charles. Interview by Nettie Major, August 8, 1965.
        Post, Marjorie. Interview by David Zeitlin, August 1964.
        Post, Marjorie Merriweather. Interviews by Nettie Major, December 1960, February 1962, March 1962, January 3, 1964, September 1964, December 30, 1964, January 3, 1965.

Columbia Center for Oral History, Columbia University Libraries, Columbia University, New York, NY
    Reminiscences of Marjorie Merriweather Post. Oral history, 1964.

Hillwood Estate, Museum & Gardens Archives, Washington, D.C.
    Frederick J. Fisher Papers
    Hillwood Archives Clipping and Periodicals Collection
    Marjorie Merriweather Post Collection
    Marvin C. Ross Papers
    Oral History Program Collection
        Beach, Walter. Interview by Stephanie Brown, November 2003.
        Beale, Betty. Interview by Stephanie Brown, January 2004.
        Brown, Peggy. Interview by Kathi Ann Brown, 1997.
        Brown, Peggy. Interview by Stephanie Brown, February 2005.
        Cannella, Betty. Interview by Nancy Harris, November 1998.
        Chapple, DeWitt. Interview by Estella M. Chung, October 8, 2012.
        Charles, Ellen. Interview by Stephanie Brown, November 13, 2003.
        Conger, Clem. Interview by Kathi Ann Brown, 1997.
        Day, Mary. Interview by Stephanie Brown, February 10, 2004.
        Del Monte, Frank. Interview by Stephanie Brown, February 17, 2004.
        Dickens, Rose. Interview by Stephanie Brown, May 2004.
        Erwin, Henry. Interview by Estella M. Chung, August 2014.
        Fern, Alan and Lois. Interview by Estella M. Chung, May 2013.
        Griffin, James, Jr. Interview by Nancy Harris, May 27, 1998.
        Handelman, Donald. Interview by Kathi Ann Brown, June 3, 1998.
        Loy, Earl. Interview by Stephanie Brown, May 2004.
        Merrill, Dina. Interview by Stephanie Brown, February 5, 2004.
        Merrill, Dina. Interview by Estella M. Chung, September 2010.
        Modig, Gus. Interview by Anne Odom and Liana Paredes, February 1999.
        Rumbough, Nina. Interview by Estella M. Chung, September 2010.
        Rumbough, Stanley. Interview by Estella M. Chung, September 16, 2011.
        Rumbough, Stanley M., Jr. Interview by Estella M. Chung, February 11, 2011.
        Russell, Ed, Jr. Interview by Estella M. Chung, September 18, 2014.
        Smith, Lisa. Interview by Estella M. Chung, August 25, 2009.
        Tucci, Michael. Interview by Estella M. Chung, November 2011.

Library of Congress, Washington, D.C.
    Joseph Edward Davies Papers, 1860–1958. Manuscript Division.
    "Mar-a-Lago, 1100 South Ocean Boulevard, Palm Beach, Palm Beach County, FL" (HABS FL-195). Historic American Buildings Survey, National Park Service, U.S. Department of the Interior, 1967. Prints & Photographs Division.

The Salvation Army National Archives and Research Center, Alexandria, VA
    The Salvation Army. *Report of Unemployment Relief Work in Greater New York, October to September 30, 1931*, [1931].

Special Collections Research Center, George Washington University, Washington, D.C.
    Marjorie Merriweather Post Papers

United States Coast Guard Museum, New London, CT
    USS *Sea Cloud* and Racial Integration in the U.S. Coast Guard. Chief Warrant Officer Professional Development.

Publications

"Acceptance of Birds Eye Frosted Foods." *Barron's*, March 30, 1936.

"American Women and Marriage." *Vogue*, March 16, 1905.

Arend, Liana Paredes. "Furnishing Hillwood." *The Magazine Antiques*, March 2003.

Baker, John Calhoun. *Directors and Their Functions: A Preliminary Study*. Boston: Division of Research, Graduate School of Business Administration, Harvard University, 1945.

Beale, Betty. *Power at Play: A Memoir of Parties, Politicians, and the Presidents in My Bedroom*. Washington, D.C.: Regnery Gateway, 1993.

"The Beginnings Are Notes Here: Post Products Celebration Last Night of 11 Held Throughout Nation." *Battle Creek Enquirer and News*, December 24, 1941.

Chung, Estella M. *Living Artfully: At Home with Marjorie Merriweather Post*. Washington, D.C.: Hillwood Museum and Gardens Foundation, in association with D Giles Limited, 2013.

Davies, Joseph E. *Mission to Moscow*. New York: Simon and Schuster, 1941.

"Dina Merrill, Actress and Philanthropist, Dies at 93." *New York Times*, May 22, 2017.

Fisher, Frederick, et al. *Hillwood Museum & Gardens: Marjorie Merriweather Post's Art Collector's Personal Museum*. Washington, D.C.: Hillwood Museum and Gardens, 2000.

Ford, Joseph Herbert. *The Medical Department of the United States Army in the World War. Volume II: Administration, American Expeditionary Forces*. Washington, D.C.: United States Government Printing Office, 1927.

"Foundation Chief Adelaide Riggs Dies." *Washington Post*, January 8, 1999.

General Foods. *Miracles with Minute Tapioca: Creamy Desserts—Fruit Pies and Puddings—Soufflés—Soups—Meat and Fish Dishes*. New York: General Foods Corp., 1948.

Kettering, Karen L. *Russian Glass at Hillwood*. Washington, D.C.: Hillwood Museum and Gardens, 2001.

Kurlansky, Mark. *Birdseye: The Adventures of a Curious Man*. New York: Doubleday, 2012.

Libbey, Theodore. *The National Symphony*. Washington, D.C.: NSO Book Project, 1995.

Major, Nettie Leitch. *C.W. Post: The Hour and the Man*. Washington, D.C.: Judd & Detweiler, 1963.

McCardle, Dorothy. "Tributes Are Paid to Marjorie Post." *Washington Post*, September 17, 1973.

Mikhalevsky, Nina. *Dear Daughters: A History of Mount Vernon Seminary and College*. Washington, D.C.: Mount Vernon Seminary and College Alumnae Association, 2001.

Museum of Modern Art. "Paintings by Leading Negro Artist at Museum of Modern Art," press release, October 3, 1944.

Nesbett, Peter T., and Michelle DuBois. *The Complete Jacob Lawrence: Jacob Lawrence Paintings, Drawings, and Murals (1935–1999). A Catalogue Raisonné*. Seattle: University of Washington Press, 2000.

Notes on Hillwood: A Guidebook. Washington, D.C.: Hillwood, 1997.

"Notice: Eleanor Close Barzin." *Washington Post*, March 25, 2007.

Odom, Anne. *Hillwood: Thirty Years of Collecting, 1977–2007*. Washington, D.C.: Hillwood Estate, Museum & Gardens, 2007.

Odom, Anne, and Wendy R. Salmond. *Treasures into Tractors: The Selling of Russia's Cultural Heritage, 1918–1938*. Washington, D.C.: Hillwood Estate, Museum & Gardens, 2009.

Postum Cereal Company Ltd. *There's a Reason*. Battle Creek, MI: Postum Cereal Company Ltd., n.d.

Pullman Company. *Private Car and Special Train Service in 1901*. Suffolk, VA: David Kennickell in cooperation with Wayne Publications, 1973.

Ross, Marvin C. *The Art of Karl Fabergé and His Contemporaries: Russian Imperial Portraits and Mementoes. Imperial Decorations and Watches*. Norman: University of Oklahoma Press, 1965.

Ross, Marvin C. *Russian Porcelains*. Norman: University of Oklahoma Press, 1968.

Rubin, Nancy. *American Empress: The Life and Times of Marjorie Merriweather Post*. New York: ASJA Press, 2002.

Skinner, LCDR Carlton. "The Lost Wartime Paintings of Jacob Lawrence." Museum of Modern Art, n.d.

Wills, Chuck. *Boy Scouts of America: A Centennial History*. New York: DK Publishing, 2009.

"The Woman's Share of the War." *Vogue*, July 1, 1917.

Wright, William. *Heiress: The Rich Life of Marjorie Merriweather Post*. Washington, D.C.: New Republic Books, 1978.

Photographic Credits

Front Cover

Photographed by Bert Morgan, Hillwood Estate, Museum & Gardens Archives, courtesy of The Bert Morgan Archive, Archive Farms, Inc.

Frontispiece

Photographed by Frank E. Geisler, Hillwood Estate, Museum & Gardens Archives

Contents

Hillwood Estate, Museum & Gardens, photographed by Edward Owen

Introduction

p. 12 Hillwood Estate, Museum & Gardens, photographed by Erik Kvalsvik; **p. 14** Alfred Eisenstaedt/The LIFE Picture Collection/Getty Images; **p. 15 above** Hillwood Estate, Museum & Gardens, photographed by Brian Searby; **p. 15 below** Post Family Papers, Bentley Historical Library, University of Michigan; **p. 18** Hillwood Estate, Museum & Gardens Archives; **p. 19** Photographed by E.B. Core, Hillwood Estate, Museum & Gardens Archives; **p. 20 left** Post Family Papers, Bentley Historical Library, University of Michigan; **p. 20 right** Photographed by Frank E. Geisler, Hillwood Estate, Museum & Gardens Archives; **p. 21** Post Family Papers, Bentley Historical Library, University of Michigan; **p. 22 above** Hillwood Estate, Museum & Gardens Archives; **p. 22 below** Post Family Papers, Bentley Historical Library, University of Michigan; **p. 23 above** Photographed by Leet Brothers, Hillwood Estate, Museum & Gardens Archives; **p. 23 below** Hillwood Estate, Museum & Gardens Archives; **p. 25** Hillwood Estate, Museum & Gardens Archives; **p. 26** Photographed by E.F. Foley, Hillwood Estate, Museum & Gardens Archives; **p. 27 left** Photographed by Ira L. Hill Studio, Hillwood Estate, Museum & Gardens Archives; **p. 27 right** Photographed by Ira L. Hill Studio, Hillwood Estate, Museum & Gardens Archives; **p. 28** Hillwood Estate, Museum & Gardens; **p. 29 left** Photographed by John Alfred Piver, Hillwood Estate, Museum & Gardens Archives; **p. 29 right** Photographed by John Alfred Piver, Hillwood Estate, Museum & Gardens Archives; **p. 30 above** Photographed by Frank E. Geisler, Hillwood Estate, Museum & Gardens Archives; **p. 30 below** Library of Congress, Prints & Photographs Division, HABS FL-195, HABS FLA, 50-PALM, 13; **p. 31 above** Library of Congress, Prints & Photographs Division, HABS FL-195, HABS FLA, 50-PALM, 23; **p. 31 below** Library of Congress, Prints & Photographs Division, HABS FL-195, HABS FLA, 50-PALM, 28; **p. 32 above** Hillwood Estate, Museum & Gardens Archives; **p. 32 below** Hillwood Estate, Museum & Gardens Archives; **p. 33** Hillwood Estate, Museum & Gardens Archives; **p. 34** Frank E. Geisler, Post Family Papers, Bentley Historical Library, University of Michigan; **p. 35** Photographed by Frank E. Geisler, Hillwood Estate, Museum & Gardens Archives; **p. 36** Rendered by Rouse & Goldstone Architects, Hillwood Estate, Museum & Gardens Archives, courtesy of Harmon H. Goldstone and Andrew Alpern; **p. 37** Photographed by J.C. Maugans, Hillwood Estate, Museum & Gardens Archives, courtesy of Harmon H. Goldstone and Andrew Alpern; **p. 38** Photographed by Mattie E. Hewitt, Hillwood Estate, Museum & Gardens Archives; **p. 39** Hillwood Estate, Museum & Gardens, photographed by Erik Kvalsvik

Business

p. 40 Hillwood Estate, Museum & Gardens, photographed by John Dean; **p. 42** Hillwood Estate, Museum & Gardens Archives, courtesy of Eliza's Quest Foods; **p. 43** Hillwood Estate, Museum & Gardens Archives, courtesy of Eliza's Quest Foods; **p. 44** Hillwood Estate, Museum & Gardens Archives, courtesy of Post Holdings; **p. 45** Hillwood Estate, Museum & Gardens; **p. 46** Hillwood Estate, Museum & Gardens; **p. 47** Postum Cereal Company Ltd. *There's a Reason*. Battle Creek, MI: Postum Cereal Company Ltd., n.d., courtesy of Eliza's Quest Foods; **p. 48** Postum Cereal Company Ltd. *There's a Reason*. Battle Creek, MI: Postum Cereal Company Ltd., n.d., courtesy of Eliza's Quest Foods; **p. 49** Post Family Papers, Bentley Historical Library, University of Michigan; **p. 50 above** Postum Cereal Company Ltd. *There's a Reason*. Battle Creek, MI: Postum Cereal Company Ltd., n.d.; **p. 50 below** Postum Cereal Company Ltd. *There's a Reason*. Battle Creek, MI: Postum Cereal Company Ltd., n.d.; **p. 51** Post Family Papers, Bentley Historical Library, University of Michigan; **p. 52 above** Postum Cereal Company Ltd. *There's a Reason*. Battle Creek, MI: Postum Cereal Company Ltd., n.d.; **p. 52 below** Post Family Papers, Bentley Historical Library, University of Michigan; **p. 53** Hillwood Estate, Museum & Gardens Archives; **p. 54** Hillwood Estate, Museum & Gardens, photographed by Brian Searby; **p. 56 above** Hillwood Estate, Museum & Gardens Archives; **p. 56 below** Photographed by French, Hillwood Estate, Museum & Gardens Archives; **p. 57 above** Photographed by French, Hillwood Estate, Museum & Gardens Archives; **p. 57 below** Hillwood Estate, Museum & Gardens Archives; **p. 58 above** Hillwood Estate, Museum & Gardens Archives; **p. 58 below** Hillwood Estate, Museum & Gardens Archives; **p. 60** Photographed by Campbell Studios, Hillwood Estate, Museum & Gardens Archives; **p. 61** Hillwood Estate, Museum & Gardens Archives; **p. 64** Hillwood Estate, Museum & Gardens Archives, courtesy of Post Holdings; **p. 65** Post Family Papers, Bentley Historical Library, University of Michigan, courtesy of Post Holdings; **p. 66** Photographed by Fred M. Hublitz, Hillwood Estate, Museum & Gardens Archives; **p. 67** Hillwood Estate, Museum & Gardens Archives; **p. 69** Hillwood Estate, Museum & Gardens Archives; **p. 70** Hillwood Estate, Museum & Gardens Archives; **p. 71 above** Hillwood Estate, Museum & Gardens, photographed by Edward Owen; **p. 71 below** Hillwood Estate, Museum & Gardens, photographed by John Dean; **p. 73** Hillwood Estate, Museum & Gardens, photographed by John Dean

Service

p. 74 Hillwood Estate, Museum & Gardens; **p. 76** Library of Congress, Prints & Photographs Division, LC-DIG-ggbain-26209; **p. 77** Hillwood Estate, Museum & Gardens, photographed by Brian Searby; **p. 78 above** Library of Congress, Prints & Photographs Division, LC-USZ62-38965; **p. 78 below** Hillwood Estate, Museum & Gardens; **p. 80** New York Times Co./Archive Photos/Getty Images; **p. 81** Hillwood Estate, Museum & Gardens, photographed by John Dean; **p. 82** Hillwood Estate, Museum & Gardens Archives; **p. 83** George Rinhart/Corbis Historical/Getty Images; **p. 84** George Rinhart/Corbis Historical/Getty Images; **p. 86** AP Photo; **p. 87** Post Family Papers, Bentley Historical Library, University of Michigan; **p. 88** Post Family Papers, Bentley Historical Library, University of Michigan; **p. 89 above** Hillwood Estate, Museum & Gardens, photographed by Edward Owen; **p. 89 below** Photographed by James R. Dunlop, Hillwood Estate, Museum & Gardens Archives; **p. 90 above** Hillwood Estate, Museum & Gardens, photographed by Brian Searby; **p. 90 below** Hillwood Estate, Museum & Gardens, photographed by Brian Searby; **p. 91** Hillwood Estate, Museum & Gardens Archives; **p. 92** Post Family Papers, Bentley Historical Library, University of Michigan; **p. 96** Hillwood Estate, Museum & Gardens, photographed by John Dean; **p. 97 above** Hillwood Estate, Museum & Gardens, photographed by John Dean; **p. 97 below left** Hillwood Estate, Museum & Gardens, photographed by John Dean; **p. 97 below right** Hillwood Estate, Museum & Gardens, photographed by John Dean; **p. 98**

© 2018 The Jacob and Gwendolyn Knight Lawrence Foundation, Seattle / Artists Rights Society (ARS), New York. Smithsonian American Art Museum, Washington, DC / Art Resource, NY; **p. 99** Photographed by the U.S. Coast Guard, Hillwood Estate, Museum & Gardens Archives; **p. 100 above** Photographed by the U.S. Coast Guard, Hillwood Estate, Museum & Archives. NH 92944 USCGC Sea Cloud (WPG-284), U.S. Naval History and Heritage Command Photograph; **p. 100 below** © 2018 The Jacob and Gwendolyn Knight Lawrence Foundation, Seattle / Artists Rights Society (ARS), New York. Santa Barbara Museum of Art, Gift of Mr. and Mrs. Burton Tremaine, Jr.; **p. 102** Hillwood Estate, Museum & Gardens, photographed by John Dean; **p. 103** Charles Del Vecchio, Post Family Papers, Bentley Historical Library, University of Michigan

Travel Luxe

p. 104 Hillwood Estate, Museum & Gardens, photographed by Erik Kvalsvik; **p. 106** Post Family Papers, Bentley Historical Library, University of Michigan; **p. 107** Post Family Papers, Bentley Historical Library, University of Michigan; **p. 108 left** Post Family Papers, Bentley Historical Library, University of Michigan; **p. 108 right** Post Family Papers, Bentley Historical Library, University of Michigan; **p. 109** Post Family Papers, Bentley Historical Library, University of Michigan; **p. 110** Hillwood Estate, Museum & Gardens Archives, courtesy of DeWitt Chapple; **p. 111** Post Family Papers, Bentley Historical Library, University of Michigan; **p. 113 above** Post Family Papers, Bentley Historical Library, University of Michigan; **p. 113 below** Post Family Papers, Bentley Historical Library, University of Michigan; **p. 114** Hillwood Estate, Museum & Gardens Archives; **p. 115 above** Edwin Levick, Post Family Papers, Bentley Historical Library, University of Michigan; **p. 115 below** Edwin Levick, Post Family Papers, Bentley Historical Library, University of Michigan; **p. 116 above** Photographed by J.C. Maugans, Hillwood Estate, Museum & Gardens Archives; **p. 116 below** Photographed by J.C. Maugans, Hillwood Estate, Museum & Gardens Archives; **p. 117** Hillwood Estate, Museum & Gardens, photographed by John Dean; **p. 118** Hillwood Estate, Museum & Gardens Archives; **p. 119** Hillwood Estate, Museum & Gardens Archives; **p. 120** Hillwood Estate, Museum & Gardens, photographed by Edward Owen; **p. 122 left** Hillwood Estate, Museum & Gardens, photographed by Edward Owen; **p. 122 right** Hillwood Estate, Museum & Gardens, photographed by Edward Owen; **p. 123** Hillwood Estate, Museum & Gardens Archives; **p. 124** Hillwood Estate, Museum & Gardens Archives; **p. 125 above** Hillwood Estate, Museum & Gardens Archives; **p. 125 below left** Hillwood Estate, Museum & Gardens Archives; **p. 125 below right** Hillwood Estate, Museum & Gardens Archives; **p. 126** Hillwood Estate, Museum & Gardens, photographed by John Dean; **p. 127** Hillwood Estate, Museum & Gardens, photographed by Edward Owen; **p. 129 above** Hillwood Estate, Museum & Gardens Archives; **p. 129 center** Post Family Papers, Bentley Historical Library, University of Michigan; **p. 129 below** Post Family Papers, Bentley Historical Library, University of Michigan; **p. 130** Hillwood Estate, Museum & Gardens Archives; **p. 131 above** Hillwood Estate, Museum & Gardens, photographed by John Dean; **p. 131 below** Hillwood Estate, Museum & Gardens Archives; **p. 133** Hillwood Estate, Museum & Gardens, photographed by Edward Owen

Photographic Credits

Giving

p. 134 Hillwood Estate, Museum & Gardens, photographed by John Dean; **p. 136** Post Family Papers, Bentley Historical Library, University of Michigan; **p. 137** Hillwood Estate, Museum & Gardens Archives; **p. 138 left** Photographed by Harris & Ewing, Hillwood Estate, Museum & Gardens, courtesy of Barbara Schmir; **p. 138 right** Hillwood Estate, Museum & Gardens Archives; **p. 139** Hillwood Estate, Museum & Gardens Archives; **pp. 140–141** Hillwood Estate, Museum & Gardens, photographed by Erik Kvalsvik; **p. 142** Hillwood Estate, Museum & Gardens, photographed by John Dean; **p. 143** Photographed by George Kalec, Hillwood Estate, Museum & Gardens Archives; **p. 144** Post Family Papers, Bentley Historical Library, University of Michigan; **p. 145 above** Hillwood Estate, Museum & Gardens Archives; **p. 145 below** Hillwood Estate, Museum & Gardens, photographed by John Dean; **p. 147** Post Family Papers, Bentley Historical Library, University of Michigan; **p. 148** Hillwood Estate, Museum & Gardens, photographed by John Dean; **p. 149** Hillwood Estate, Museum & Gardens Archives; **p. 150 above** Hillwood Estate, Museum & Gardens, photographed by John Dean; **p. 150 below** Hillwood Estate, Museum & Gardens, photographed by John Dean; **p. 152** Hank Walker/The LIFE Picture Collection/Getty Images; **p. 153** Hank Walker/The LIFE Picture Collection/Getty Images; **p. 154** Hillwood Estate, Museum & Gardens, photographed by John Dean; **p. 155 above** Hillwood Estate, Museum & Gardens, photographed by Edward Owen; **p. 155 below** Hillwood Estate, Museum & Gardens, photographed by Edward Owen; **p. 156 left** Hillwood Estate, Museum & Gardens Archives; **p. 156 right** Hillwood Estate, Museum & Gardens, photographed by Stanley Rumbough; **p. 157** Hillwood Estate, Museum & Gardens Archives; **pp. 158–159 all** Hillwood Estate, Museum & Gardens Archives; **p. 160** Hillwood Estate, Museum & Gardens, photographed by Erik Kvalsvik; **p. 161 above** Hillwood Estate, Museum & Gardens, photographed by Edward Owen; **p. 161 below** Hillwood Estate, Museum & Gardens, photographed by Edward Owen; **p. 162** Post Family Papers, Bentley Historical Library, University of Michigan; **p. 163** Hillwood Estate, Museum & Gardens, photographed by Erik Kvalsvik; **p. 165** Post Family Papers, Bentley Historical Library, University of Michigan

Legacy

p. 166 Hillwood Estate, Museum & Gardens, photographed by Erik Kvalsvik; **p. 168 above** Hillwood Estate, Museum & Gardens, photographed by Erik Kvalsvik; **p. 168 below** Hillwood Estate, Museum & Gardens, photographed by Erik Kvalsvik; **p. 169** Hillwood Estate, Museum & Gardens, photographed by Erik Kvalsvik; **p. 171** Hillwood Estate, Museum & Gardens Archives; **p. 172** Hillwood Estate, Museum & Gardens, photographed by Erik Kvalsvik; **p. 173** Hillwood Estate, Museum & Gardens, photographed by Erik Kvalsvik; **p. 174** Hillwood Estate, Museum & Gardens, photographed by Erik Kvalsvik; **p. 175** Hillwood Estate, Museum & Gardens, photographed by Erik Kvalsvik

Back Cover

Hillwood Estate, Museum & Gardens, photographed by Erik Kvalsvik

Hillwood Collection Objects

Contents

Tea and coffee service by Boin-Taburet, France, ca. 1889
Bequest of Marjorie Merriweather Post, 1973
12.303

Introduction

Miniature of C.W. Post
Gift of Mrs. Augustus Riggs, 1988
53.61

Portrait of Adelaide and Eleanor Close, 1910–1919
Bequest of Marjorie Merriweather Post, 1973
52.20

Business

Cereal bowls in Hillwood's collection
Bequest of Marjorie Merriweather Post, 1973
26.155.8; 26.152.16; 26.151.11; 26.149.41

Postum advertisement, artwork by Carolyn Haywood, 1927
Museum Purchase, 2013
2013.11

The Dangerous Servants: Evils of Coffee, Tobacco and Alcohol, G.W. Peters, ca. 1913
Gift of General Foods, 1978
51.232

The Dangerous Servants: Evils of Coffee, Alcohol and Tobacco by Charles F. Church, 1913
Gift of General Foods, 1978
51.172

Royal Doulton and Company, porcelain with the monogram of C.W. Post
Gift of Eleanor Close Barzin, 1974
26.187

Breakfast service by Shelley Potteries
Bequest of Marjorie Merriweather Post, 1973
26.153

Service

Marjorie Post Close by August Benzinger
Gift of Eleanor Close Barzin, 1996
51.238

Set by Wedgwood & Sons to raise money for an Allied charity, 1917
Bequest of Marjorie Merriweather Post, 1973
26.34

Suffragette suit
Bequest of Marjorie Merriweather Post, 1973
48.12.1

The Cross of Honor award by the Flag Association to Marjorie Post in 1933
Bequest of Marjorie Merriweather Post, 1973
18.81

Imperial Porcelain Factory vase, dating to 1836
Bequest of Marjorie Merriweather Post, 1973
25.324

Limoges service made for Ambassador and Mrs. Davies, Brussels, 1939
Gift of Mrs. Augustus Riggs, 1975
24.204

Needlework honoring the *Sea Cloud*'s World War II service
Bequest of Marjorie Merriweather Post, 1973
43.65.1-2

Navigator's jacket, USS *Sea Cloud* IX 99, World War II
Gift of Pamela Nichols Howe, 2018
2018.12

Legion of Honor medal and miniatures, 1957
Bequest of Marjorie Merriweather Post, 1973
18.78.1-5

Travel Luxe

Model of the *Hussar V*/*Sea Cloud* presented to Nedenia Hutton (Dina Merrill) by Captain Lawson
Bequest of Dina Merrill Hartley
2018.40.1

Plate, by Lenox Company, showing the *Sea Cloud* with black hull
Gift of Dina Merrill Robertson, 1975
26.201

Plate, by Lenox Company, showing the *Sea Cloud* with white hull after 1939
Museum Purchase, 2004
26.281

Cartier box with photograph of the *Sea Cloud*
Bequest of Marjorie Merriweather Post, 1973
12.395

Sea Cloud shoes by Bob, Inc.
Bequest of Marjorie Merriweather Post, 1973
49.28

Sea Cloud glassware by T.G. Hawkes and Company, Corning, New York, 1935
Bequest of Marjorie Merriweather Post, 1973
23.481

Sea Cloud table linens by unknown maker
Gift of Mrs. W.M. Fralic, 1991
45.91.2; 45.91.4

Merriweather airplane napkins
Bequest of Marjorie Merriweather Post, 1973
2018.4.1-3

Merriweather carry-on
Gift of Dina Merrill Hartley, 2010
2010.24.3

Giving

Figurine of prima ballerina
Anna Pavlova
Bequest of Marjorie
Merriweather Post, 1973
26.59

Silver Fawn, awarded by the
Boy Scouts to one woman
a year
Bequest of Marjorie
Merriweather Post, 1973
18.84

Plaquette of Mount Vernon
Seminary, 1937
Bequest of Marjorie
Merriweather Post, 1973
12.237

Medal from Mount Vernon
for distinguished service to
alma mater, 1937
Bequest of Marjorie
Merriweather Post, 1973
14.155

Heart-shaped pendant from
the New York Club alumni of
Mount Vernon, by Tiffany &
Co., ca. 1960
Bequest of Marjorie
Merriweather Post, 1973
17.26

Plate by Kornilov Brothers
Factory, ca. 1900
Bequest of Marjorie
Merriweather Post, 1973
25.161.1

Plate by Imperial Porcelain
Factory, 1886
Bequest of Marjorie
Merriweather Post, 1973
25.316

Potpourri vases by Sèvres,
1757
Bequest of Marjorie
Merriweather Post, 1973
24.78.3-4

Draped vases by Sèvres,
1758-78
Gift of Mrs. Augustus Riggs,
1974
24.186.1-2

Index

Page numbers in *italics* refer to illustrations. "MMP" refers to Marjorie Merriweather Post.

Alix of Luxembourg, Princess, 101
Anna Pavlova, figurine of, *134*, 195
Astor, Vincent, 94

Baker's Chocolate, 62, 70
Battle Creek, Michigan, 14, 16, 41, 172
Battle Creek High School, Michigan, 148–49, *158–59*
Beale, Betty, 18, 34, 138, 151
Belgium, 20, 29, *91*, 93
   see also Brussels
Benzinger, August: portrait of MMP, *74*, 194
Birds Eye Frosted Foods, 62–63, 66, 68
Bob, Inc.: *Sea Cloud* shoes, *122*, 194
Boin-Taburet: silver tea and coffee service, *5*, 194
Boulders, Greenwich, Connecticut, 17, 24, 28, *32*, 51, 59
Boy Scouts of America, 138, 139, *139*, 142, *143*, 143–44
   Silver Fawn award, *142*, 143, 195
breakfast service (Shelley Potteries, England), *71*, 194
Brown v. Board of Education Supreme Court ruling (1954), 95–96
Brussels: U.S. embassy, 29, *92*, 93
Burden mansion, Manhattan, 28, 29
Burmeister & Wain, 112

Cadillac Series 75 limousine, 128
Camp Post, Texas, 139, 142–43
Camp Post, Virginia, 142
Camp Topridge, near Lake Placid, New York, 27–28, 33, 72, 101, 109, 128
Campbell, Edmund, 156
Cannella, Betty (financial secretary), 13, 135, 167, 170, 173
Carmichael, Leonard, 146
Cartier box with photograph of the *Sea Cloud*, *120*, 194
cereal bowls, *40*, *73*, 194
Charles, Ellen (granddaughter), 24, 27, 29, 38, 135
Charles of Luxembourg, Prince, 101

Chester, Colby, 59, 62, 63
Chester, Genie, 109
Christian Science, 16, 19, 41, 171
Chrysler limousine, 127
Church, Charles F.: *Evils of Coffee, Tobacco and Alcohol*, 46
Close, Adelaide (daughter), 19, *19*, 24, *25*, *26*, *27*, *29*, 109, *147*
   portrait by Tartoué, *28*, 194
Close, Edward Bennett (first husband), 17, *18*, 19, *19*, 59, 84, 107
Close, Eleanor (daughter), 19, 24, *25*, *26*, *27*, *28*, *29*, 109, *147*
   portrait by Tartoué, *28*, 194
Conger, Clem, 36
Congressional Record, 38, 101, 174
Cox & Stevens, *111*, 112
Cross of Honor (United States Flag Association), 79
   Amelia Earhart, 38, 77, 79, *80*
   MMP, 79, *81*, *82*, 194

The Dangerous Servants: Evils of Coffee, Tobacco and Alcohol, 45, 46, 194
Davies, Joseph (third husband), 22, 99, 123, *124*, *125*
   ambassador to Soviet Union and Belgium, 20, 33, 68, 84, 85–86, *86*, 87, 93
   marriage to MMP and divorce, 20, 122, 167
   Mission to Moscow, 84, 93
   relationship with MMP, 20, 83–84, 126
Day, Mary, 136
Deibert, John, 167
Del Monte, Frank (chauffeur), 128
Derham Crown Chrysler limousine, 127
Derham Custom Body Company, Rosemont, Pennsylvania, 127
Duveen, Sir Joseph, 29

Earhart, Amelia, 38, 77, 79, *80*
Eddy, Mary Baker: *Science and Health*, 16
Eisenhower, Dwight D., 37, 102, 151

Eisenhower, Mamie, 170–71
Erwin family, 167

Fern, Alan, 170
Fleischman Floral Company, Chicago, 54, *58*
Frosted Foods
   see Birds Eye Frosted Foods

General Foods Corporation, 63, 66, 68, 70, 72
   see also Postum Cereal Company
Grape-Nuts, 13, *40*, 46, 62, *65*, 66, 70, 107
Great Depression, 79, 81–82, 144
Greenwich Country Club, Connecticut, 75
Gregory, Elizabeth, 41
Gripsholm cruise liner, 130, 132

Handelman, Donald (financial manager), 27, 135, 167
Harding, Ann, 93
Health Center Hospitals, 138
Hillwood, Roslyn, Long Island, 28, *38*, 101, 148
Hillwood, Washington, D.C., 13, 14, 27, 36, 38, 89, 103, *152–53*, 167
   entertaining
      balls, 151
      lunch and dinner parties, 36, *67*, 69, 72, 138, 164
      menus from 1960s, *67*, *69*
      tea and garden parties, 101, *103*, 135
   as a future museum, 33–34, 167, 170
   gardens, 13, 38, *157*, 167, 171, *173*, *174*, *175*
   monument to MMP in the rose garden, 171–72, *172*
   motor court with Eros sculpture, *39*
   renovations made, 167, 170
   rooms
      dressing room suite and office, 66, 89, 101
      entry hall, *12*, *166*, 170
      French drawing room, *163*, 168–69

French porcelain room, *160*
library, *104*, 128, *167*, 170
massage room, *140–41*
staff, 13, 27, 37, 128, 135, *167*, 170, 171–72
Hillwood Estate, Museum & Gardens, 13, 34, 167, 172–73, 174, *175*
Hogarcito, Palm Beach, Florida, 28, *34*, *35*
Hoxie, Gordon, 17
Hussar (motor boat), 111
Hussar (private railcar), 107, 109–11, *110*
Hussar IV (schooner), 111, *111*, 112–14
  interiors, 112–13, *113*, 117, 120
Hussar V (yacht, later renamed *Sea Cloud*), *104*, 111–12, 114, *114*, *115*, 116–17, *118–19*, 120–22, 126
  interiors, 114, *116*, 117, 120
  model presented to Nedenia Hutton, *104*, 194
Huston, Walter, 93
Hutton, Edward Francis ("E.F.," second husband), 19, *20*, *21*, 27, 59, 79, *114*, *118–19*, 120
  boats, 110–12, 114, 116, 120
  marriage to MMP and divorce, 19, 59, 66, 122
  Postum Cereal Company involvement, 59, 62, 63, 66
  private railcar, 107, 109
  travels, 24, 107, 109, 114, 120–21
Hutton, Nedenia (Dina Merrill) (daughter), 13, 19, *20*, 27, 194
  travels on *Hussar/Sea Cloud*, 24, 26, *118–19*, 120–22
  see also Merrill, Dina
E.F. Hutton Emergency Food Depot, 81

"I Will Share" campaign, 79
Imperial Porcelain Factory
  plate, *155*, 195
  vases, 87, *88*, *89*, 194
Instant Postum, 46, *48*, 62

Jell-O gelatin, 62, *67*, *69*, 72
Johnson, Lady Bird, 156

Johnson, Lyndon B., 37, 156

Kayser, Elmer Louis, 146
Kellogg, Dr. John Harvey, 41
Kennedy, Jacqueline, 37, 137–38
Kennedy, John F., 37
Kennedy, Rose, 37
Kirov ballet, 138
Knickerbocker, Cholly, 75
Kornilov Brothers Factory: plate, *154*, *155*, 195

La Vita Inn, Battle Creek, Michigan, 41, 43, 55
Lady Baltimore (motor boat), 111
Lake Merriweather, Virginia, 138, 138–39, 142
Lawrence, Jacob, 96, 98, *98*
  Captain Skinner, 98
  Decommissioning the Sea Cloud, 99, *100*
  Migration of the Negro series, 96, 98
Legion of Honor medal and miniatures, *102*, 194
Lenox Company: *Sea Cloud* plates, *117*, 194
Leopold III, King of Belgium, *91*, 93
Limoges service made for Ambassador and Mrs. Davies, *90*, 194
Long Island University, *147*, 147–48
  C.W. Post College, 147, *147*, *152–53*
  Sigma Alpha Epsilon fraternity, 147, *156*, *157*
  Marjorie Post May Hall, 148

Major, Nettie, 77, 85, 130
Mar-A-Lago, Palm Beach, Florida, 27, 28, *30–31*, 128
Marie Adelaide of Luxembourg, Princess, 101
Marie Gabrielle of Luxembourg, Princess, 101
Marjorie Merriweather Post Foundation, 173
Marjorie Merriweather Post Memorial Causeway, Palm Beach, 172
Marjorie Post Hutton Canteen for Women and Children, New York City, 81–83
Maxwell House Coffee, 62, 72
May, Herbert (fourth husband), 23, *23*, 132, 137–38
McCardle, Dorothy, 128
Merrill, Dina (daughter), 13, 19, 24, 37, 62, *70*, 128, *147*
  building of *Hussar/Sea Cloud*, 114, 117, 121
  on houses and estates, 13, 28–29, 167
  marriage to Cliff Robertson, *70*, 72, 171
  on MMP, 19, 20, 23, 24, 26, 79, 167, 173
  see also Hutton, Nedenia
Merriweather (private plane), 14, 128, *129*, 130, *131*
  carry-on, *133*, 194
  interiors, *129*, *130*
  napkins, *131*, 194
Merriweather Post Dining Hall, Camp Bedford, New York State, 139
Merriweather Post Pavilion of Music, Columbia, Maryland, 164, *165*
Minute Tapioca, 62, 70
Mission to Moscow
  book, Davies (1941), 84, 93
  film, Warner Bros. (1943), 38, 93
Mitchell, Howard, 151, 157
Modig, Gus (butler), 171–72
Mortimer, Charles, 63, 66, 68
Moscow: U.S. embassy (Spaso House), 29, *83*, 88, 84, 85
Mount Vernon Seminary and Junior College, Washington, D.C., 16–17, 144, 146–47, *149*
  heart-shaped pendant given to MMP, 146, *150*, 195
  medal given to MMP for distinguished service, *148*, 195
  Merriweather House, 146
  New York Club, 144, 146, *150*, 195
  plaquette, *145*, 195
  Post Hall and Library, 146
Museum of Modern Art, 96, 98
Music for Young America series of concerts, 154, 156–57, 160

National Conference of Christians and
    Jews Brotherhood Award, 101–2
National Society of Arts and Letters
    awards, *138*
National Symphony Orchestra (NSO),
    149, 151, 154, 156–57, 160, 164
  Merriweather Post Contest, *162*, 164
National Trust for Historic
    Preservation, 170
Naval Reserve Yacht Owners
    Distinguishing pennant, 99, *99*, 101
navigator's jacket, USS *Sea Cloud*,
    97, 194
needlework honoring *Sea Cloud*'s
    World War II service, *96*, 194
New York State Suffrage Party, 77
New York Yacht Club, 114, 120
Nixon, Richard, 37, 151

Packard Twelve Chassis, 128
Pavlova, Anna, figurine of, *134*, 195
Plymouth City Gate, England, *108*
Post, Caroline Lathrop (grandmother), 54
Post, Charles Rollin (grandfather), 54
Post, Charles William ("C.W.," father),
    53, *147*
  funeral, 54–55, *56–58*
  ill-heath and suicide, 13, 16, 18,
      41, 51, 53, 54
  marriages, 14–15, 17
  miniature portrait, *15*, 194
  monogrammed porcelain (Royal
      Doulton and Company), *54*, 194
  Postum and the Postum Cereal
      Company, 14, 41, 43, 45, 46–49,
      51, 53, 55, 59
  travels, 105–7, 111
Post, Ella Letitia Merriweather
    (mother), 14–16, *15*, 17, 18, 24, 41,
    55, 105, *106*
Post, Leila Young (stepmother), 17, 51,
    53, 55
Post, Marjorie Merriweather
  as an ambassadress
    Belgium, 20, 29, 93
    Soviet Union, 20, 29, 33, 68, 84,
        85–91, *86*, *87*, 93

  biographical details
    birth and early life, 14–16
    Christian Science beliefs, 16, 19, 171
    on C.W.'s death, 53, 54, *58*
    dancing, love of, 20, 23, 130,
        132, 135, *136*
    daughters *see* Close,
        Adelaide; Close, Eleanor;
        Hutton, Nedenia
    death, funeral, and memorials,
        38, 170–72
    divorces, 13, 18, 19, 23, 59,
        66, 122, 167
    education, 16–17, 144, *145*, 146, 174
    generosity, 19, 135, 139, *140–41*,
        149 *see also* philanthropy and
        fundraising *below*
    grandchildren, 24, 26, 27, 29,
        38, 128, 135
    on her parents, 15–16, 17
    knitting, 38, *74*, 75, 102
    as Marie Antoinette, *2*, 35
    marriages, 13, 17, *18*, 18–20, 23, 24,
        59, 83–84, 122, 126, 132, 167
    media attention, 13, 18, 55, 77,
        83–84, 85, 86, 105, 109, 122
    personality, 13–14, 26, 27, 83, 93
    pets, 14, *14*, 24, *28*
  as a businesswoman, 24,
      27, 38, 41, 174
    on the board of General Foods,
        63, 66, 68, 72
    early involvement in the company,
        41, 43, 45, 55
    running the company, 55, 59, 62,
        63, 66, 68, 70, 72
    takes over company on father's
        death, 18, 19, 41, 55
    uses General Foods products,
        67, *69*, *71*, 72
  clothes and accessories, *2*, 35, 151
    Sea Cloud shoes (Bob, Inc.),
        122, 194
    suffragette suit, *78*, 194
  collections, 5, 13, 29, 33–34, 36,
      93–94, *154*, 170
    18th century French art and

      furniture, 29, 33, *160*, 163, *168–69* *see also* Sèvres porcelain
    jewelry, 13, 83, 93
    porcelain, 13, 29, 36, *90*, *160*,
        161, 194, 195
    Russian decorative art, 13, 20, 29,
        33, 87, *88*, *89*, 154, *155*, 195
    tableware, 40, 71, 73, 77, 194
  houses and estates, 13, 19, 28–29
    General Foods products served,
        71, 72
    running households, 13, 14,
        17–18, 27, 36–37
    staff, 13, 17, 27, 37, 121, 128, 135, 167,
        170, 171–72, 173
    see also Boulders; Burden
        mansion; Camp Topridge;
        Hillwood, Roslyn, Long Island;
        Hillwood, Washington, D.C.;
        Hogarcito; Mar-A-Lago;
        Tregaron; triplex apartment
  philanthropy and fundraising, 13, 19,
      23, 24, 28, 34, 138, 174, 194
    boy scouts, 138–39,
        139, 142–44, *143*
    educational activities, 23, 28,
        33–34, 83, 135, 144, 146–49,
        151, 154, 156–57
    during the Great Depression,
        79, 81–83, 144
    Long Island University, *147*, 147–48
    Mount Vernon Seminary, 144,
        146–47, *148*, 149, *150*, 195
    music and ballet, 135, 136–38, *137*,
        149, 151, 154, 156–57, 160, 164
    Music for Young America,
        154, 156–57, 160
    National Symphony Orchestra, 149,
        151, 154, 156–57, 160, 164
    in wartime, 19, 38, 75–76,
        77, 101–2, *103*
    Washington Ballet and Ballet Guild,
        135, 136–38, *137*, 164
  public service
    as an ambassadress
        see ambassadress *above*
    awards and decorations, 79, *81*, *82*,

Index

101–2, *102*, *142*, 143, *148*, *156*, 157, 194, 195
business involvement
    see businesswoman *above*
honors Amelia Earhart, 38, 77, 79, *80*
politics, interest and involvement in, 26, 29, 37–38, 76–77, 86, 151, 156
supports women's suffrage, 76–77, *78*
scrapbooks and albums, *22*, 77, *91*, *93*, 105, 106, *107–9*, 115, *118–19*, 122, *123*, 126
transport
    boats, 111–12, 130, 132 *see also Hussar IV*; *Hussar V*; *Sea Cloud*
    cars and other vehicles, 127–28, 132
    plane, 14, 128, *129*, 130
    private railcar, 107, 109–11, *110*
    stagecoach, 105, 106, *108*, *109*
travels, 24, 45, 107, 111, 120
    Belgium, 20, 29, *91*, *93*, 130, 132
    cruises, *22*, 114, 122, *123*, 126, 130, 132
    Cuba, 126
    England, 105–6, *108–9*, 132
    Galapagos Island, 121
    honeymoons, *22*, 122, *123*, 130, 132
    Soviet Union, 20, 29, 33, 68, 84, 85–91, *86*, *87*, *93*
    scrapbooks, *22*, *91*, *93*, 106, *108–9*, *118–19*, 122, *123*
    Yosemite National Park, 106, *107*
wealth, 13, 72, 79, 85
photographs and portraits
    1900s and 1910s, *10*, *18*, *19*, *25*, *60*, *74*, *145*, 194
    1920s, *2*, *20*, *21*, *26*, *27*, *35*
    1930s, *22*, *80*, *82*, *83*, *86*, *87*, *114*, *118–19*, *123*
    1940s, *22*, *99*, *124*, *125*
    1950s and 1960s, *14*, *23*, *103*, *138*, *139*, *143*, *147*, *149*, *152–53*, *156*, *158–59*
Post, Reverend Roswell, 54
Post Toasties cereal, 46, 62, *64*, 70
Postum (coffee substitute), 13, 41, *42*, 43, *43*, 45, 46, 62, 68, 70, 72, 194
    see also Instant Postum
Postum Cereal Company (later General Foods Corporation), 14, 41, 43, 46
    advertising and publicity, *42*, 43, *43*, *45*, *45*, *46*, *64*, *65*, 194
    Cabinet, 45, 47–49, 53, 59, *61*
    dispute over ownership after C.W.'s death, 55
    distribution system, 62
    expansion, 59, 62–63, 66
    factory premises, 46, *47*, *48*, *49*, *50*
    listed on Stock Exchange, 62
    MMP in charge after death of C.W., 18, 19, 41, 55, 59, 62, 63, 66
    Post Addition (housing development), 46, *52*, 172
    treatment of staff, 46–47, 48–49, 51, 55, 59, 66, 68
    see also Grape-Nuts; Postum
Pullman Company private railcars, 107, 110, 111

Randolph, Jennings, 174
Red Cross, 75, 102
Robertson, Cliff, *70*, 72, 171
Rogers, Robert, 164
Rolls Royce Coupe de Ville, 127–28
Roosevelt, Eleanor, 79, *82*
Roosevelt, Franklin D., 37, 68, 84, 85
Roosevelt, Selwa, 151
Ross, Marvin (curator), 170
Royal Doulton and Company: C.W.'s monogrammed porcelain, *54*, 194
Rumbough, Stanley (grandson), 128
Russell, Ed, Jr., 109
Russia, 20, 68, 85–91, *86*, 93
    MMP's identification card, *87*
    MMP's Russian collection, 13, 20, 29, 33, *87*, *88*, *89*, *154*, *155*, 195
    see also Moscow; Soviet Union

Salvation Army
    food stations, 81
    E.F. Hutton welfare boxes, 81, *84*
    Unemployment Relief Work, 79, 81

Samuels, Mitchell, 146
Sandwich Glass Company, Massachusetts, 87
Sanka decaffeinated coffee, 62, 72
Scampi (pet schnauzer), 14, *14*
Schiff, Mortimer, 138
Sea Cloud (yacht), 13, 19, 24, 63, 94, 98, 122, 126–27, 194
    box by Cartier, *120*, 194
    glassware, *127*, 194
    model presented to Nedenia Hutton, *104*, 194
    plates (Lenox Company), *117*, 194
    shoes by Bob, Inc., *122*, 194
    table linens, *126*, 194
    see also Hussar V; USS *Sea Cloud* IX 99
Sèvres porcelain, 13, 29, 36
    draped vases, *161*, 195
    potpourri vases, *161*, 195
Shelley Potteries, England: breakfast service, *71*, 194
silver tea and coffee service (Boin-Taburet), *5*, 194
Skinner, Carlton, 95, 96, 98, *98*, *99*, 101
Smithsonian Institution, 170, 172–73
Somers, Elizabeth, 146
Soviet Union, 20, 29, 33, 68, 84
    see also Russia
Spaso House, Moscow (U.S. embassy), 29, 33, 68, 84, 85
Special Car Club of the New York, New Haven and Hartford Railroad Company, 107
SS *C.W. Post* (Liberty ship), 101
Stalin, Joseph, 85, 86
stock market crash (1929), 62
Sugar Crisp cereal, 70, 72
Sutherland, Duke of, 132
Sutton Place, Surrey, England, 132
Swans Down Cake Flour, 62, 70
Symington, Lloyd, 149

Tartoué, Pierre: portrait of Adelaide and Eleanor Close, 24, *28*, 194
tea and coffee set (Wedgwood & Sons), *77*

Topridge *see* Camp Topridge
Tregaron, Washington, D.C., 28
triplex apartment, 2 East 92nd Street,
 Manhattan, 28–29, *36, 37*
Truman, Harry S., 37

United States cruise liner, 132
USS *Sea Cloud* IX 99 (weather ship),
 94–95, 96, *96, 98,* 98–99, *100,*
 101, 194
 navigator's jacket, *97,* 194

Van Vleck, Natalie J., 63, 66
Vanderbilt, W.K., 94
Vettlesen, George, 114
Vickers Viscount model 786 airplane,
 128 *see also* Merriweather
Vietnam War, 38, 101, *103*
Vogel, Fred, 117, 120, 146

Walter Reed Army Hospital,
 Washington, D.C., 38, 101
Washington Advisory Committee
 on the Arts, National Cultural
 Center, 164
Washington Ballet (Washington School
 of Ballet), 136–38, *137,* 164
Washington Ballet Guild, 135
Wedgwood & Sons: tea and coffee set,
 77, 194
William Baumgarten & Company,
 112, *113*
Wilson, Woodrow, 76–77
Windsor, Duke and Duchess of, *125,* 126
women's suffrage, 76–77, *78*
World War I, 59
 base hospital in France, 76, *76*
 MMP's relief efforts, 19, 75–76
World War II, 20, 84, 85, 93–94, 144
 navigator's jacket, *97,* 194
 needlework honoring *Sea Cloud*'s
  World War II service, *96,* 194
 Sea Cloud offered to U.S. Navy,
  94–95, *96, 98, 99,* 194
  see also USS *Sea Cloud*

Yosemite National Park, 106, *107*